SOFT-COMPUTING IN
CAPITAL MARKET

SOFT-COMPUTING IN CAPITAL MARKET

Edited by

Jibendu Kumar Mantri

BrownWalker Press
Boca Raton

Soft-Computing in Capital Market

BrownWalker Press
Boca Raton, Florida
USA • 2014

ISBN-10: 1-62734-503-5
ISBN-13: 978-1-62734-503-3

www.brownwalker.com

Cover image @Cutcaster.com/Adrian Sawvel

"*The power of God is with you at all times; through the activities of mind, senses, breathing, and emotions; and is constantly doing all the work using you as a mere instrument.*"

— *Bhagavad Gita*

....

To my Father

But for whom nothing could have been possible.

My special thanks & gratitude to

Mr. Jeff Young
Publisher, Universal-Publishers,
Who has directly or indirectly helped and extended his support in bringing the book
to the present shape.

....

My affections to

My daughter Lori
For her inspirations and suggestions

Contents

Preface

Computational Finance, an exciting new cross-disciplinary research area, depends extensively on the tools and techniques of computer science, statistics, information systems and financial economics for educating the next generation financial researchers, analysts, risk managers, and financial information technology professionals. This new discipline, sometimes also referred to as "Financial Engineering" or "Quantitative Finance" needs professionals with extensive skills both in finance and mathematics along with specialization in computer science. Therefore, to fulfill the need of applications of this offshoot of the technology, this book is in print which is an edition of plethora of collections from cross disciplinary research.

This edited book covers most of the recent and advance research and practical areas in computational finance i.e. starting from traditional fundamental analysis using algebraic and geometric tools to the logic of science to explore information from financial data without prejudice. Utilizing various methods, the researchers of computational finance aim to determine the financial risk with greater precision that certain financial instruments create.In this line of interest, twelve papers dealing with this new techniques and /or novel applications related to computational intelligence, such as statistics, econometrics, neural-network and various numerical algorithms are included in this volume.

In Chapter-1, the research study is being predicted for the stock price of activate companies in Tehran Stock Exchange (Iran) using General Regression Neural Network (GRNN) and Linear Regression (LR). At first, 10 macro economic variables and 30 financial variables are considered and then using Independent Components Analysis (ICA) results are shown that has input obtained from seven final variables which includes three macro-economic variables and four financial variables. The findings presented two models for stock price prediction. The results have shown that artificial neural network method is more efficient than linear regression method.

In recent years, many researchers have introduced various methodologies and theories to explain and analyze stock market data. However, Chapter-2 tries to explain that the stock market is a very complex system. The complexity of the stock market increases the difficulty of testing any hypothesis relating to the market. For instance, the linear time series models are used for presenting stock market data rarely produce satisfactory results. In this study, the application of wavelet transform (WT) on identifying structure break for stock market data is explored. In doing so, this study hopes to acquire a better understanding of the information adaptation process by focusing on using time scale analysis to study structure break behavior of stock market through decomposing stock market into a scale domain. Results indicate that WT manage to uncover structure breaks behavior in monthly Amman Stock Exchange (ASE) Index from 1998 until 2009. In addition, these structure breaks represent some of the economic and financial events that affect ASE.

The purpose of Chapter-3 is to define a conceptual model representing the stock market in the micro level. This model is essentially based on cognitive behavior of the investors. In order to validate this new model, an artificial stock market simulator is built based on agent-oriented methodologies. The proposed simulator includes the market supervisor agent who executes transactions via an order book and various kinds of investor agents depending to their profile. The target of this simulation is to understand the influence of psychological character of an investor and the effects of his neighborhood on his decision-making and their impact on the market in terms of price fluctuations. Interactions between investors and information exchange during a transaction reproduce the market dynamics and organize the multi-agent based pricing. The resulting simulation system is a tool able to numerically simulate financial market operations in a realistic way. Simulation experiments are being performed to observe stylized facts of the financial times series and to show that the psychological attitudes have many consequences on the stock market dynamics. These experiments show that representing the micro level led to observe emergent socio-economic phenomena at the macro level.

Chapter-4 proposes a fuzzy approach for evaluation of composite financial stability index and fuzzy Markov model for analysis and forecast of financial situation. The methods are demonstrated through application of factual and estimated financial and macroeconomic information of the Azerbaijan Republic.

In Chapter-5, the authors try to evaluate the performance of DEoptim on a high-dimensional portfolio problem. The setup is the same as in the R Journal article Ardia et al. (2010); namely minimizing the portfolio CVaR under an upper bound constraint on the percentage CVaR contributions. Because the resulting optimization model is a non-convex programming problem with multiple local optima, DEoptim is more apt in solving this problem than gradient-based methods such as optim and nlminb.

Chapter-6 aims to develop a forecasting methodology on sector success evaluation (SSE) relating to job creation potential which is denoted with the difference of company establishment and liquidation quantities in this study. Artificial neural network system (ANN) is used for identifying expected job creation potential of different sectors with respect to financial ratios such as liquidity, leverage, activity, profitability and growth ratios. The proposed system is carried out in three main sectors of Turkey (agriculture, construction and manufacturing). The relevant data concerning financial ratios is collected from Istanbul Stock Exchange data set and data concerning job creation potential is gathered from the Union of Chambers and Commodity Exchanges of Turkey. The results reveal that ANN is a successful decision making tool that can help managers on expected success of sectors, compare expected and real job creations and make their strategic planning more effectively. Furthermore, it is identified that "fixed assets turnover" as an activity ratio that has the highest impact on sectorial success and the changes should be frequently followed. In contrast, "current assets/total assets (%)" and "net profit margin growth rate (%)" have the lowest effectiveness on sectorial success.

In Chapter-7, the author compares nicely the performance of Black (1976), Vasicek (1977) and CIR (1985) models as benchmarks with feed forward and recurrent artificial neural networks (ANNs) in pricing Brazilian IDI calls options using daily data for the period from January 2003 to September 2008. It is the first study that evaluates the performance of ANNs in pricing Brazilian interest rate options which is one of the major emerging markets. The author measures forecast performance for all the estimated models based on summary measures of forecast accuracy. Nevertheless, he performed parametric and nonparametric statistical tests as AGS, MGN and SIGN for competing forecast models. According to the statistical tests and summary forecast measurements, ANN is superior to Black, Vasicek and CIR models in IDI calls option pricing and there are no differences between feed forward and recurrent architectures in terms of accuracy when pricing these options. The founding results suggest that ANNs may have an important role to play in pricing interest rate options for which there is either no closed-form model or the closed-form model is less successful as in Brazilian case.

In Chapter-8, an attempt is made in predicting the Shanghai Composite Index returns and price volatility on a daily and weekly basis. Here two different types of prediction models namely the Regression and Neural Network models are used for prediction of task where multiple technical indicators are included in the models as inputs. The performances of the two models are compared and evaluated in terms of directional accuracy. Their performances are also rigorously compared in terms of economic criteria like Annualized Return Rate (ARR) from simulated trading. Here, both trading with and without short selling has been considered and the results show in most cases, trading with short selling leads to higher profits. Also, both the cases with and without commission costs are discussed to show the effects of commission costs when the trading systems are in actual use.

Chapter-9 explores the use of variants of Self Organizing Maps to simulate agent's interaction in social systems. The efforts were mainly concentrated to model agents learning and psychological relationships as well as the way latter can affect the system general behavior. Lastly, the authors have developed a suitable environment to simulate economic systems dynamics, totally based on models inspired on the approach of self-organization in cortical brain models.

In Chapter-10, a GMDH-type neural network and genetic algorithm is developed for stock price prediction of cement sector in Iran. For stocks price prediction by GMDH type-neural network, the authors are have used Earnings Per Share (EPS), Prediction Earnings Per Share (PEPS), Dividend Per Share (DPS), Price-Earnings ratio (P/E) and Earnings-Price ratio (E/P) as input data and stock price as output data. For this work, data of ten cement companies is gathered from Tehran Stock Exchange (TSE) in decennial range (1999-2008). GMDH type neural network is designed with 80% of the experimental data. For testing the appropriateness of the modeling, reminder of primary data are entered into the GMDH network. The last results are very encouraging and congruent with the experimental results.

In Chapter-11, the authors emphasize on the problem of estimation of volatility of Indian Stock market. It begins with volatility calculation by Auto Regressive Conditional Heteroscedasticity (ARCH) & Generalized Autoregressive Conditional Heteroscedasticity (GARCH) models for financial computation. At last the accuracy of using Artificial Neural Network for this is examined and concluded that ANN can be used as a better choice for measuring the volatility of stock market.

The last Chapter-12, aims at applying different methods i.e GARCH, EGARCH, GJR-GARCH, IGARCH and ANN models for calculating the volatilities of Indian Stock markets. Fourteen years of data of BSE Sensex and NSE Nifty are used to calculate the volatilities. The performance of data exhibits that there is no difference in the volatilities of Sensex and Nifty estimated under the GARCH, EGARCH, GJR-GARCH, IGARCH and ANN.

I hope the disseminated and collected information will be handy and useful to the financial researchers, analysts, risk managers, practitioners and mostly to the students' community delving in this area.

Dr. Jibendu. K. Mantri

CHAPTER 1

A Comparison Analysis for Prediction Stock Price: GRNN and LR Models

Prof.Reza Gharoie Ahangar

Islamic Azad University, Tehran, Iran
Member of International Economic Development Research Center
(IEDRC)

A Comparison Analysis of Modeling Stock Price Prediction: GRNN and LR Models

Abstract

This study predicted the stock price of activate companies in Tehran Stock Exchange (Iran). For reaching this purpose, General Regression Neural Network (GRNN) and Linear Regression (LR) have implemented. At first, 10 macro economic variables and 30 financial variables selected and then using Independent components Analysis (ICA) obtained seven final variables, which including three macro economic variables and four financial variables. The findings presented two models for stock price prediction. The results have shown that artificial neural network method is more efficient than linear regression method.

Key Words: Prediction, Financial Market, Artificial Neural Network, Stock Price

1- Introduction

The important characteristic of developed countries is that their money and capital market is active and dynamic. On the other hand, in any economic system, a group with more activity and proper saving earn more for the future (Ritanjali & Panda, 2007). How to use the savings can have positive or negative effects for the community. If these savings direct with a proper mechanism to production line, besides the efficiency it can bring to the owners of capital as the main supply also it will be useful to establish investment projects in economy (Widrow et al, 1994). If this money enters to unhealthy economic flow, it will have some inappropriate effects for the community. It has seen in most countries where the volume of liquidity in the hands of the people is a lot , the most important task for the country's economic officials is guiding, absorbing and creating conditions to increase the efficiency of these monetary resources for the whole community (Chen & Dua, 2008). One of the most important tools, which have the ability to absorb this liquidity, is "Stock Exchange". In this issue, stock exchange and buying and selling mechanism play an important role, because the owners can operate their capital with expected return by purchasing stock, and on the other hand ,they can have participation in supplying finance resources for the country's industry (Manne, 1966). Owners of small capitals are not able to get good returns from their investment and not the size of today's economy will allow them to have the power to produce alone or to move the wheel of community's economy. But if an appropriate mechanism collects these small assets, high efficiency can bring to the community; therefore, stock exchange is the economic institutions of society in developed countries and its operations is one of the important indicators that reflects economic- social conditions of these countries. Any insecurity in the stock market could lead to huge economic crisis.

The financial forecasting or stock market prediction is one of the hottest fields of research lately due to its commercial applications owing to the high stakes and the kinds of attractive benefits that it has to offer (Ritanjali & Panda, 2007). Unfortunately, stock market is essentially dynamic, non-linear, complicated, nonparametric, and chaotic in nature (Tan et al., 2005). The time series are multi-stationary, noisy, random, and have frequent structural breaks (Oh & Kim, 2002; Wang, 2003) . In addition, stock market's movements are affected by many macro-economical factors such as political events, firms' policies, general economic conditions, commodity price index, bank rate, bank exchange rate, investors' expectations, institutional investors' choices, movements of other stock market, psychology of investors, etc (Miao et al., 2007; Wang, 2003). The ability to accurately predict the future is fundamental to many decision processes in planning, scheduling, purchasing, strategy formulation, policy making, and supply chain operations and stock price. As such, forecasting is an area where a lot of efforts have been invested in the past (Armstrong, 1988). Yet, it is still an important and active field of human activity at the present time and will continue to be in the future

Forecasting has been dominated by linear methods for many decades. Linear methods are easy to develop and implement, and they are also relatively simple to understand and interpret. However, linear models have serious limitation in that they are not able to capture any nonlinear relationships in the data. The approximation of linear models to complicated nonlinear relationships is not always satisfactory. In the early 1980s, Makridakis et al (1982), organized a large-scale forecasting competition (often called M-competition) where a majority of commonly used linear methods were tested with more than 1,000 real time series. The mixed results show that no single linear model is globally the best, which may be interpreted as the failure of linear modeling in accounting for a varying degree of nonlinearity that is common in real world problems. Artificial neural networks are one of the technologies that have made great progress in the study of the stock markets. The most important feature of neural networks is to analyze the mass of information about issues that they are not known, the economic issues are just such situation. Usually stock prices can be seen as a random time sequence with noise, artificial neural networks, as large-scale parallel processing nonlinear systems that depend on their own intrinsic link data, provide methods and techniques that can approximate any nonlinear continuous function, without a priori assumptions about the nature of the generating process (Pino et al., 2008). It is obvious that several factors are effective on future stock price and the main weak point in this surrey is that all of them considered a few limit factors in future stock price and using linear methods, Regarding that fact, although previous studies highlighted the problem to some extent, none of them provide a comprehensive model to estimate the stock price. If one estimates the prince and provides a model for it to eliminate uncertainties to a large extent, it can help to increase the investments in stock exchange. Conducting the scientific surveys to obtain a suitable and desirable model to estimate the stock price is the best task. The aim of this study is to predict stock price using classical prediction methods (linear regression) and neural networks to identify the most effective method in predicting stock prices.

2- Literature Review

In this section, we consider other studies in relation to classical and neural network issues. Refenes et al., (1994) compared neural networks performance with regression models by modeling the behavior of stocks via neural networks. In this study, neural networks are considered as an alternative to classical statistical techniques and these networks have been used to predict the stocks of large companies. It is shown that neural networks have better performance than the statistical techniques, and forecast more accurately and provide a better model. Statistical models based on ARIMA (p, d, and q) model are as time series methods. It is shown that neural networks explain and describe better in predicting the behavior of stock prices and it can model the environmental conditions better than regression model. Kimand & Han (2000) in their study proposes genetic algorithms (GAs) approach to feature the discrimination and the determination of connection weights for artificial neural networks (ANNs) to predict the stock price index. Olson & Mossman (2003) have used accounting ratios by neural networks and linear regression to predict stock output in Canada. The results of this study showed that the neural network back propagation method is superior to linear regression, both in classifying outputs and also in terms of predictive power. Hamid & Iqbal (2004) presented a primer for using neural networks for financial forecasting. They compare volatility forecasts from neural networks with implied volatility from S&P 500 Index futures options using the Barone-Adesi and Whaley (BAW) American futures options pricing model. Abbaspour (2004) has performed a study to predict the stock price of Iran Khodro in

Tehran stock exchange with the use of artificial neural network. The data used in this study include daily data in the period of 2001 to 2002.Variables affecting Iran Khodro's stock prices and exchange rates include oil prices, (P/E) ratio and stock trading volume. The results indicate the priority of artificial neural network to forecast prices by the box-Jenkins. Allen & Yang (2004) examined the deviation of the UK total market index from market fundamentals implied by the simple dividend discount model and identified other components that also affect price movements. Enke & Thawornwong, (2005) introduced an information gain technique used in machine learning for data mining to evaluate the predictive relationships of numerous financial and economic variables. Neural network models for level estimation and classification are then examined for their ability to provide an effective forecast of future values. Cao et al., (2005) have used artificial neural networks in order to move the stock price changes of the Chinese market. In this way the neural network compared with the linear regression method and has concluded that the neural network serves better than the regression method. Raei & FallahPour (2006) have done a research to predict stock returns in Tehran stock exchange by the artificial neural networks and multi-factor models. Daily stock price of Behshahr Industries Development Corporation was selected as the sample. Multivariate linear regression is used for processing multi-factor model and multi-layer Perceptron is used for neural networks. The results show the superiority of the artificial neural network model to multifactor model. Wang (2007) integrated new hybrid asymmetric volatility approach into artificial neural networks option pricing model to improve forecasting ability of derivative securities price. Rashid (2007) investigated the dynamic association between daily stock index returns and percentage trading volume changes. To proceed with this, linear and nonlinear Granger causality tests are applied to the Karachi Stock Exchange (KSE) data. Chang & Liu (2008) in their study used an integrated system, CBDWNN by combining dynamic time windows, case based reasoning (CBR), and neural network for stock trading prediction. Hsu & Hsieh (2008) employed a two-stage architecture for better stock price prediction. Zhang & Wu (2008) proposed an improved bacterial chemo taxis optimization (IBCO), which is then integrated into the back propagation (BP) artificial neural network to develop an efficient forecasting model for prediction of various stock indices. Chen & Du (2009) adopted the operating rules of the Taiwan stock exchange corporation (TSEC) which were violated by those companies that were subsequently stopped and suspended, as the range of the analysis of this research. De-Faria & Gonzalez (2009) in their work performed a predictive study of the principal index of the Brazilian stock market through artificial neural networks and the adaptive exponential smoothing method, respectively. Araújo (2010) presented a hybrid intelligent methodology to design increasing translation invariant morphological operators applied to Brazilian stock market prediction. Daim et al., (2011) evaluated the effectiveness of neural network models which are known to be dynamic and effective in stock-market predictions. The models analyzed are multi- layer perceptron (MLP), dynamic artificial neural network (DANN) and the hybrid neural networks. Chang (2011) in his study used the artificial neural networks (ANN), decision trees, the hybrid model of ANN and decision trees (hybrid model), the three common algorithm methods used for numerical analysis, to forecast stock prices. The author compared the stock price forecasting models derived from the three methods, and applied the models on 10 different stocks in 320 data sets in an empirical forecast. Dai et al., (2012) in their research, a time series prediction model by combining nonlinear independent component analysis (NLICA) and neural network is proposed to forecast Asian stock markets.

3- Objectives

The present study attempts to undertake the best method of forecasting between artificial neural network and classical linear regression methods to determine stock price for companies listed in Tehran Stock Exchange. For reaching this objective, we consider;

I) Determine the main variables to estimate future stock price of companies acting in stock exchange.

II) Price estimation using two methods of artificial neural network and linear regression and comparison of these two methods' results.

4- Research Methodology
4-1- Sample Unit

The sample of the present study includes all companies, which were activated in Tehran stock exchange during 2004-2010. Therefore, those companies whose symbol was not active during this period were omitted and finally, 100 companies were chosen. The scope of subject in this study includes the consideration of the relationship between macro economic and financial variables with stock future price.

4-2- Data Collection Method

In this study, we used 10 macro economic variables and 30 financial variables to study their effects on stock future price. Data related to macro economic variables were collected through Central Bank yearbook, economic reports and balance sheet of Central Bank and Monetary and financial Research Center of Iran Central Bank and data related to companies financial variables collected through companies financial statements send informational Agency of Tehran(Iran) stock exchange.

4-3- Methodology Steps

a)   Identifying related factors and omitting additional variables (among macro economic and financial variables) through the analysis of independent components.
b)   Modeling and estimating stock future price through the linear regression equation.
c)   Modeling and estimating stock future efficiency using General regression neural network.
d)   Comparison of result related to these methods.

4-3-1- Independent Components Analysis (ICA)

To estimate financial time series, it is necessary to use a set of continuous descriptive input variables among a very huge set of primary inputs. It is difficult to choose a significant and suitable subset of input variables. In several scientific fields, it is difficult to find a reasonable transfer for a huge set of multi-data. Our purpose is to use a technique to summarize independent components of time series in a set of variables which is named independent components Analysis (ICA). This method will decrease the number of descriptive variables by decreasing a set of financial and economic information into smaller subsets of independent components and maintaining the suitable information. Removing the random elements from each data set will facilitate the identification of relationship between independent components and stock indexes. Independent components Analysis are process to summarize a new set of statistical independent components in a guide vector. These components will show some estimations of data main resource. This process supposes a matrix of time series which includes a compound process; so that, this process will analyze the independent components by creating a matrix when we enter them, and identify the related and unrelated components and provide us with the best matrix of estimative variables.

This technique will summarize as follows:

- This technique will summarize independent components of time series in a set of variables.
- This technique will find a way to change data with the minimum statistical dependency among the summarized components into a linear data.
- If two random variables are unrelated, they will not be independent.
- This technique is so special for analysis and estimation which uses two matrixes of data covariance and data changes by increasing the arrangement of linear and non-linear regression

4-3-2- Linear Regression

If researchers want to estimate the dependent variable by one or more independent variables, they will use a linear regression model. This model will be shown as follows;Amount of P for each set of data will result in minimum μ .When ever we use standard scores instead of raw variables in the analysis, P regression coefficients will be shown as B.

Linear regression can be a method to estimate a set of time series. Average of financial and macro economic variables of identified resources in the beginning of each year are independent variables in these estimations. Dependent variables Q are the real output of the company in estimation model, which depend on price data of all stocks in our sample. Dependent variable will be estimated using regression step method (OLS). All independent variables will enter to the regression equation. These independent variables with P-values more than 5% will be omitted in estimation period and at last, we will choose a subset of independent variables. Olson & Mossman state that variables of 3 to 7 independent variable will show the best estimations for this period. According this study if step solution method chooses more than eight independent variables, P–value will be decreased to 3% or 4%, and if step solution method chooses one or two variables, P- value will be increased to 10% to include more variables.

$$Q_{j,t} = \sum_{i=1}^{k} P_{i,t} * F_{j,i,t-1} + u_{j,t} \qquad (1)$$

K = The number of independent variables
P = Regression coefficient of independent variable I in month t
$F_{j,i,t-1}$ = Independent variable I for stock j at the end of previous period (month t-1).
$U_{j,t}$ = Error terms for each regression
$Q_{j,t}$ = Price of (dependent variable) stock j in month t.

4-3-3- General Regression Neural Network
General Regression Neural Network (GRNN) can approximate any arbitrary function from historical data. The major strength of GRNN compared to other ANNs is that its internal structure is not problem dependent.

Topology of GRNN

- GRNN consists of four layers:
- The first layer is responsible for reception of information.
- The input neurons present the data to the second layer (pattern neurons).
- The output of the pattern neurons are forwarded to the third layer (summation neurons).
- summation neurons are sent to the fourth layer (output neuron)

We can summarize this model as:

- This model will consider a few non- linear aspects of the estimation problem.
- This network model will be taught immediately, and will be suitable for scattered data.
- First, data will be clustered to decrease the needed layers in hidden layer.
- This model enables to solve any problems in monotonous functions.
- This model can not ignore non-related inputs with out the main revisions in the main algorithm.

5- Factors for Comparison of Two Methods

In time series, conforming of estimation model to data pattern is very important. We can obtain the conformity of estimation method with data pattern by calculating estimation error during the time period. For example, when a technique of evaluation estimates the periodical and seasonal alternations in time series, then estimation error will show the disordered or random component in time series. Mean Square Error (MSE) index is obtained through dividing total error differences square by time series. Mean Absolute Percentage Error (MAPE) is an index, which will be used whenever estimation of error based on percent is more suitable. Determination coefficient (R^2) is the most important factor, which can explain the relationship between two variants

6- Choosing Final Variables among Primary Variables

40 financial and macroeconomic variables will enter independent components analysis method:

A. Macroeconomic Variables

Growth rates of industrial production
Interest rate
Inflation rate
Exchange rate
Rate of return on stock public
Unemployment rate
Oil price
Gross Domestic product (GDP)
Money supply 1 (M1)
Money supply 2 (M2)

B. Financial Variables
Book value per share
Sales per share
Earning per share
Cash flow per share
Inventory turnover rate
Annual average volume of daily trading relative to annual average total market capitalization
Dividend yield
Dividend payout ratio
Dividend per share

Total of sales to total assets
Bid – ask spread
Market impact of a trade
Price per share
Trading volume
Turnover rate
Commission rate
Indicator variables for the day of the week effect
Holiday effect
January month
Amortized effective spread
Price history
Past return
Size of firm
Ratio of total debt to stockholder's equity
Pastor measure
Ratio of absolute stock return to dollar volume
Market depth
Ratio of net income to book equity
Operating income to total assets
Operating income to total sales

Independent Components Analysis (ICA) method chooses variables with minimum statistical dependency and explanation strength, and then we chose 40 variables.

C. Financial Variables
Earning per share
Size of firm
Ratio of total debt to stockholder's equity
Operating income to total sales

D. Macroeconomic Variables
Inflation rate
Money supply 1 (M1)
Growth rates of industrial production

7- Results

Here, we show the results of two methods and the models created by linear regression and neural network methods and comparison of the models' results using the above-mentioned factors.

7-1- Estimation of Linear Regression Model

Table 1: Model Summary

Durbin-Watson	Std. Error of The Estimate	Adjusted R Square	R Square	R
2,013	83,487569	0,211	0,279	0,368

A   Predictors: (Constant), EXCHANGE, DEPT, EPS, SOF, INFLATION, M1,B Dependent Variable: Stock Price

Table 2: Table of ANOVA

Model	Sum Squares	df	Mean Square	F	sig
1 Regression Residual Total	381258,653 287923,471 326214,368	7 1117 1123	441,257 382,186	5,0 09	0,000a

a. Predictors: (Constant), EPS, SOF, income, inflation, M1, Dept, ratio

Table 3: Table of Coefficients

Model	Un-standardized Coefficients		Standardized Coefficients	t	sig
	B	Std. Error	Beta		
1 (Constant)	-14,61	39,216		-2,498	0,459
ratio	2,009	0,843	2,138	3,181	0,001
inflation	7,162	3,728	0,179	2,772	0,005
income	-0.208	0.096	-0,022	-0,532	0,066
Dept	0.0309	0,223	0,031	1,991	0,042
SOF	-0,0001	0,001	0,027	2,107	0,047
EPS	0,189	0,005	0,184	2,987	0,001

a. Dependent Variable: stock price

$$Y=-14.61+2.009X_1+7.162X_2+0.0309X_3-0.0001X_4+0.189X_5 \qquad (2)$$

Y: stock price
X_1: Growth rate of industrial products
X_2: Inflation rate
X_3: Ratio of total liabilities to stockholders pay
X_4: Company's degree
X_5: Earning per share

As it is observed financial variable of operational income to total selling are not mentioned in the model, because of a variable to be meaningful and mentioned in the model, "t" should be more than 1.98 and "Sig" less than 0.05, respectively. Therefore, the significance level for this variable is more than 5% and t-value is (-0.532), so this variable will not be mentioned in the model.
According to the tables, which calculated by algebra method, multi correlation factor (R) is 0.368. That is, 0.368 correlations between independent variables and dependent variables. This means that independent variables which remained in regression equation have 0.368 significant relationships with stock price.Determination coefficient (R^2) or (Pearson's correlation coefficient) shows a ratio of total dependent variable changes, which are calculated by dependent variables of the equation. So, in dependent variables could estimate 0.279 variance of dependent variable (price). Moreover, according the B standard coefficient one can say growth rate variable of industrial products (Beta = 2.138) in a significant level 0.001 is the most descriptive for dependent variable value or stock price.

7-2- Estimation of General Regression Neural Network Model

To estimate General Regression Neural Network Model, we consider seven variables obtained from dependent components analysis as input (P) and stock price as output (T). Also, we calculated spread = 0.8326, because spread of more than one will cause in hyper fitting of network and a larger region of input to output vector, and its very small value will cause in increase of estimation error. In a way that function will have a high slope and neuron which weights are more similar to its input will have more outputs than other neurons. In this network, member of input vector (P) will be calculated for all neurons and will be calculated for transfer function (sigmoid function) and the output will be gained after multiplying in weights vector and adding to bias, and this output will be a vector. We used a three-layer general regression neural network which had seven neurons in internal layer and 14 neurons in middle layer and one neuron in external to design. After using learning algorithm and network education of 37 educational periods, network error graph is as follows.

7-2-1- Model One

Is an estimated model which is not educated and has its own real error?

$$Y=-8.11+ 1.83X_1-0.000011X_2+7.16X_3+2.07X_4-.00008X_5+0.957X_6+0.243X_7 \tag{3}$$

7-2-2- Model Two
- Which is obtained through using learning algorithm in model One which has the minimum error.
- LM learning algorithm was chosen which has the most adaptability to all survey aspects.
- Value of SPREAD = 0.8326 was used because spread value of more than one will case in hype fitting in network and a larger region of input to output vector, and its very small value will cause in increase of estimation error.
- We used a three–layer general regression neural network, which had seven neurons in internal layer, 14 neurons in middle layer and one neuron in external layer to design.

$$(4)$$

$$Y=-11.07+4.11X1-0.000009X2+6.74X3+1.31X4-0.0007X5+0.39X6+0.131X7$$

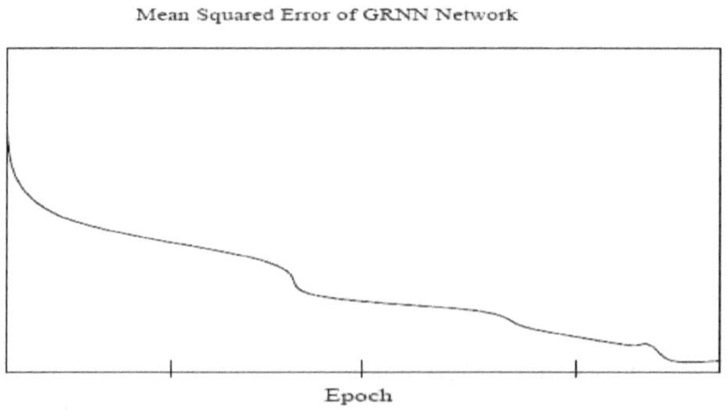

Fig1: Mean Squared Error of GRNN Network

8- Conclusion
8-1- Comparison of two Methods Results

As it is shown in the table below, value of Mean Square Error, Mean Absolute Percentage Error and Determination Coefficient will be decreased significantly after using training in neural network, which will be shown the increase of estimation factor in trained neural network.

Table 4: Compare of two methods

Factors	R^2	MAPE	MSE
GRNN	0,71	1,42	76,2
LR	0,368	3,73	97,6

After using LM algorithm and network training, above statistics will be changed as follows;

Table 5: Compare of two methods after using LM algorithm

Factors	R2	MAPE	MSE
GRNN	0,98	0,78	31,6

In this survey, we chose 100 companies of high quality in Tehran stock exchange, and according to results we understand that artificial neural network method is better than linear regression method in estimation. Models based on neural networks can appropriately simulate the behavior of stock prices and offer a model which is closer to reality than classic methods. Thus, this study shows the superiority and priority of the non-linear models on linear models. The result of this analysis indicates that investors can use scientific methods to predict stock price, and so their investment can be successful in the Stock Market. According to the results of research, stock prices can be predicted with minimal error using artificial neural network. So, the investors using the inputs listed in the pages before can be easily obtained, and being familiar with MATLAB software can predict stock price of the companies present in stock exchange.

References

[I] Abbaspour, M., (2004). Price prediction of Iran Khodro Stock in Tehran Stock Exchange using neural networks, Unpublished doctoral Thesis.

[II] Allen, D. E. & Yang, W. (2004); Do UK stock prices deviate from fundamentals? *Mathematics and Computers in Simulation*, Volume 64, Issue 3-4, Pages 373-383.

[III] Araújo, R.D.A., (2010). Hybrid intelligent methodology to design translation invariant morphological operators for Brazilian stock market prediction. *Neural Networks*, Volume 23, Issue 10, Pages 1238-1251.

[IV] Armstrong, J. S. (1988). Research needs in forecasting. *International Journal of Forecasting*, Volume 4, Pages 449-465.

[V] Cao, Q., Leggio, K. B., & Schniederjans, M.J. (2005); A comparison between Fama and French's model and artificial neural networks in predicting the Chinese stock market, *Computers & Operations Research*, Volume32, Issue 10, pages2499- 2512.

[VI] Chang, P. & Liu, C. (2008); A neural network with a case based dynamic window for stock trading prediction; *Expert Systems with Applications*, Volume 36, Issue 3, Part 2, Pages 6889-6898.

[VII] Chang, T. S., (2011). A comparative study of artificial neural networks, and decision trees for digital game content stocks price prediction. *Expert Systems with Applications*, Volume 38, Issue 12, Pages 14357-15598.

[VIII] Chen, W. S. & Du, Y. K., (2009); Using neural networks and data mining techniques for the financial distress prediction model, *Expert Systems with Applications*, Volume 36 Issue 2, Pages 14846-14851.

[IX] Dai, W., Wu, J. V., & Lu, C. J., (2012). Combining nonlinear independent component analysis and neural network for the prediction of Asian stock market indexes. *Expert Systems with Applications*, Volume 39, Issue 4, Pages 4444-4452.

[X] Daim, T.U., Guresen, E., & Kayakutlu, G., (2011). Using artificial neural network models in stock market index prediction. *Expert Systems with Applications*, Volume 38, Issue 8, Pages 10389-10397.

[XI] De-Faria, E.L. & Gonzalez, J.L., (2009); Predicting the Brazilian stock market through neural networks and adaptive exponential smoothing methods, *Expert Systems with Applications*, Volume 36, Issue 10, Pages 12506-12509.

[XII] Enke, D. & Thawornwong, S. (2005); The use of data mining and neural networks for forecasting stock market returns, *Expert Systems with Application*, Volume: 29, Issue: 4, Pages: 927-940.

[XIII] Hamid, S. A., & Iqbal, Z. (2004); Using neural networks for forecasting volatility of S&P 500 Index futures prices, *Journal of Business Research*, Volume 57, Pages 1116–1125.

[XIV] Hsu, S. H. & Hsieh, J. A. (2008); A two-stage architecture for stock price forecasting by integrating selforganizing map and support vector regression, *Expert Systems with Applications*, Volume 36, Issue 4, Pages 7947-7951.

[XV] Kimand, K. & Han, I. (2000); Genetic algorithms approach to feature discretization in artificial neural networks for the prediction of stock price index, *Expert Systems with Applications*,Volume 19, Issue 2, Pages 125–132.

[XVI] Makridakis, S., Anderson, A., Carbone, R., Fildes, R., Hibdon, M,. Lewandowski, R., Newton, J., Parzen, E., & Winkler, R. (1982). The accuracy of extrapolation (time series) methods: Results of a forecasting competition. *Journal of Forecasting*, Volume 1, Issue 2, Pages 111-153.

[XVII] Manne, H. G (1966). Insider Trading and the Stock Market. Harvard University, USA.

[XVIII] Miao, F. Chen, Z. and Zhao, G. (2007) Stock price forecast based on bacterial colony RBF neural network, *Journal of QingDao University*, Volume 20, Issue 2, Pages 50–54 (in Chinese).

[XIX] Oh, K.J. and Kim, K.-J. (2002), Analyzing stock market tick data using piecewise non linear model, *Expert System with Applications* Volume 22, Issue 3, Pages 249–255.

[XX] Olson, dennis and Mossman, Charls (2003), neural network forecasts of Canadian stock returns using accounting ratios, *International journal of foresting*, Volume 19, Issue 3, Pages 453-465.

[XXI] Pino, R. Parreno, J. Gomez A. and Priore, P. (2008) Forecasting next-day price of electricity in the Spanish energy market using artificial neural networks, *Engineering Applications of Artificial Intelligence*, Volume 21, Issue 1, Pages. 53–62.

[XXII] Raei, B and Fallahpour, S., (2006). Financial Distress Forcasting Using Artificial Neural Networks, *Journal of Financial Research (Iran Publication)*. Volume 17, Issue 1, Pages 39-69.

[XXIII] Rashid, A., (2007). Stock prices and trading volume: An assessment for linear and nonlinear Granger causality. *Journal of Asian Economics*, Volume 18, Issue 4, Pages 595-612.

[XXIV] Refenes,A. Zapranis,A. & Francis, G. ,(1994) " Stock Performance Modeling Using Neural Networks(A Comparative Study With Regression Models)," *Neural Networks*, Volume 7, Issue 2, Pages 374-388.

[XXV] Ritanjali Majhi and Panda, (2007); Stock market prediction of S&P 500 and DJIA using bacterial foraging optimization technique. In 2007 *IEEE congress on evolutionary computation* (CEC 2007) (pp. 2569–2579).

[XXVI] Tan, T. Z., Quek, C., & Ng, G. S. (2005). Brain inspired genetic complimentary learning for stock market prediction. In *IEEE congress on evolutionary computation*, 2–5th September (Vol. 3, pp. 2653–2660).

[XXVII] Wang, Y. (2003). Mining stock prices using fuzzy rough set system, *Expert System with Applications*, Volume 24, Issue 1, Pages 13–23.

[XXVIII] Wang, Y. (2007); Nonlinear neural network forecasting model for stock index option price: Hybrid GJR GARCH approach, *Expert Systems with Applications*, Volume 36, Issue 1, Pages 564-570.

[XXIX] Widrow, B., Rumelhart, D., & Lehr, M. A., (1994). Neural networks: Applications in industry, business and science, *Communications of the ACM. New York, NY, USA*, Volume 37, Issue 3, Pages 93-105.

[XXX] Zhang, Y. & WU, L.,(2008); Stock market prediction of S&P 500 via combination of improved BCO approach and BP neural network, *Expert Systems with Applications*, Volume 36, Issue 5, Pages 8849-8854.

CHAPTER 2

A Structure Break Identification in Stock Market Data by Using Wavelet Transform

Sadam Al Wadi, Mohd Tahir Ismail, & Samsul Ariffin Abdul Karim

De School of Mathematical Sciences, Universiti Sains Malaysia, Fundamental and Applied Sciences Department, Universiti Teknologi Petronas, Bandar Seri Iskandar, Malaysia

Structure Break Identification in Stock Market Data by Using Wavelet Transform

Abstract

In recent years, many researchers have introduced various methodologies and theories to explain and analyze stock market data. However, the stock market is a very complex system. The complexity of the stock market increases the difficulty of testing any hypothesis relating to the market. For instance, the linear time series models are used for presenting stock market data rarely produce satisfactory results. In this study, the application of wavelet transform (WT) on identifying structure break for stock market data will be explored. In doing so, this study hopes to acquire a better understanding of the information adaptation process by focusing on using time scale analysis to study structure break behavior of stock market through decomposing stock market into a scale domain. Results indicate that WT manage to uncover structure breaks behavior in monthly Amman Stock Exchange (ASE) Index from 1998 until 2009. In addition, these structure breaks represent some of the economic and financial events that affecting ASE.

1. Introduction

According to Elfouly et al. (2008), the wavelet transform (WT) has been a popular and widely used methodology for the past twenty years. It has been used in various fields such as finance, mathematics, medicine and engineering. This method offers a systematic way to analyze time series starting from the time domain and into the scale (or frequency) domain. In addition, WT has several properties that can perform various functions. For instance, it is able to adapt itself to capture features across a large range of frequencies and hence can be used to extract components of time series such as trend, seasonality, business cycle and noise.

A structure break refers to changes with large magnitudes and is characterized by abrupt changes. In the stock market, structure break is an unexpected shift accrued in the stock market data (Gencay, 2002). However, in most time series applications the focus has always been on detecting small changes. Furthermore, observed measurements often contain information related to perturbations in the environment and the changes in the structure. The detection of structure break does not seem as clear as the expectations. Therefore, researchers have devoted a lot of attention to investigate approaches for the detection of structure breaks in practical applications (Eddie et al., 2010).

In the context of stock markets, structure breaks indicate important events and one of it is the introduction of financial innovations in a financial market whereby it will induce a structural break. In addition, in the context of stock price index, the restructuring of the composition of constituent shares in a market index will bring about a structural break. Then the implementation of new regulations will cause a structure break in both the supply of commodities and demand (Eddie et al., 2010). Therefore by studying and analyzing structural breaks will reveal significant and fundamental findings that will provide the necessary information to policy-makers to make relevant future plans.

Moreover, the detection of structure breaks in the stock market data is a key issue for investors to obtain insight into the data and to study the movements in the stocks purchased and sold during the past years. The information made available by the detection of the structure breaks will help investors to make the necessary decisions to protect their investments in the future. In this regard, Wavelet Transform (WT) and Fast Fourier Transform (FFT) will be used to determine which method is more effective to detect structure breaks in the stock market data from the Amman stock exchange (ASE). Applications of wavelet transform in stock market problem have been discussed in details by Karim et al. (2011).

The organization of this paper starts with introduction. Then the literature review is presented in Section 2. After that, the methodology is discussed extensively in Section 3. Later in Section 4 the data is described and follow by results on the jump point detection in Section 5. While in Section 6 some important events are identified in the corresponding to the jump points. Finally, the conclusion is presented in Section 7.

2. Literature review

2.1. Applications for Detecting Structure Breaks

In the literature, different approaches are suggested for the detection of structure breaks. Studies which discuss applications for financial time series observations are Laville and Teyssiere (2006), Strikholm (2006) and Hillebrand and Schnabl (2006). Laville and Teyssiere (2006) have revealed that some major changes which match events can be detected by applying mathematical methods to multivariate series of returns from real and artificial financial markets. While, Strikholm (2006) has determined the number of breaks in piecewise linear structural break models by studying the US index of real interest rate series by using a sequential method. Then Hillebrand and Schnabl (2006) have focused on the volatility of the Yen/Dollar exchange rate in order to test for a structural break in the effectiveness of Japanese foreign exchange intervention using GARCH method and change point detection. For more examples refer to Ip et al. (2004) and Ito (2003).

In addition, Lombard (1988) applied FFT in order to detect structure breaks. However, FFT suffered from many problems, for example, it loses the information about the location of a particular frequency. In the other words, the jumps are detected without a time domain. Thus, it is impossible to tell when a particular event took place. FFT constructs the data as a curve without considering the fluctuations very effectively in the data.

In order to overcome the disadvantages of FFT, Muller (1992) suggested boundary kernels in nonparametric approach to estimate the location of a structure break and its jump size. It is critical to choose the fit bandwidth while applying this method. This is crucial since the choice of a small bandwidth will lead to unclear change point locations, while the choice of a large bandwidth will not pick up change points with relatively small jump sizes. In this regard, it is pertinent to note that WT has some desirable properties that can be applied in structure break detections. For example, Ip et al. (2004) used WT to detect structure breaks in the daily exchange rate of the US dollar against the Deutsche Mark from 1989 to 1991, with convincing results in which all the points detected reflect political impacts and strong economic and financial influences. WT is very important method in the stock market area; therefore, the next subsection provides the definition of WT and FFT.

3. Methodology

This section will introduce Wavelet Transform (WT) and Fast Fourier Transform (FFT).

3.1. Wavelet Transform Functions

WT is used to divide time series observations into two series in the wavelet domain by creating low frequency sub series (approximation coefficients) using the scale function, and high-frequency sub series (detailed coefficients) using the wavelet function.

The approximation coefficients are obtained through a low-pass filter (L_oF-D) and produce a low frequency from the original signals and are associated with the scale function. It contains the main features and the most important information of the WT. The approximation coefficients are considered the key for WT's applications and it represents the trend. In most cases approximation coefficients should be around $N/2$ signals (Misiti, 2007).

The detailed coefficients are constructed from the difference between two successive approximations which represent the high frequency components via the high-pass filter (H_oF-D) (Aggrawal et al., 2008). In most cases, the detailed coefficients should also be around $N/2$, where N are the original signals. Basically, in the first level of the decomposition, the signals are divided into approximations and detailed coefficients. After that, the approximation coefficients themselves are divided into a second level of approximations and detailed coefficients and so on. This process continues until the required level of decomposition is achieved. Figure 1 shows the wavelet decomposition process until level two (Aggarwal et al., 2008):

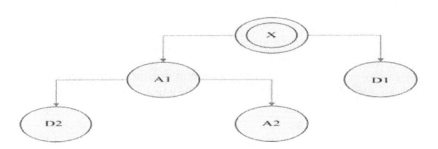

▶   *Figure 1.* **WT decomposition until level two.**

Figure 2 illustrates the decomposition process for two levels. The successive approximation series of X (original signals) is A_1 and the successive approximation series of A_1 is A_2 and so on. Basically, the range of A_1 is the highest and A_2 is the lowest among the approximation sub series and A_2 contains the most significant information. The details sub series D_2 consists of useful higher-frequency information and the information of the time localization of the sharp movements are contained in D_1. In any decomposition level, when the approximation coefficients are added to the details coefficients, signals can be reconstructed. The following equation illustrates the reconstruction, mathematically, until level two. (Aggarwal et al., 2008):

$$X = A_1 + D_1 = A_2 + D_2 + D_1.$$

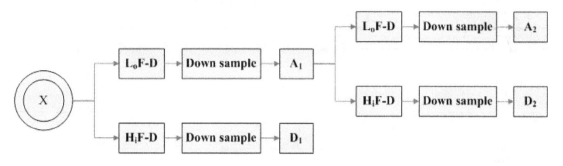

Figure 2. **The second scale signal decomposition.**

The decomposed signals can be reconstructed back to the original time domain signal without losing any information, a process known as inverse WT. Figure 3 illustrates the reconstruction (Yu et al., 2000).

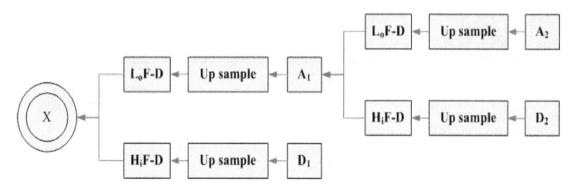

Figure 3. **The Reconstruction of the approximations and the details coefficients.**

WT uses a basic function which is called the mother wavelet. The mother wavelet can be obtained by dilation and translation processes. These processes are usually used to capture the features that are local in time and frequency. The dilation process allows the mother wavelet to cover different frequency ranges as the scaling parameter changes. The mother wavelet must satisfy some mathematical conditions (Gencay et al., 2002). As mentioned earlier, WT is disseminated into two types, continuous and discrete. The following sections describe these types.

In this paper we utilized Daubechies wavelet function (DWF) for structure break detection. This function having compact support or narrow window function is suitable for local analysis of the signal. These wavelet types are compactly supported. Moreover, DWF are widely used in statistics and finance application and represents a development and improvement of the Haar Wavelet Transform (Haar) in terms of frequency-domain characteristics and arbitrary regularity together with vanishing moments property. (Misiti et al., 2007). Indeed, DWF has advantages better than the other WT functions such as; Haar, Coiflet and Symelet. Therefore the following table provides a comparison between the most popular WT functions.

Table 1. Properties of Orthogonal WT

Property	Haar	Daubechies	Symelet	Coiflet
Arbitrary regular		✓	✓	✓
Orthogonal and compact support	✓	✓	✓	✓
Symmetry	Symmetric	Asymmetric	Near-Symmetric	Near-Symmetric
Existing of the scale function	✓	✓	✓	✓
Orthogonal analysis	✓	✓	✓	✓
Bio-orthogonal analysis	✓	✓	✓	✓
Continuous transformation	✓	✓	✓	✓
Discrete transformation	✓	✓	✓	✓
Exact reconstruction	✓	✓	✓	✓
Fast algorithm	✓	✓	✓	✓
Explicit expression	✓			

Mathematically DWT can be defined by the following function (Chiann and Moretin, 1998):

$$\psi_{j,k}(t) = 2^{\frac{j}{2}} \psi(2^j t - k), \; j, k \in Z; \; z = \{0, 1, 2, \ldots\}. \tag{1}$$

Where ψ is a real valued function having compactly supported, and $\int_{-\infty}^{\infty} \psi(t)dt = 0$. Generally, the WT were evaluated by using dilation equations, given as:

$$\phi(t) = \sqrt{2}\sum_k l_k \phi(2t - k), \tag{2}$$

$$\psi(t) = \sqrt{2}\sum_k h_k \phi(2t - k). \tag{3}$$

Father and mother wavelets were defined by the last two equations (2) and (3) where $\phi(t)$ represents the father wavelet, and $\psi(t)$ represents the mother wavelet. Father wavelet gives the high scale approximation components of the signal, while the mother wavelet shows the deviations from the approximation components. This is because the father wavelet generates the scaling coefficients and mother wavelet evaluates the differencing coefficients. Father wavelet defines the lower pass filter coefficients (h_k). High pass filters coefficients (l_k) are defined in Daubechies (1992) as:

$$l_k = \sqrt{2} \int_{-\infty}^{\infty} \phi(t)\phi(2t-k)dt, \qquad (4)$$

$$h_k = \sqrt{2} \int_{-\infty}^{\infty} \psi(t)\psi(2t-k)dt. \qquad (5)$$

There are no a specific formula for dWT. Usually, dWT is represented by the square gain function of their scaling filter; the square gain function is defined in Gencay et al. (2002) as:

$$g(f) = 2\cos^l(\pi f) \sum_{l=0}^{\frac{l}{2}-1} \binom{\frac{l}{2}-1+l}{l} \sin^{2l}(\pi f). \qquad (6)$$

Where l is positive number and represent the length of the filter. For more details and examples refer to Gencay et al. (2002), Motohiro (2008), Zbigniew (2001), Daubechies, (1992), Chiann and Moretin (1998) and Manchanda et al. (2007).

3.2 Fourier Transform

Fourier transform (FT) is an operation to transfer the set of complex valued function to other function; which is known as frequency domain. Consequently, the FT is similar the other operation in mathematics. We discuss one type of FT which is the Discrete Fourier Transform (DFT).Janacek and Swift (1993) have defined Discrete Fourier transforms (DFT) for discrete points N as:

$$X(K) = \sum_{n=0}^{N-1} X(n)W_n^{kn}. \qquad K = 0,1,...,N-1. \qquad (7)$$

Where $X(n)$ is the time series data, $W_n = e^{\frac{-j\pi 2}{N}}$. Moreover, the inverse discrete Fourier transform (IDFT) was defined by:

$$X(n) = \frac{1}{N} \sum_{k=0}^{N-1} X(k)W_N^{-kN}, \quad n = 0,1,...,N-1. \qquad (8)$$

Consequently, FFT and inverse Fast Fourier Transform (IFFT) directly depend on the DFT and IDFT respectively. FFT and IFFT are two algorithms which designed from the previous equations DFT and IDFT respectively. For more details and examples refer to Gencay (2002).

It is well known that, WT covers the limitations of FFT with respect to non-stationary time series data (Li, 2003; Gencay et al., 2002; Cascio, 2007). Table 2 illustrates all the similarities and dissimilarities between the two transforms:

Table.2. *Similarities and Dissimilarities between WT and FFT*

	FFT	WT
Speed	Fast algorithm	Fast algorithm
Data Stationarity	Suitable with stationary data only	Suitable with stationary and non-stationary data
Information Loss during decomposition	Some information loss	No information loss
Self-similar detecting	Not Applicable	Applicable
Localization	Localized in frequency only	Localized in time and frequency
Information Isolation	Some information is isolated during the decomposition	No information isolation
Function Basis	Based on sine and cosine functions	Based on the Mother and Father wavelet functions
Data Filtering	No filter inside the function.	Contains filters (wavelet filter and scale filter)
Volatility Localization	Cannot determine the local volatility	Can determine local volatility

Based on the Table 1, the FFT, WT will be used to analyze the stock market data in the case study in order to generate these dataset. The information from the dataset will provide a basis to argue that the WT is a more efficient application to use in analyzing ASE data than FFT and the structure break can be detected very well using WT. Therefore, the next section presents the dataset from ASE on. The review has revealed the importance of studying these transforms and comparing them in the context of the objectives of this study.

4. Data Set

The data under study are the monthly data from the ASE. The purpose of the experiment is to illustrate the effectiveness of WT in detecting structure breaks from December 1998 to July 2009. The monthly data is used because we believe that the structure breaks can be observed specifically across time if low frequency data is used. Figure 4 shows the distribution of the stock market data with 128 observations. It is noticeable that most of the structure breaks occur in the ASE after the observation number 60 (November 2003) since there are plenty of up-down movements in the data behavior.

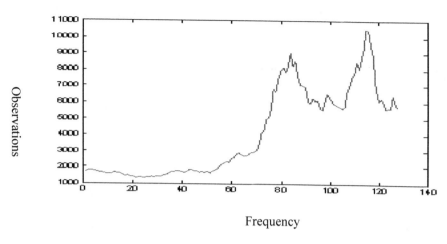

Frequency

Figure 4. **Monthly data from ASE**

5. Structure Break Identification

In this section, the detection of structure breaks using FFT and WT will be illustrated.

5.1. Identifying Structure Breaks by Using FFT

Figure 5 illustrates the periodogram or the plot of the estimation power spectrum versus frequency using FFT method. Based on this figure, it can be concluded that FFT suffers from many problems. Firstly it loses the information about the location of a particular event and as a result we cannot capture the structure break since it represents the data as a function of position. Secondly, the structure breaks are detected without consideration for the time domain. Thus, it is impossible to tell when a particular event took place. Thirdly, FFT constructs the data as a curve without considering the fluctuations very effectively in the data. This curve which is inherent on the x-axis can hardly capture the structure breaks and interpret the financial behavior. Consequently we can conclude that FFT has failed to detect the structure breaks in ASE in a comprehensive manner.

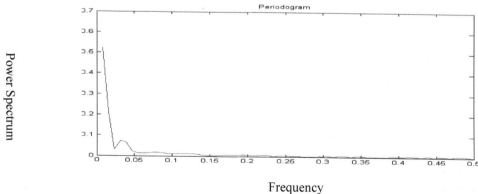

Frequency

Figure 5. **Power spectrum estimation (peridogram).**

Thus in order to obtain a comprehensive detection of the structure breaks in this case study, it is suggested that we apply WT to identify the structure breaks in the dataset.

5.2. Identifying Structure Breaks Using WT

It is clear that when compared to Figure 5, Figure 6 provides a more detailed and comprehension detection of the structure breaks and thus illustrates the superior ability of Daubechies wavelet transform (dWT) to detect structure breaks.

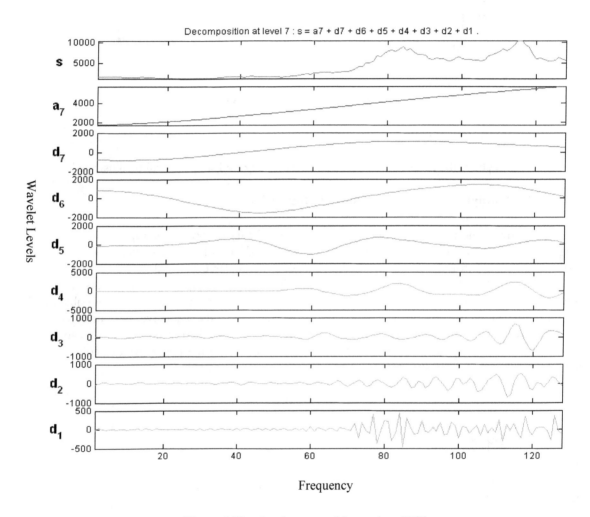

Figure 6. **Wavelet decomposition using dWT.**

Figure 6 represents the decomposition of the data until level 7 using dWT $(2^j = 128\ observations, j = 7$ levels). It shows the fluctuations in the ASE from 1998 to 2008. It is noticeable that the fluctuations can be detected clearly in d_1 which is the first level of the details coefficients. As the decomposition of the data moves from d_1 to d_7, it is clear that the monthly data becomes progressively smoother since the amount of data will be decreased automatically. And this process goes on until d_7 (level 7 in the details coefficients). The irregular values have been eliminated resulting in the smooth level obtained in d_7.

6. Result and Discussion

In the section the numerical comparison between FFT and WT via dWT will be discussed extensively. From Figure 6, it can be notice that the data exhibits structure breaks around observation numbers 60 (November 2003), 70 (September 2004), 80 (July 2005), 120 (November 2008), which are clearly shown in d_4. These structure breaks are caused by some significant events such as:

1- Political factors (Iraq war) which forced a lot of the investors to leave Iraq for the border countries (e.g. Jordan).

2- Government policies aimed to encourage economic growth.

3- An attractive investment climate in the Kingdom. In 2006 a lot of shares owned by non-Jordanians represented between (44.5% - 45.5%) of the ASE capitalization.

4- The increasing profitability of public shareholding companies.

5- Enhancing the qualitative technological infrastructure for the ASE.

6- Increasing investor confidence in the ASE which contributed to a better performance.

The effects of these events on the value of the shares purchases and shares sold will be presented later in Table 3.It is noticeable that there are many notations in the structure breaks when using WT. It can be seen that a structure break occurs after observation 40 (March 2002 refer to d_5 in Figure 6). Moreover, many structure breaks occur after the year 2004. This is because we can notice that there are very high fluctuations around this period. This high volatility period indicates the possibility of structural breaks occurring during this period and continuing until 2009.

In 2002 the Jordanian government has purposed new economic policies in order to enhance the investment climate in Jordan, encourage economic growth, enhance productivity of public shareholding companies, and enhance qualitative technological developments and investors' confidence in the ASE (Al-sharkas, 2004).The main reason why the ASE experienced a high level of fluctuations from 2004-2009 is because the number of non Jordanian investors increased (Al-sharkas, 2004). Generally, there are 10 reasons to attract non-Jordanian investors to invest in Jordan. They are its unique and strategic location, stable political environment, free market oriented economy, package incentives and exemptions to encourage investment, access to major international markets, free trade zones and industrial estates, qualified and competitive human resources, world class infrastructure and communications, attractive investment climate and high quality of life.

Therefore, precisely because of the measures taken by the Jordanian government as highlighted above, in the period from 2004 to 2006, the investments are unbalanced (sometimes positive and sometimes negative). Moreover, in February 2006 the investments become more balanced and continue until August 2006. However, in August 2006 the investments show a negative balance, but in September the non Jordanian investments have already increased and consequently, the investments fluctuate from time to time. This instability in the investments effect the ASE from 2002 to 2009 and this is clearly indicated in the decomposition of the dataset using dWT as illustrated in Figure 6 through the detection of structure breaks and high volatility. Table 3 below illustrates the incidences of high volatility and their causes in the ASE for the period of 2006 to 2009

Table 3. *Non-Jordanian investments in the ASE*

Year	Shares purchased to Non-Jordanians	Shares sold to Non-Jordanians
January-2006	JD157.6 million	JD198.2 million
February-2006	JD166 million	JD158.6 million
March-2006	JD218.2 million	JD135.1 million
April-2006	JD177.1 million	JD155.5 million
May-2006	JD278.4 million	JD254.3 million
June-2006	JD151.3 million	JD98.6 million
July-2006	JD162.7 million	JD160.1 million
Augest-2006	JD188.3 million	JD229.1 million
September-2006	JD154.2 million	JD114.0 million
October-2006	JD95.1 million	JD77.2 million
November-2006	JD96.3 million	JD98.3 million
December-2006	JD125.5 million	JD96.9 million
January-2007	JD134.8 million	JD117.3 million
February-2007	JD363 million	JD376.1 million
March-2007	JD255.1 million	JD65.6 million
April-2007	JD159.6 million	JD90.1 million
May-2007	JD208.5 million	JD129.5 million
June-2007	JD144.3 million	JD111 million
July-2007	JD505.9 million	JD480.3 million
Augest-2007	JD142.1 million	JD102.6 million
September-2007	JD262.5 million	JD252.4 million
October-2007	JD277.9 million	JD190.9 million
November-2007	JD198.9 million	JD172.4 million
December-2007	JD144.5 million	JD147.2 million
January-2008	JD195.3 million	JD178.9 million
February-2008	JD193.1 million	JD187.6 million
March-2008	JD262.4 million	JD259.9 million
April-2008	JD392.4 million	JD346.5 million
May-2008	JD344.0 million	JD304.2 million
June-2008	JD633.5 million	JD557.9 million
July-2008	JD836.9 million	JD788.4 million
Augest-2008	JD448.7 million	JD403.9 million
September-2008	JD357.8 million	JD327.1 million
October-2008	JD248.7 million	JD216.1 million
November-2008	JD184.4 million	JD256.0 million
December-2008	JD122.4 million	JD83.6 million
January-2009	JD163.1 million	JD158.1 million
February-2009	JD302.1 million	JD288.4 million
March-2009	JD304.2 million	JD298.0 million
April-2009	JD252.8 million	JD256.6 million
May-2009	JD295.7 million	JD255.4 million
June-2009	JD212.3 million	JD206 million
July-2009	JD94.7 million	JD121.3 million
Augest-2009	JD73.9 million	JD85.4 million

Where, JD: Jordanian Dinar

It should be noted that the data before 2006 is not available on the ASE website. Based on Table 3 the value of shares purchased and sold by Non-Jordanians in January 2006 totaled JD157.6 million. In March 2006 there was a significant increase, while in April 2006 there was a decrease. This is followed by an increase in May 2006. And from June 2006 to September 2006, it was stable and then in October 2006 the investments decreased by a significant amount. However, in February 2007 value of shares purchased by non-Jordanians increased significantly then decreased from March 2007 to May 2007. However, in June 2007 the value of shares purchased by non-Jordanians increased tremendously, which caused a structure break. In 2008 investments became unstable, especially from March 2008 to May 2008. Then in July 2008 investments started to increase significantly followed by a decrease until December 2008. Similarly, in 2009 there are periods of volatility, for example investments increased from July 2009 to September 2009 followed by a decrease in November 2009. Consequently, investment and specifically, non-Jordanian investment is the main variable which affected the ASE and we also notice that before 2004 investment is very low and there is a very small structure break or no structure breaks. For more details about investment in the ASE refer to AL-Shubiri (2010).

7. Conclusion

In this paper we have presented the analysis, results and discussion regarding the decomposition of the monthly stock market data of the ASE using two models, that is, FFT and WT via dWT. From the results of the decomposition of the datasets, it is apparent that firstly, WT (Figures 6) is a far better method to use compared to FFT (refer to Figure 5) in identifying the structure breaks in the ASE. Secondly, by using WT we are able to detect and identify the period of volatility from 2004 to 2009 as a time where significant structure breaks occur due to the instability in investments. Thirdly, the information made available by WT is very useful for investors in order to take care of their investments for the future. In this regard, the factors of future events are very important in the stock market field.

References

[I] Aggarwal, K. S., Saini, M. L. & Kumar A. (2008). Electricity Price Forecasting in Ontario Electricity Market Using Wavelet Transform in Artificial Neural Network Based Model. *International Journal of Control, Automation, and Systems*, 6, 639-650.

[II] Al-sharkas, A., (2004). The Dynamic Relationship between Macroeconomic Factors and the Jordanian Stock Market. *International Journal of Applied Econometrics and Quantitative Studies*, 1, 97-114.

[III] AL- Shubiri, F. N. (2010). Analysis the Determinants of Market Stock Price Movements: An Empirical Study of Jordanian Commercial Banks. *International Journal of Business and Management*, 5, 137-147.

[IV] Cascio, L. (2007). Wavelet Analysis and Denoising: New Tools for Economists. Department of economic. Working paper No. 600. ISSN 1473-0278.

[V] Chiann, C & Morettin P. (1997). A Wavelet Analysis for Time Series, *Journal of Nonparametric Statistics*, 10, 1 - 46.

[VI] Daubechies, I. (1992). *Ten Lectures on Wavelets*, SIAM and Philadelphia.

[VII] Eddie, C.M. Carisa, K.W. & Ip, W-C. (2010). Jump Point Detection For Real Estate Investment Success. *Physica A*, 389, 1055-1064.

[VIII] Elfouly H.F., Mahmoud I. M., Dessouky I. M. M., and Deyab S. (2008). Comparison between Haar and Daubechies Wavelet Transformations on FPGA Technology. *International Journal of Computer and Information Engineering*, 2, 37-42.

[IX] Gencay, R., Seluk F. & Whitcher, B. (2002). *An Introduction to Wavelets and Other Filtering Methods in Finance and Economics.* Academic Press, New York.

[X] Hillebrand, E. & Schnabl, G. (2006). A Structural Break in the Effects of Japanese Foreign Exchange Intervention On Yen/Dollar Exchange Rate Volatility, *Working paper Series*, No 650, European Central Bank.

[XI] Ip, W.C., Wong, H., Xie, Z. & Luan, Y. (2004). On Comparison of Jump Point Detection For An Exchange Rate Series. *Science in China Series A. Mathematics*, 47, 52-64.

[XII] Ito, T. (2003). Is Foreign Exchange Intervention Effective? The Japanese Experience in the 1990s, in: Paul Mizen (Ed.), Monetary History, Exchange Rates and Financial Markets. *Essay in Honour of Charles Good hart*, 2, 126-153.

[XIII] Janacek, G. And Swift, L. (1993). *Time Series Forecasting, Simulation and Applications.* Ellis Hoewood Limited. England.

[XIV] Karim, S.A.A, Karim, B.A., Ismail, M.T., Hasan, M.K and J. Sulaiman. Applications of Wavelet Method in Stock Exchange Problem. Journal of Applied Sciences, 11 (8): 1331-1335.

[XV] Lavielle, M. & Teyssière, G. (2006). Detection of Multiple Change-Points in Multivariate Time Series, *Lithuanian Mathematical Journal*, 46, 287-306.

[XVI] Li, D. (2003). *Empirical Study of Investment Behaviour in Equity Markets Using Wavelet Methods.* Ph.D theses. Rensselaer Polytechic Institute Troy, New York.

[XVII] Lombard, F. (1988). Detecting Change Points by Fourier Analysis, *Technometrics*, 30, 305-310.

[XVIII] Manchanda, P. Kumar, J. and Siddiqi, A.H. (2007). Mathematical Methods for Modeling Price Fluctuations of Financial Time Series. *Journal of Franklin Institute.* 344, 613-363.

[XIX] Misiti, M., Misiti, Y., Oppenhiem, G., & Poggi, J. (2007). *Wavelets and Their Applications.* Great Britain and united state. ISTE Ltd.

[XX] Motohiro, Y. (2008). Measure *Business* Cycle: A Wavelet Analysis of Economic Time Series. *Economics Letter*, 100, 208-212.

[XXI] Muller, H.G. (1992). Change-Points in Nonparametric Regression Analysis, *Annals of Statistics*, 20, 737-761.

[XXII] Strikholm, B. (2006). Determining the Number of Breaks in A Piecewise Linear Regression Model, Sse/Efi Working Paper Series in Economics and Finance, No. 648.

[XXIII] Yu, I. K., Kim, C. & Song, Y. H. (2000). A Novel Short-Term Load Forecasting Technique Using Wavelet Transform Analysis. *Electric Power Components and Systems*, 28, 537-549.

[XXIV] Zbigniew, R. (2001). Wavelet Methods in (Financial) Time Series Processing. *Physica A.* (296): 307-319

CHAPTER 3

Design of Cognitive Investor Making Decision for an Artificial Stock Market Simulation: A Behavior-based Approach

Lamjed Ben Said, Zahra Kodia, & Khaled Ghedira

De SOIE/ISG,41, Rue de la Liberte, Cite Bouchoucha
Le Bardo, 2000 Tunis, Tunisia

Design of Cognitive Investor Making Decision for an Artificial Stock Market Simulation: A Behavior-based Approach

Abstract

The stock market is considered as a dynamic and complex system which incorporates a large number of actors where everyone is trying to make benefits. Many approaches are used to describe and to understand the market dynamics. The purpose of this paper is to define a conceptual model representing the stock market in the micro level. This model is essentially based on cognitive behavior of the investors. In order to validate our model, we build an artificial stock market simulator based on agent-oriented methodologies. The proposed simulator includes the market supervisor agent who executes transactions via an order book, and various kinds of investor agents depending to their profile. The target of this simulation is to understand the influence of psychological character of an investor and the effects of his neighborhood on his decision-making and their impact on the market in terms of price fluctuations. Interactions between investors and information exchange during a transaction reproduce the market dynamics and organize the multi-agent based pricing. The resulting simulation system is a tool able to numerically simulate financial market operations in a realistic way. Simulation experiments are being performed to observe stylized facts of the financial times series and to show that the psychological attitudes have many consequences on the stock market dynamics. These experiments show that representing the micro level led us to observe emergent socio-economic phenomena at the macro level.

Keywords: Computational finance, Artificial intelligence, Multi-agent based simulation, Cognitive and behavioral modeling, Stock market.

1 Introduction

The complexity of financial market still represents a wide field of research and applications [20]. A large number of researches are undertaken in order to model the mechanism of pricing in the stock market and to better comprehend the investor behavior while taking decision. A study of the state of the art led us to observe an evolution of approaches used to describe and to understand the stock market dynamics. First, we distinguish numerical approach during the eighties such as [11] and [7]. Then, we notice in the nineties the use of multi-agent based approach to model and to simulate stock market dynamics (e.g., see [16], [1], [14], [15], [19] and [13]). Finally, we identify behavioral multi-agent based simulation during the recent years like [9]. To deal with the complexity of the stock market, we use the agent approach which offers the possibility to model and to study two granularity levels of the market: the micro and the macro level. At the micro level, it gives the opportunity to observe the individual behavior of each actor. At the macro level, the agent approach represents a powerful tool to observe the emergent results of interactive and cooperative systems. A Multi-Agent System (MAS) is a set of software or human agents that communicate and cooperate together to achieve a common objective [5]. The foundation for such system is the variety of types of interactions that constitute its

42

dynamics. Main advantages of the multi-agent oriented approach can be summarized into the following points: (1) considering individual behavior, (2) taking into account the actions and interactions, (3) studying the emergence of collective phenomena. This approach allows us to describe and to give for each entities the basic mechanisms to decide for itself when, how and why a particular action must be made [3].We introduce a novel model representing the stock market and essentially based on cognitive behavior of the investors. Our artificial stock market includes the market supervisor agent essentially responsible for executing transactions via an order book and a several kinds of investor agents depending to their profile. We take into account three pairs of behavioral attitudes.

In fact, investor decision making constitute a complex process which is based on cognitive and rational paradigm and biased by behavioral attitudes. Interactions between investors and information's exchange during a transaction reproduce the market dynamics and organize the multi-agent based pricing. This paper is structured as follows. The second section describes the cognitive and behavioral investor model. This model takes into consideration economic and financial concepts in the existing literature. In the third section, we define the multi agent based pricing performed by the market supervisor agent. We describe also interactions and relationships between the various actors and we explain information exchange during a transaction. In the fourth section, we present experiments undertaken through our simulator and we expose statistical results and the imitation attitude effects. Finally, in the fifth section, we conclude the paper and we summarize future works.

2 Cognitive and behavioral investor's model

We describe in this section the investor behavior while taking the decision of selling or buying. Our artificial stock market is composed of: (1) a set of investor agents corresponding to their behavioral profile, (2) a Market Supervisor agent responsible of conducting transactions and controlling the dynamics of the stock market.For the behavioral investor's model, we take into account three pairs of behavioral attitudes: (1) Pessimism / optimism, (2) Speculation /Caution and (3) Mimetism / Leadership. Each investor agent A_i is identified by an index i and is characterized by his *MarketExperience$_i$* which represents its experience degree. We consider two investor experience levels: 0 for novice investor agent which has low experience and 1 for expert and professional investor. The A_i behavioral profile, *Behavior$_i$*, is defined by three-dimensional vector (*OptimismV$_i$*, *SpeculationV$_i$*, *MimetismV$_i$*). Each component of this vector describes a behavioral attitude which can be either checked or reversed (represented respectively by +1 and -1). For example, A_j who has its *Behavior$_j$* $\equiv$ (+1, +1, +1) is an optimist speculator mimetic investor, whereas if its *Behavior$_j$* $\equiv$ (-1, -1, -1), this agent is pessimist, cautious and leader. We note that all possible combinations are taken into consideration in our model.

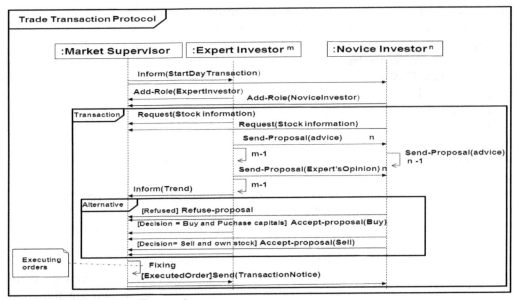

Fig. 1. Trade Transaction Protocol.

Figure 1 shows the Trade Transaction Protocol via an Agent UML sequence diagram. It specifies the sequence of messages that are exchanged along with their corresponding event occurrences on the actors' lifelines of our artificial stock market. This sequencing diagram represents the confrontation of supply and demand for stocks by novice and expert investors. This confrontation takes place so that each actor transacts under his own criteria via the Market Supervisor. The latter does not act as a centralized entity but as a meeting place used by investors to interact and realize stocks' exchanges. We use FIPA-ACL (Agent Communication Language) specifications to encode the messages' content. The first message is sent by the Market Supervisor and informs investors that the transaction day is open. The add-Role message announces the presence of investors. It determines also the role played by the sender: expert investor role or novice investor role. Expert investor and novice investor send a request message asking for stock information. Market Supervisor replies for each message by collecting the needed information. If an investor gives a buy order, he must own in advance the capital corresponding to the amount of his purchase. In opposition, if he gives a sell order, he must own in advance the corresponding stocks. We assume that the transactions may include one or more stocks. After taking decision, expert investor can either give advice or recommend a stock to other expert investors and novice investors through a Send-Proposal message. He communicates also the stock trend to the Market Supervisor via an inform message. The novice investor can also give advices to other investor playing novice investor role. Three choices are then possible for investors: (1) if the decision is to hold, investor refuses the proposal, (2) if the decision is to buy and the investor purchases stocks, he accepts buying and he sends a buy order via an Accept-Proposal message and (3) if the decision is to sell and the investor owns stocks, he accepts selling and he sends a sell order. We define a market order as a request to trade a specific quantity of a stock at any price. Every 30 seconds during a trading day, Market Supervisor executes the fixing by matching sell and buy orders and calculating the market price of the considered stock. Then, a notification (send message) is transmitted to the correspondent senders of executed orders.

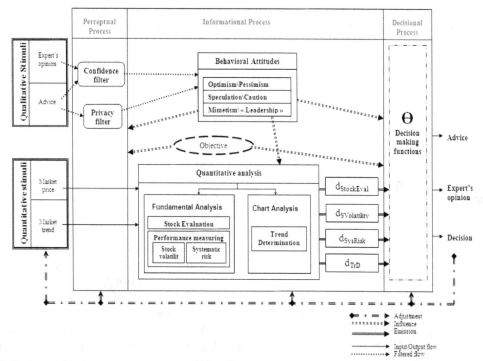

Fig.2. Cognitive behavioral investor's model and his interactions within the stock market.

Initially, every investor agent A_i disposes of a number of randomly S_0 stocks and a fixed determined *Wealth_i*, the liquidity that it owns to invest in stock market. Each step of simulation, based on quantitative and qualitative stimuli, the investor agent takes the decision of buying, selling or doing nothing and actualizes its *Portfolio_i* (the set of stocks that it disposes).

The cognitive and behavioral model that we propose is divided into three components. Figure 2 shows the links, the inputs and the outputs of these components.

2.1 Perceptual Process

The Perceptual Process (PPr) in our model represents the first step in making decision mechanism which guarantees the information mining and filtration. Investor agent receives various kinds of qualitative stimuli and quantitative stimuli. The stimuli affect the investor agent decisions of buying or selling. Their effects are weighted according to the investor agent behavioral profile described through the three pairs of behavioral attitudes considered in our model.

We assume that market trend and market price are determinant and basic parameters in investor making decision. These two elements, which constitute the quantitative stimuli, are neither affected by the investor profile nor by the perceptual process. Consequently, they are transmitted directly to the informational process.In addition, investor can give and receive advice or opinion of its neighbors. We take into consideration two qualitative stimuli. The agent takes into account the received message on condition it is filtered through the privacy filter and / or the confidence filter.

Confidence Filter receives as input qualitative stimuli: expert's opinions and advices. Expert's opinion is a message transmitted by agent having *MarketExperience_i* equals to 1 and defines the recommendation to buy or to sell a specific stock. Whereas, advice represents a stock judgment transmitted by any investor agent to its acquaintance. Every qualitative stimulus until circulating in the market has a degree of conviction named *CDegree*. The qualitative information is taken into consideration whenever a confidence threshold is reached. The confidence threshold called *Th_ConfidenceSensibility*$_i$ is depending of the investor behavioral profile (*BP*$_i$) and is calculated as bellow:

$$Th\_ConfidenceSensibility_i = \frac{1}{\exp(\frac{BP_i}{3})}$$

with $BP_i = OptimismV_i + SpeculationV_i + MimetismV_i$.

If the confidence degree of a message (*CDegree*) is lower than the confidence threshold (*Th_ConfidenceSensibility*$_i$), this message is taken into account. Otherwise, the receiver refuses the message and ignores it. The purpose of the *Privacy Filter* consists in considering the sender of the message instead of its content. Investors are influenced by their observation of the choice of other without knowing if it can be benefic or not. In our model, advices can be considered although they are not confident. We use a dynamic network of trusted neighbors of the agent A_i, the *CNeighborNet*$_i$. This network is inspired from the six degrees of separation concept [17] and is applied to the field of stock market neighborhood. If the transmitter of an advice does not belong to this network, the message will be filtered (not considered). We assume that the cardinal of *CNeighborNet*$_i$ is less than or equal to six investors for novices (agents having *MarketExperience*$_i$ equals 0) and it does not exceed two for experts (agents having *MarketExperience*$_i$ equals 1). At the beginning of the simulation, the *CNeighborNet*$_i$ is randomly chosen. Every step of simulation, A_i updates its *CNeighborNet* with deleting the transmitter of a "wrong" advice which provides deficit and replacing it by a randomly chosen agent. On the privacy filter, if the sender of the message is part of trust network of the receiver, the message is accepted. Otherwise, the message is refused.

As shown in Figure 2, the PPr is influenced by the investor behavioral attitudes. In fact, the optimistic investor agent, which has a confidence in the outcome, does not react the same way as the pessimistic investor agent. We assume that a speculator investor presents a lower *Th_Confidence Sensibility*$_i$ than a cautious investor who checks up a large number of messages received. Besides, an imitator investor agent reproduces unconsciously the reaction of its entourage of investors. It follows and is aligned with the overall trend of the market. Whereas, the leader holds the dominant market position and take initiatives to buy or sell stocks. Subsequently, the imitator PPr is more extended for the leader one. Indeed, the number of persons composing *CNeighborNet*$_i$ of an imitator investor is larger compared to the leader who has confidence in a few number of investors.

2.2 Informational Process

Informational Process (IPr) treats qualitative and quantitative stimuli filtered by the perceptual process. Investor agent ought to buy stocks which are deemed undervalued. It might sell the stocks which are considered overvalued. We consider in our model three analyses related to fundamental analysis and chart analysis: (1) stock evaluation, (2) performance measuring and (3) Trend determination. Each kind of analysis provides signals to buy or to sell the stock considered.

We assume that the investor A_i aims a single objective during a trading day named *Objective*$_i$. The objectives taken into account by our model are the security of the capital, profitability and speculating and finally liquidity and availability. The objective influences all processes of the model and determines the schedule for the investor, *Periodicity*$_i$. The latter represents the period during which it remains inactive on our artificial stock market but listening to its environment. This period ranges from 1 to 20 steps. If the investor aims to secure its capital, its frequency is relatively large compared to those who seek opportunities to capitalize on speculating. While the schedule for the investor who opts for liquidity and availability is regular.

The first analysis, *Stock Evaluation*, is based on the constant-growth model (known as Gordon Shapiro model). This model only requires data from one period and a growth rate estimated by an investor [18]. In order to evaluate one stock, the model purposes the formula [12]:

$$P_{SEval} = \frac{Div}{K - g_i}$$

where Div is the expected dividend of the next period, K is the discount rate and g_i is the growth rate. To determine the growth rate of dividends, we base our model on two parameters: (1) the growth rate for future dividends named g_i and (2) the discount rate K. We enrich the Gordon Shapiro model to take into account non-constant growth of dividends. Indeed, dividends growth is often non-linear. It is high at the beginning of the period but it tends to slow down thereafter. We propose in this case to divide the period into several sub-periods with constant growth rates for each sub-period. We define a high growth rate initially and a lower one in the following sub-periods. This idea enables us to apply the Gordon Shapiro model for each sub period. Once active, each investor calculates its growth rate at the step of simulation after its *Periodicity$_i$* using the following formula:

$$g_i = \frac{1}{\ln(step * (1 + \eta))}$$

with η : randomly chosen parameter.

The discount rate depends on investor behavioral profile and more specifically on the speculation/caution attitude. If the agent is speculator, it accepts risks to maximize its benefit and chooses an important rate which range from 0.3 to 0.8. However, the cautious investor agent chose a rate situated between 0.1 and 0.3.

After calculating P_{SEval}, the agent compares it with the actual stock price in the market named P_{SMar}. The latter is provided by the Market Supervisor agent. The signal provided by this analysis is calculated as bellow.

$$d_{StockEval} = \begin{cases} +1 \text{ if } P_{SEval} \succeq P_{SMar} \\ -1 \text{ otherwise.} \end{cases}$$

The second analysis, *Performance Measuring*, is based on calculating stock volatility and systematic risk. This analysis provides two signal namely $d_{SVolatility}$ and $d_{SysRisk}$. The overall risk of a stock is determined by the magnitude of the fluctuations related to this stock as measured by

volatility. Higher is the volatility, are higher the risk and the benefit. We estimate volatility at the step t by the following formula:

$$V_t = \frac{\max P_{SMar} - \min P_{SMar}}{\frac{\max P_{SMar} + \min P_{SMar}}{2}}$$

When deciding whether or not to buy a given stock, investor agent ought to be made aware of the amount of volatility risk currently associated with the investment. The speculator investor agent decides to buy a stock even if it presents a high rate of risk, something unacceptable by the cautious investor agent.

In addition, we used the notion of systematic risk which is defined by a given coefficient β. This coefficient indicates how the expected return of a stock or portfolio is correlated to the return of the financial market as a whole. It is calculated by the Market Supervisor agent. A β of less than 1 means that the stock is less volatile than the market. A β of greater than 1 indicates that the security's price is more volatile than the market.

The third analysis consists on the *Trend Determination*. The trend of our artificial stock market is determined and diffused by the Market Supervisor agent. It represents the average trends calculated by all expert investors having *MarketExperience$_i$* equals to 1 (which marks expert investors). If the trend is upward, it implies that the stock value should continue to rise. The market presents an *uptrend*. If investors perceive that the following value outside the market price, they notice a sign of rising.Otherwise, it announced a reversal of trend *downtrend* and causes a signal to sell. In our model, we are guided by the Points and Figure Charting known as PFC [4]. The latter is a simplistic method which represents the changes of the stock price without taking into consideration the passage of time. The aim of this method is to determine the best time to buy and sell stocks. This method is sensitive to the determination of two parameters namely the "box" (also named square) and the threshold inversion. The box is unit price determining the minimum change of stock price to draw a symbol (cross or round) on the vertical axis. More the box six is lower, more the graph will be sensitive. The higher box size filters more minimal changes of the stock price. In fact, this variation is measured in terms of boxes, thus setting the box which will directly affect signal of buy or sell (Figure 3(c)).

PFC is based on the following principles:
- The crosses are used to represent the movement of higher prices.
- The rounds are used to mark the movements of decline.
- No significance is attached to the element of time.
- No importance is given to small changes in the way.
- It requires that the market price changes with a significant amount determined in advance so that it is represented on the graph.

When the price goes below the support line (the higher line in Figure 3.(a)), the trend is downward. In this case, the market presents a downtrend. If the price goes above the resistance line (the lower line in Figure 3.(a)), the investor admits a signal that announces the purchase of market downturn. Indeed, the volume of transactions increases when a value announces a turnaround. This turnaround is even deep than the volumes are higher.

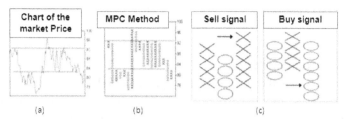

Fig. 3. The chart analysis. (a) Chart of the market price. (b) MPC Method. (c) Sell and Buy signal done by PFC.

The parameters taken into account in PFC method are also influenced by the speculation/caution attitude. Cautious investor agent proceeds with prudence and prefers to take every detail into account before buying or selling. Thus, it chooses a box with a small size contrary to speculator who chooses a box with a large size.

2.3 Decisional Process

The *Decisional Process* (DPr) represents the ultimate component of decision making mechanism. The DPr aim is to provide a final decision based on the IPr outputs. In fact, investor agents' decision making takes place after the four tests relative to: stock evaluation, stock volatility, systematic risk and trend determination. Each test gives out a signal to buy, sell or do nothing. The final decisional signal D is calculated as follows:

$$D = \alpha * d_{StockEval} + \lambda * d_{SVolatility} + \gamma * d_{SysRisk} + \delta * d_{TrD}$$

We notice that the parameters α, λ, γ and δ are generated randomly under the condition that their sum is equal to 1. Therefore, D ranges from -1 (which indicates buying) to +1 (which indicates selling) and just represents a signal. We note that D will be transformed to an order expect if $|D| >$ Th_RunTr_i. Th_RunTr_i defines a threshold for which the agent A_i runs a transaction following its decision-making. We assume that the Th_RunTr_i related to the cautious investor is lower than the one considered by the speculator investor. D can also be diffused as a qualitative stimulus with $CDegree_{Msg}$ (confidence degree) equals to decisional parameter moderator related to trend determination, δ. The latter is chosen due to the fact that the chart analysis is the most reliable method for trading in stock market.

3 Multi-agent based pricing

3.1 Artificial stock market dynamics

We assume that the stock market is represented by a social network where information circulates randomly among heterogeneous set of investors. Investors are influenced by their observations of the choices of others. The stronger the social signal, the more they are influenced. Information concerning stocks is available permanently for all investors. Their interactions form the stock price. We neglect the external factors as financial crushes due to crisis, wars and climatic disasters. In addition, we admit that the buying and selling are accomplished immediately and closed out the same day. More explicitly, if an investor gives a purchase order, he must own in advance the capital corresponding to the amount of his purchase. In opposition, if he gives a sell order, he must own in advance the corresponding stocks.We assume that the transactions may include one or more stocks.

The investor agent is accepted in the market if and only if it verifies the following conditions during the simulation:

- The agent has a wealth not null.
- The agent leaves the market if he loses its liquidity and does no more stocks in its portfolio.
- The agent can issue an order to buy only if its liquidity has corresponding to the total amount, so it can issue an order to sell a number of shares only if he has in the corresponding quantity of stocks in its portfolio.

3.2 Market Supervisor Agent

Market Supervisor agent plays a crucial role in stock market. It offers the following actions: (1) launching of the stock market transactions, (2) publication of information related to stocks for investors, (3) matching orders of sale and purchase and execution of transactions via the fixing, (4) updating stock information and (5) calculating the market trend. We present the Fixing Order algorithm that is the basis of operation of the stock market. This algorithm implements the principles of orders execution. It seeks to determine a market price that allows the greatest number of transactions (lines 13-16). It is used to determine a price called fixing by comparing sorted buy and sell orders book (lines 10-11-13). The fixing must meet a number of rules to ensure equality between all Investor agents and transparency in the artificial market.

1. **FIXING Algorithm**
2. Input
3. S: the list of stocks considered in our market
4. BOBook: the list of Buy Orders related to each stock (two-dimensional array)
5. SOBook: the list of Sell Orders related to each stock (two-dimensional array)
6. Output
7. Transactions: the list of buy and sell executed orders
8. ExecutionMessage: ACL message that indicates that the order is executed
9. Begin
10.   For each Stock S of the stock market Do
11.   Sort(BOBook[S], 'ascendant');
12.   Sort(SOBook, 'descendant');
13.   While(NotEmpty(SOBook) AND NotEmpty(BOBook)) Do
14.   If First(BOBook[S]).Price<Last(SOBook[S]).Price) Then
15.   Send(ExecutionMessage, BOBook[S].sender);
16.   Send(ExecutionMessage, SOBook[S].sender);
17.   RunTr(First(BOBook[S]), Last(SOBook[S]));
18.   Else
19.   Delete(First(BOBook[S]));
20.   End If
21.   End While
22.   End for
23.   End

4 Experiments

Figure 4 represents our simulator which is composed of: (1) Simulator graphics for observing stock market dynamics, (2) Stocks' attractivity map: Stock exchange map and (3) Control and launching parameters. Our simulator is implemented using the MadKit platform [8] using java programming language.

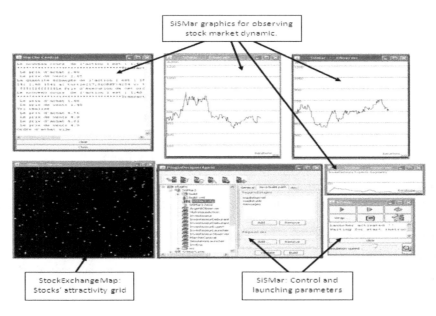

Fig. 4. Artificial stock market simulator and control tools.

The fact that Madkit has a specific environment modeling with an organizational architecture rather than specific agent architecture or a specific model of interaction, responds well to our needs in modeling which is based on an organizational structure for investors. The implementation of interaction with messages allows great flexibility in the content of interactions, whether transfer of states between investors in the stock market (beginning of a trading day) or processes of passive observation (advice to buy or sell) or consultation (Stock price).

4.1 Statistical results

In this section, we present some statistical results which show that many facts of real stock markets are reproduced with our model.

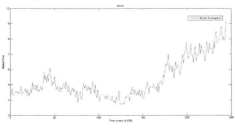

Fig. 5. Market price volatility.

Initially, we introduce in our artificial market a stock with an initial price equals to 2.20 units. This stock presents an upward trend on the market and has β indicator (systematic risk) equals to 0.6. Figure 5 shows the market price volatility under our artificial market. We notice that the upward movements are longer than those of downward. This reflects a resistance to downtrend pressure on the bull market.

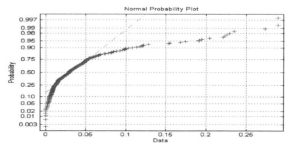

Fig. 6. Normal probability plot of logarithmic return.

In Figure 6, we present a normal probability plot of price return. We are typically concerned about whether the price return is distributed according to a normal distribution, since many of the statistical inference procedures that we use require the assumption of normality of the returns. For comparing, the solid line represents the cumulative distribution of the standard normal distribution $N(0,1)$. The price returns are plotted against a theoretical normal distribution. We remark that the points form an approximate straight line at the beginning. Departures from this straight line indicate departures from normality.

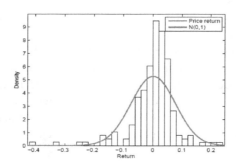

Fig. 7. Fat tails (Leptokurtosis) of the distribution of returns.

Price returns exhibit fatter tails than the standard normal, or Gaussian, distribution and presents a kurtosis equals to 5.52. A remarkable Leptokurtosis behavior can be seen in Figure 7. This figure presents the price returns distribution compared to a theoretical normal distribution having the same mean and variance.Furthermore, financial time series usually exhibit a characteristic known as volatility clustering, in which large changes tend to follow large changes, and small changes tend to follow small changes. In fact, large shocks of either sign are allowed to persist, and can influence the volatility forecasts for several periods.

Said, Kodia, & Ghedira

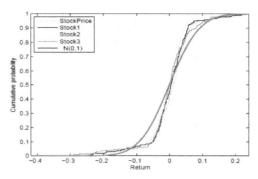

Fig. 8. Cumulative distribution functions of Returns.

Volatility clustering, or persistence, suggests a model where successive perturbations, although uncorrelated, are nonetheless serially dependent. Figure 8 plots the cumulative distribution function (CDF) of the four stocks return and shows a comparison between normal distribution and the CDF of returns of stocks. We observe a crossover to the normal distribution which happens for empirical financial data.

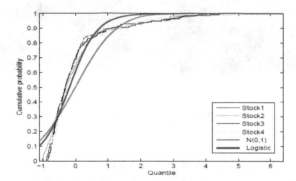

Fig. 9. Normal probability plot of the absolute value of logarithmic return.

A normal probability plot represents useful tool for assessing of data. Many statistical approaches make the hypothesis that the underlying distribution of the data is normal, so this plot can provide some assurance that the hypothesis of normality is not being violated, or provide an early warning of a problem with your assumptions. We could notice that on Figure 9 there is clear evidence that the underlying distribution is not normal. Hence, our behavioral model is able to reproduce stylized facts observed in real stock market and to assure no predictability of future price developments and an efficient price formation.

4.2 Imitation attitude effects

This experiment studies the effect of market leader and its influence on its neighbor and the variation of the stock value. During this experiment, we consider four stocks. To observe this behavioral attitude, we have designed and developed a graphical tool to see the attractiveness of each agent and detect the behavior of investors respond to fluctuations in market prices (StockExchangeMap). On this grid, each stock is represented in a corner by a blue dot. Expert investor agents having *MarketExperience* equals to 1 are drawn by red dots while novice investor having *MarketExperience*

53

equals to 0 are drawn by green dots. The coordinates of an investor are calculated that the position $P(x, y)_i$ is the barycenter of the four points representing the stocks considering the weight as the amount of each stock owned in *Portfolio$_i$*.

We begin to observe a population of 20 expert investor agents and 180 novice investor agents (Figure 10). We suppose that the size of the *CNeighborNet$_i$* is 2 for expert and 6 for novice investors. we observe after 55825 steps of simulation (which is approximately 50 days) that experts take advantage of the market towards the most volatile and most efficient stocks (trends visible by encircled areas) while novices can not follow the trend of the market. The advice exchanged between novices skew market behavior.

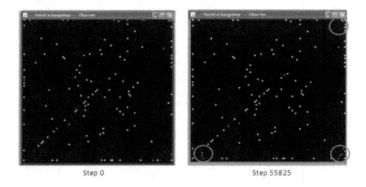

Step 0   Step 55825

Fig. 10. The behavior of investors with a population of 20 expert investor agents and 180 novice investor agents.

By increasing the number of expert investor agents to 40 and keeping the same number of novice investor agents, we observe the change of the investors' behavior. We note the disappearance of many expert investor agents (red dots) and novice investor agents (green dots) perceived through the area surrounded after 55605 simulation steps.

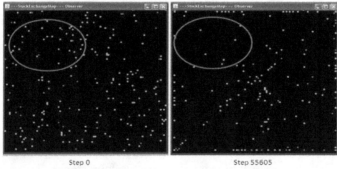

Step 0   Step 55605

Fig. 11. The behavior of investors with a population of 40 expert investor agents and 180 novice investor agents.

We note that novice investor agents follow the behavior of expert agents and are trying to sell the stock represented in the map by the upper left corner (Figure 11).What we are emphasizing here is that it is possible to reproduce realistic market evolutions through our behavioral cognitive model.

5 Conclusion and future works

This paper proposes a simulation model for artificial stock market. The objective is to use multi-agent system in order to check the influence of psychological character of an investor on his decision making process. The architecture proposed for the multi-agent system is based on the perceive-reason-act model, but with the addition of behavioral attitudes. Our contribution is to consider the stock market as a social organization of autonomous actors with dependents heterogeneous beliefs and different behavioral attitudes. Different perspectives can be considered in our work. The first is to refine the model and enrich its implementation with including new cognitive concepts. Learning techniques and fuzzy logic can be used respectively to explore the memory effect and the uncertainty at various levels in the stock market. More specifically, the decisional process of our model can be described by the representation based on reinforcement learning via a markovian decision process. Whereas, the perceptual process may include components which are based on fuzzy sets such as threshold triggers and inhibitor sets.

References

[I] Arifovic J.,1996. The behavior of the exchange rate in the genetic algorithm and experimental economies,Journal of Political Economy, vol 104, p.510-541.

[II] BenSaid L. and T. Bouron, 2001. Multi-agent simulation of virtual consumer populations in a competitive market. Seventh Scandinavian Conference on Artificial Intelligence: SCAI'01, Frontiers in Artificial Intelligence and Applications : edition IOS Press, Odense, Denmark, p. 31-43.

[III] Dessalles J. and al, 2007. Emergence in multi-agent systems: conceptual and methodological issues. Agent-based modelling and simulation in the social and human sciences, Oxford: The Bardwell Press, p. 327-355.

[IV] Dorsey T., 2007. Point & figure charting: The essential application for forecasting and tracking market prices, Wiley Trading, 3rd Edition.

[V] Ferber J., 1995. Les systmes multi-agents, vers une intelligence collective, InterEditions.

[VI] Gode D. and Sunder S., 1993. Allocative efficiency of markets with zero intelligence traders. Journal Of Political Economy, p. 119-137.

[VII] Grossman S. and Stiglitz J., 1980. On the impossibility of informationally efficient markets, American Economic Review, vol. 70, p. 393-408.

[VIII] Gutknecht O. and Ferber J., 2000. The madkit agent platform architecture, Agents Workshop on Infrastructure for Multi-Agent Systems, p. 48-55.

[IX] Hoffmann A. and al., 2007. Social simulation of stock markets: Taking it to the next Level, Journal of Artificial Societies and Social Simulation, 10(2), p. 7.

[X] Jennings, Nicholas R. An Agent-Based Approach for building Complex Software Systems, Communications of the ACM, 44(4), 35-41, April 2001.

[XI] Karaken J. and Wallace N., 1981. On the indeterminacy of equilibrium exchange rates, Quarterly journal of economics, vol. 96, p. 207-222.

[XII] Lally M., 1988. The gordon-shapiro dividend growth formula and inflation. Accounting & Finance, 28(2), p. 45-51.

[XIII] LeBaron B., 2000. Agent-based computational finance: suggested readings and early research, Journal of Economic Dynamics and Control, vol. 24, p. 679-702.

[XIV] Lettau M., 1997. Explaining the facts with adaptive agents: the case of mutual fund flows,Journal of Economic Dynamics and Control, vol. 21, p.1117-1148.

[XV] Lux T. and Marchesi M., 1998. Volatility clustering in financial markets : A microsimulation of interactive agents,Third Workshop on Economics and Interacting Agents, Ancona.

[XVI] Margarita S. and Beltratti A., 1993. Stock prices and volume in an artificial adaptive stock market,International Work-Conference on Artificial Neural Networks (IWANN'93), p. 714-719.

[XVII] Milgram S., 1967. The small world problem. Psychology Today, vol. 1.

[XVIII] Peyrard J., 2001. La Bourse. Edition Vuibert, collection Entreprise, 9th edition.

[XIX] Routledge B., 1994. Artificial selection: genetic algorithms and learning in a rational expectations model. Technical Rapport, GSIA, Carnegie Mellon, Pittsburgh, Pennsylvania.

[XX] Arthur W.B., Durlauf S.N., Lane D.A.: The Economy as an Evolving Complex System II. Santa Fe Institute, Addison-Wesley, Volume 27, p.15-44 (1997)

CHAPTER 4

Fuzzy Model for Analysis and Forecasting of Financial Stability

G. C. Imanov

Institute of Cybernetics, NASA

Fuzzy Model for Analysis and Forecasting of Financial Stability

Abstract

The current paper proposes a fuzzy approach for evaluation of composite financial stability index, and fuzzy Markov model for analysis and forecast of financial situation. The methods are demonstrated through application of factual and estimated financial and macroeconomic information of the Azerbaijan Republic.

Keywords: fuzzy logic inference, fuzzy Markov model, financial stability index.

1. Introduction

Analysis and forecasting of financial situation are very important issues for the governments for ensure sustainable socioeconomic development of the state. Today the problem of financial stability of the state is a global problem. Starting from the beginning of the 90s of the XX century scientists constructed some early warning systems, among which we can underline the works of G. Kaminsky, C. Reinhart "The Twin Crisis: The Causes of Banking and Balance of Payments Problem" [1], M. Goldstein, G. Kaminsky, C. Reinhart "Assessing Financial Vulnerability" [2], D. Reagle, D. Salvatore "Forecasting Financial Crisis in Emerging Market Economies" [3]. In the paper [1] the links between banking and currency crisis, the macroeconomic background of the crisis, anatomy of crisis and its indicators are analyzed [2]. Book [2] presents a comprehensive battery of empirical tests on the performance of alternative early warning indicators for the emerging-market economies that should prove useful in the construction of a more effective global warning system. Not only are the authors able to draw conclusions about which specific indicators have sent the most reliable early warning signals of currency and banking crisis in emerging economies, they can also test the out-of-sample performance of the model during the Asian crisis and find that it does a good job of identifying the most vulnerable economies. In addition, they show how the early warning system can be used to construct a "composite" crisis indicator to weigh the importance of alternative channels of cross-country "contagion" of crisis, and to generate information on the recovery path from crisis. In the paper [3] annual data for six financial indicators was gathered and compared with the critical levels found. In these works statistical and probabilistic models were used for evaluation of composite financial stability index. However, as can be seen from these investigations all indicators, which are analyzed in these works are fuzzy. In this paper we try to construct a fuzzy model for forecasting the index of the financial stability in Azerbaijan. To solve this problem, we mainly used information of IMF, WB, Journal of Institutional Investor, data provided by the Central Bank of Azerbaijan.

The process of modeling incorporates three stages:
- Selection of indicators and information processing;
- Assessment of composite financial stability index;
- Forecasting of the level of financial state.

2. Information processing and evaluation of the composite financial stability index

For fuzzy modelling of the financial crisis we used indicators and threshold, which are proposed in [1]. They are noted in Table 1. Indicators of Table 1 enable one to define terms, such as *stable, threshold, crisis*, as well as intervals of the linguistic variable "financial state" for the country, which is illustrated in Table 2. In Table 1 for variables such as international reserves, exports, terms of trade, deviations of the real exchange rate from the trend, commercial bank deposits, output and the stock market index, credit rating for which a decline in the indicator increases the probability of crisis, the threshold is below the mean value of the indicators. Terms values were used as percentile of distribution, which was equal to the arithmetic mean of the values available from other studies [1], [2].

Table 1. Indicators of the Early Warning System of the Financial Crisis

Optimal thresholds (percentile):

			Banking crisis	Currency crisis
1	M2 multiplier;	- MMV	89	90
2	Domestic credit / nominal GDP;	- DOC	88	90
3	Real interest rate on deposits;	- RIR	88	80
4	Ratio of lending rate to deposit rate	- LED	88	87
5	Excess real M1 balance	- EMB	89	88
6	M2 (in US dollars) / reserves (in US dollars)	- MRE	90	90
7	Bank deposits	- CBD	15	20
8	Exports (in US dollars)	- EXP	10	10
9	Imports (in US dollars)	- IMP	90	80
10	Credit rating	- CRA	11	11
11	Terms of trade	- TRA	10	19
12	Real exchange rate	- PRE	10	10
13	Reserves	- INR	10	20
14	Domestic-foreign interest rate differential on deposits	-IRD	89	81
15	Output	- OUT	10	14
16	Stock prices (in US dollars)	- SMI	15	10
17	Overall budget balance / GDP	- BUD	10	14
18	Current account balance a share of GDP	- CAB	20	14
19	Current account balance a share of investment	- CAI	15	10
20	Short-term capital inflows	- SCI	85	89
21	Foreign direct investment (FDI)	- FDI	16	12

22	General government consumption / GDP	- GGC	90	88
23	Central bank credit to the public sector / GDP	- CBC	90	90
24	Net credit to the public sector / GDP	- NCR	88	80

Table 2. Terms of linguistic variables of the financial state and its intervals (percentile)

No	Indicators	Stable			Threshold			Crisis		
1	INR	100.00	57.50	15.00	20.00	15.00	10.00	15.00	8.00	1.00
2	EXP	100.00	55.00	10.00	12.50	10.00	7.50	10.00	5.50	1.00
3	TRA	100.00	57.25	14.50	19.00	14.50	10.00	14.50	7.75	1.00
4	DRE	100.00	55.00	10.00	12.50	10.00	7.50	10.00	5.50	1.00
5	CBD	100.00	58.75	17.50	20.00	17.50	15.00	17.50	9.25	1.00
6	OUT	100.00	56.00	12.00	14.00	12.00	10.00	12.00	6.50	1.00
7	SMI	100.00	56.25	12.50	15.00	12.50	10.00	12.50	6.75	1.00
8	CBC	1.00	45.50	90.00	87.50	90.00	92.50	90.00	95.00	100.00
9	CRA	100.00	55.50	11.00	8.50	11.00	13.50	11.00	6.00	1.00
10	CAB	1.00	9.00	17.00	14.00	17.00	20.00	17.00	58.50	100.00
11	CAI	1.00	6.75	12.50	10.00	12.50	15.00	12.50	56.25	100.00
12	DOC	1.00	45.00	89.00	88.00	89.00	90.00	89.00	94.50	100.00
13	IRD	1.00	43.00	85.00	81.00	85.00	89.00	85.00	92.50	100.00
14	EMB	1.00	44.75	88.50	88.00	88.50	89.00	88.50	94.25	100.00
15	FDI	1.00	7.50	14.00	12.00	14.00	16.00	14.00	57.00	100.00
16	GGC	1.00	45.00	89.00	88.00	89.00	90.00	89.00	94.50	100.00
17	IMP	1.00	43.00	85.00	80.00	85.00	90.00	85.00	92.50	100.00
18	LED	1.00	44.25	87.50	87.00	87.50	88.00	87.50	93.75	100.00
19	MMV	1.00	45.25	89.50	89.00	89.50	90.00	89.50	94.75	100.00
20	MRE	1.00	45.50	90.00	87.50	90.00	92.50	90.00	95.00	100.00
21	NCR	1.00	42.50	84.00	80.00	84.00	88.00	84.00	92.00	100.00
22	BUD	1.00	6.50	12.00	10.00	12.00	14.00	12.00	56.00	100.00
23	RIR	1.00	42.50	84.00	80.00	84.00	88.00	84.00	92.00	100.00
24	SCI	1.00	44.00	87.00	85.00	87.00	89.00	87.00	93.50	100.00

Table 3. Azerbaijan financial and macroeconomic indicators for 2007.09-2008.08

	1	2	3	4	5	6	7	8	9	10	11	12
INR	3135.7	3237.4	3370.4	4015.2	3929.8	4015.5	4256.9	4315.5	4323.4	5225.7	5223.7	5338.2
EXP	324	503.9	641.8	596.7	626.2	571.6	346.2	2313.4	11011.9	2619.7	17189.3	3025.2
TRA	-168.7	-9.9	63.3	-112.2	132.6	130.9	-71.7	1741.2	10473.9	1998.9	16372.3	2419.7
DRE	93.4	92.4	92.7	95.1	96.5	98	97.2	100.3	102.6	103	102.5	105
CBD	3403.8	3539.17	3612.43	3762.44	3697.74	4293.81	4293.88	4432.43	4667.35	5067.03	5010.77	5023.24
OUT	1211.16	2748.88	2126.87	3340.74	2392.76	2414.15	3559.3	3101.66	3946.76	3043.55	3979.33	2321.98
SMI	79.93	85.93	93.93	92.11	93.66	96.81	105.1	109.95	123.24	134.05	133.9	115.08
CBC	0	0	0	0	0	0	0	0	0	0	0	0
CRA	40	40	40	40	40	40	40	40	40	40	40	40
CAB	0.41	0.57	0.59	0.28	0.64	0.59	0.42	0.82	0.78	0.49	0.46	0.72
CAI	1.08	1.98	2.02	1.2	3.96	2.95	2.66	3.89	3.66	2.6	2.36	2.35
DOC	0.11	0.13	0.14	0.05	0.03	0.02	0.04	0.09	0.25	0.03	0.05	0.04
IRD	11.91	12.17	12.12	12.12	11.97	12.21	12.39	0	0	0	0	0
EMB	30.7	54.3	100	91.32	82.6	74.79	111.68	114.78	85.48	4.12	-13.03	0
FDI	0.16	0.09	0.09	0.06	0.09	0.08	0.05	0.07	0.06	0.04	0.05	0.09
GGC	10	10	10	10	10	10	10	10	10	10	10	10
IMP	492.7	513.8	578.5	708.9	493.6	440.7	417.9	572.2	538	620.8	817	605.5
LED	1.4	1.4	1.4	1.4	1.4	1.6	1.8	1.7	1.5	1.5	1.5	1.74
MMV	1.88	1.91	1.91	1.72	1.84	1.94	1.83	1.89	1.96	1.85	1.85	1.77
MRE	18.1	16.9	17	17.6	16.5	18.6	16.8	19.2	20.2	19.3	20.7	16
NCR	21	21	21	21	21	21	21	21	21	21	21	21
BUD	0.02	0.02	0.02	0.02	0.02	0.02	0.02	0.02	0.02	0.02	0.02	0.02
RIR	10.76	10.2	8.78	9.26	9.26	8.45	7.49	7.32	8.26	10.49	10.79	9.48
SCI	1.5	1.5	1.5	1.5	1.5	1.5	1.5	1.5	1.5	1.5	1.5	1.5

For the assessment of the composite financial stability index we used fuzzy logic inference. As input data we used Azerbaijan financial and macroeconomical indicators for 2007.09 – 2008.08 (Table 3). Note that the CBC indicator is missing in Azerbaijan financial statistics. That is why we used 23 indicators.

First of all we expressed indicators in percentiles (Table 3).

At the next stage we fuzzified indicators and constructed membership functions. For this purpose we defined three terms of linguistic variables (stable, threshold and crisis) and in fuzzification process there was used Gaussian function of normal distribution (Figure 1). Then rules determining financial state index (FSI) were constructed. Using method of composition we obtained the aggregated fuzzy set, which is area of values of the fuzzy variable – FSI (Figure 2). Using the centroid method we carried out the defuzzification and found meaning of FSI = 24.98, which corresponded to the stable state. From Figure 2 it can be seen that 66.6 parts of support of the fuzzy set are in stable state and 33.3 parts are in the threshold state.

The problem was solved for the 12 months in 2007-2008 and the results show that in all the periods the indicators **CAB**, **CAI**, **FDI** were in *crisis* state.

Table 4. Azerbaijan financial and macroeconomic indicators for 2007.09 – 2008.08.(in percentiles)

	1	2	3	4	5	6	7	8	9	10	11	12
INR	26.61	28.85	31.78	45.96	44.08	45.97	50.42	50.85	50.91	57.53	57.51	58.35
EXP	40.59	41.15	41.59	41.44	41.54	41.37	40.66	46.85	58.08	47.81	64.56	49.09
TRA	40.7	41.2	41.44	40.88	41.66	41.65	41	46.79	58.22	47.61	64.49	48.95
DRE	31.68	27.89	29.02	38.14	43.45	49.15	46.11	52.63	55.54	56.04	55.41	58.57
CBD	27.68	31.32	33.29	37.32	35.58	50.54	50.54	51.78	53.89	57.47	56.97	57.08
OUT	16.33	47.94	35.15	53.37	40.62	41.06	54.87	51.73	57.53	51.33	57.75	39.16
SMI	26.66	32.18	39.54	37.86	39.29	42.19	49.81	51.42	55.5	58.81	58.76	53
CBC	0	0	0	0	0	0	0	0	0	0	0	0
CRA	40	40	40	40	40	40	40	40	40	40	40	40
CAB	34.04	50.2	50.89	20.58	52.62	50.89	35.07	58.83	57.45	42.32	39.22	55.38
CAI	23.95	39.8	40.51	26.07	58.22	52.29	50.59	57.81	56.46	50.24	46.49	46.32
DOC	52.34	54	54.83	42.14	37.17	34.69	39.65	50.69	63.93	37.17	42.14	39.65
IRD	54.3	54.53	54.49	54.49	54.35	54.57	54.73	31.12	31.12	31.12	31.12	31.12
EMB	38.7	47.39	54.74	53.67	52.6	51.64	56.17	56.55	52.95	28.92	22.61	27.4
FDI	64.48	52.19	52.19	40.79	52.19	50.44	35.52	46.05	40.79	30.26	35.52	52.19
GGC	10	10	10	10	10	10	10	10	10	10	10	10
IMP	39.07	42.19	50.58	57.01	39.21	31.39	28.02	50.27	45.77	52.67	62.33	51.91
LED	35.46	35.46	35.46	35.46	35.46	52.71	60.26	56.48	46.79	46.79	46.79	57.99
MMV	51.42	53.84	53.84	15.47	44.54	56.27	42.11	52.23	57.89	46.96	46.96	27.54
MRE	50.09	37.17	38.26	44.81	32.8	51.91	36.08	54.1	57.74	54.46	59.56	27.34
NCR	21	21	21	21	21	21	21	21	21	21	21	21
BUD	0.02	0.02	0.02	0.02	0.02	0.02	0.02	0.02	0.02	0.02	0.02	0.02
RIR	57.18	54.58	44	50.22	50.22	39.4	26.05	23.69	36.76	55.93	57.32	51.24
SCI	1.5	1.5	1.5	1.5	1.5	1.5	1.5	1.5	1.5	1.5	1.5	1.5

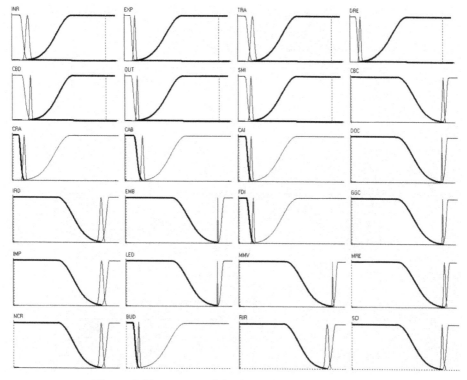

Figure 1. Fuzzy sets of the input indicators of the model

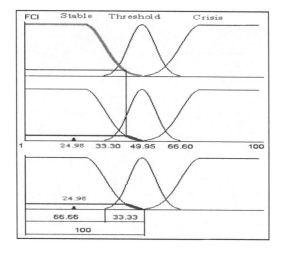

Figure 2. Fuzzy set of the FSI

Table 5. Input indicators values for the model for September 2007 (in percentiles)

Indicators		Month 1	Term
International reserves	- INR	26.61	E1
Exports	- EXP	40.59	E1
The terms of trade	- TRA	40.7	E1
Real exchange rate	- DRE	31.68	E1
Commercial bank deposits	- CBD	27.68	E1
Output	- OUT	16.33	E1
Stock prices	- SMI	26.66	E1
Central Bank credit to the public sector / GDP - CBC		0	E1
Credit rating	- CRA	40	E1
Current account balance / GDP	- CAB	34.04	E3
Current account balance / Investment	- CAI	23.95	E3
Domestic credit / GDP	- DOC	52.34	E1
Domestic-foreign interest rate differential on deposits	- IRD	54.3	E1
Excess real M1 balance	- EMB	38.7	E1
Foreign direct investment / GDP	- FDI	64.48	E3
General government consumption / GDP		10	E1
Import		39.07	E1
=Ratio of lending rate to deposit rate		35.46	E1
M2 multiplier	- MMV	51.42	E1
M2 / reserves	- MRE	50.09	E1
Net credit to the public sector / GDP	- NCR	21	E1
Overall budget balance / GDP	- BUD	0.02	E1
Real interest rate on deposits	- RIR	57.18	E1
Short-term capital inflows / GDP	- SCI	1.5	E1

3. Fuzzy Markov model forecasting the state of the composite financial stability index

Fuzzy Markov model is expressed by the following equation:

$$U_x^{(n)} = U_x^{(0)} \circ M^{(n)}, \qquad (1)$$

where $U_x^{(0)}$ is the initial state vector describing the probability of the state composite financial stability index; $U_x^{(n)}$ is the probability vector of the state composite financial stability index in the n periods; $M^{(n)}$ is the transition matrix, whose elements represent grade of membership of the transition going from one state to another; $\circ$ is the union and intersection operator.

For the solution of the equation (1) we used hypothesis, which is described in [4] and [5]. In our case initial vector of probability of the state is evaluated from composite financial stability index, which we obtained by applying fuzzy logic inference. It is necessary to underline that we assumed equal grade of importance for all the indicators.

As can be seen from Table 3, out of 23 input indicators only 3 indicators are in the crisis state. If the probabilities of getting each indicator in the crisis state are equivalent, then the probability that the financial system is in the crisis state is equal to 0.13 (3/23). Thus, the probability that the system is in the threshold state is 0.87.Distribution of the probability consists of 3 events - S1 (stable), S2 (threshold), S3 (crisis), defined in the following table:.

Table 6. Distributions of the probability.

Number of indicators	Probability of the indicators at the crisis state
1 – 3	0 – 0.13
4 – 6	0.17 – 0.26
7 – 12	0.30 – 0.52
13 – 23	0.57 – 1

This table gives us a possibility of defining the distribution of the probability of occurrence of the following four states of the Financial Stability Index:

Very high stability (VH)1 – 0.87;
High stability (H) 0.87 – 0.74;
Low stability (L) 0.74 – 0.48;
Very low stability (VL) 0.48 – 0.

The corresponding membership functions for the fuzzified values of (VH), (H), (L) and (VL) are defined as follows:

$$\mu_{VH} = \frac{0}{0.87} + \frac{0.154}{0.88} + \frac{0.308}{0.89} + \frac{0.462}{0.9} + \frac{0.615}{0.91} + \frac{0.769}{0.92} + \frac{0.923}{0.93} +$$
$$+ \frac{1}{0.935} + \frac{0.923}{0.94} + \frac{0.769}{0.95} + \frac{0.615}{0.96} + \frac{0.462}{0.97} + \frac{0.308}{0.98} + \frac{0.154}{0.99} + \frac{0}{1} \quad (1)$$

$$\mu_{H} = \frac{0}{0.74} + \frac{0.154}{0.75} + \frac{0.308}{0.76} + \frac{0.462}{0.77} + \frac{0.615}{0.78} + \frac{0.769}{0.79} + \frac{0.923}{0.8} +$$
$$+ \frac{1}{0.805} + \frac{0.923}{0.81} + \frac{0.769}{0.82} + \frac{0.308}{0.85} + \frac{0.615}{0.83} + \frac{0.462}{0.84} + \frac{0.308}{0.85} + \quad (2)$$
$$+ \frac{0.154}{0.86} + \frac{0}{0.87}$$

$$\mu_{L} = \frac{0}{0.48} + \frac{0.077}{0.49} + \frac{0.154}{0.5} + \frac{0.231}{0.51} + \frac{0.308}{0.52} + \frac{0.385}{0.53} + \frac{0.462}{0.54} +$$
$$+ \frac{0.538}{0.55} + \frac{0.615}{0.56} + \frac{0.692}{0.57} + \frac{0.769}{0.58} + \frac{0.846}{0.59} + \frac{0.923}{0.6} + \frac{1}{0.61} +$$
$$+ \frac{0.923}{0.62} + \frac{0.846}{0.63} + \frac{0.769}{0.64} + \frac{0.692}{0.65} + \frac{0.615}{0.66} + \frac{0.538}{0.67} + \frac{0.462}{0.68} +$$
$$+ \frac{0.385}{0.69} + \frac{0.308}{0.7} + \frac{0.231}{0.71} + \frac{0.154}{0.72} + \frac{0.077}{0.73} + \frac{0}{0.74}$$

$$\mu_{VL} = 0/0 + 0.0417/0.01 + 0.0833/0.02 + 0.125/0.03 + 0.167/0.04 + 0.208/0.05 + 0.25/0.06 +$$
$$+ 0.292/0.07 + 0.333/0.08 + 0.375/0.09 + 0.417/0.1 + 0.458/0.11 + 0.5/0.12 + 0.542/0.13 +$$
$$+ 0.583/0.14 + 0.625/0.15 + 0.667/0.16 + 0.708/0.17 + 0.75/0.18 + 0.792/0.19 + 0.833/0.2 +$$
$$+ 0.875/0.21 + 0.917/0.22 + 0.958/0.23 + 1/0.24 + 0.958/0.25 + 0.917/0.26 + 0.875/0.27 +$$
$$+ 0.833/0.28 + 0.792/0.29 + 0.75/0.3 + 0.708/0.31 + 0.667/0.32 + 0.625/0.33 + 0.583/0.34 +$$
$$+ 0.542/0.35 + 0.5/0.36 + 0.458/0.37 + 0.417/0.38 + 0.375/0.39 + 0.333/0.4 + 0.292/0.41 +$$
$$+ 0.25/0.42 + 0.208/0.43 + 0.167/0.44 + 0.125/0.45 + 0.0833/0.46 + 0.0417/0.47 + 0/0.48$$

Using the fuzzy probabilities defined above, we construct the following transition matrix of probability:

$$M^{(1)} = \begin{pmatrix} VL & VH & VH \\ H & VL & H \\ L & L & VH \end{pmatrix} \quad (3)$$

This matrix is not universal, as it is constructed based on the expert information and it depends on the financial situation of the state.

A forecast of the financial state is based on two hypotheses: (1) financial state is worsening and (2) financial state is improving. As can be seen below, the first hypothesis is formed by the matrix $M^{(1)}$ and the second is

formed by the matrix $M^{-1} = \begin{pmatrix} VH & VL & VL \\ H & H & L \\ L & L & VH \end{pmatrix}$.

Initial state vector $U_x^{(0)}$ defined with the help of financial stability index, which is evaluated by means of fuzzy logic inference. In our case, financial stability index includes 3 indicators, which are in the crisis state, that is why the probability that the system stays in the stable state is equal to 0.87. Probabilities for the threshold and crisis state are equal respectively to 0.07 and 0.06. Thus, the fuzzy initial state vector is

$$U_x^{(0)} = (VH, VL, VL) = (0.87, 0.07, 0.06).$$

Using the value of $U_x^{(0)}$ and M^{-1}, we calculate the value of vector $U_x^{1} = U_{(x)}^{(0)} \circ M^{(1)}$ for the next period:

$$U\,'_x = (VH\,,VL\,,VL\,) \circ \begin{pmatrix} VL & VH & VH \\ H & VL & H \\ L & L & VH \end{pmatrix} \quad (4)$$

By applying logical multiplication we have

$$(VH \wedge VL) \vee (VL \wedge H) \vee (VL \wedge L) = VL \vee VL \vee VL = VL$$
$$(VH \wedge VH) \vee (VL \wedge VL) \vee (VL \wedge L) = VH \vee VL \vee VL = VH$$
$$(VH \wedge VH) \vee (VL \wedge H) \vee (VL \wedge VH) = VH \vee VL \vee VL = VH$$

By replacing the matrix M^1 in (4) with matrix $\overline{M}^1$, we obtain

$$\overline{U\,'_x} = (VH\,,VL\,,VL\,) \circ \begin{pmatrix} VH & VL & VL \\ H & H & L \\ L & L & VH \end{pmatrix}$$

By applying logical multiplication:

$$(VH \wedge VH) \vee (VL \wedge H) \vee (VL \wedge L) = VH \vee VL \vee VL = VH$$
$$(VH \wedge VL) \vee (VL \wedge H) \vee (VL \wedge L) = VL \vee VL \vee VL = VL$$
$$(VL \wedge VL) \vee (VL \wedge L) \vee (VL \wedge VH) = VL \vee VL \vee VL = VL$$

Crisp value of logical variables defined by (2), by choosing probability with maximum membership function value:

$$U\,'_x = (VL,VH,VH) = \big([0,0.41],\,[0.94,0.99],\,[0.94,0.99]\big) \quad (5)$$
$$\overline{\overline{U\,'_x}} = (VH,VL,VL) = \big([0.94,0.99],\,[0,0.41],\,[0,0.41]\big)$$

Membership functions defined in (2) are used to calculate these values (5). Intervals correspond to the maxima of the membership functions μ_{VH} and μ_{VL}. Fuzzy probabilities are calculated for the following events: financial situation is (1) stable, (2) is in the threshold state, and (3) is in the crisis state. As was mentioned in Section 2, during evaluation of the financial stability index with the help of fuzzy inference method, it was determined that three indicators were in the crisis state: Current Account Balance/GDP (CAB), Current Account Balance/Investment (CAI), and Foreign Direct Investment/GDP (FDI). It means that the government should pay special attention to these indicators in order to improve them. The results obtained with fuzzy inference are used as the input data $U_x^{(0)}$ to the forecasting problem.

Fuzzy-Markov forecasting model is better at long-term forecasting than short-term [6]. We think that in both cases transition matrix must be constructed with participation of highly qualified experts, because the results of the forecasting depend on the transition matrix.

Conclusions

In this paper fuzzy logic inference system is used for evaluation of composite finance stability index (FSI) of the state. Fuzzy Markov model has been used to predict the possible value of FSI for the subsequent month. In this study it is assumed that the importance degree of the indicators is equal. In future it is intended to define different degrees of importance for each indicator.

References

[I] M. Goldstein, G. Kaminsky, C. Reinhart. Assessing Financial Vulnerability, Institute for International Economics, USA Washington 2000, p. 152.

[II] G. Kaminsky, C. Reinhart. The Twin Crisis: The Causes of Banking and Balance-of-Payments Problems, The American Economic Review, USA Washington 1999, pp. 473-500.

[III] D. Reagle, D. Salvatore. Forecasting Financial Crisis in Emerging Market Economies. Open Economies Review, 2000, pp. 247-259.

[IV] L.A. Zadeh, Linquistic Approach and its Application in Decision Analysis, Directions in Large-Scale Systems – Book, Plenum Press, pp. 339-357, 1975.

[V] C.W. Cheong, A.L. Hui, V. Ramachandran, Web Server Workload Forecasting – Fuzzy Linquistic Approach, IJCIM, Vol.9, No.3, Sept.-December, 2001, pp. 36-44.

[VI] J. Xuepeng, X. Zhisheng, D. Yunyun, L. Xiangbing, Application of Fuzzy-Markov Method in China Fire Forecasting by 55-year, Proceeding of the 2006 International Symposium of Safety Science and Technology, Changsha, China, Oct.24-27, 2006, pp. 952-956.

CHAPTER 5

Large Scale Portfolio Optimization with DEoptim

Kris Boudt
Vrije Universiteit Brussel VU University Amsterdam

David Ardia
Laval University

Katharine M. Mullen
UCLA

Brian G. Peterson
DV Trading

Large Scale Portfolio Optimization with DEoptim

Abstract

This chapter evaluates the performance of DEoptim on a high-dimensional portfolio problem. The setup is the same as in the *R Journal* article Ardia *et al.* (2010); namely minimizing the portfolio CVaR under an upper bound constraint on the percentage CVaR contributions. Because the resulting optimization model is a non-convex programming problem with multiple local optima, DEoptim is more apt in solving this problem than gradient-based methods such as optim and nlminb.

1. Introduction

The R package DEoptim of Ardia et al. (2011) implements several Differential Evolution algorithms. DE belongs to the class of genetic algorithms which use biology-inspired operations of crossover, mutation, and selection on a population in order to minimize an objective function over the course of successive generations. More details on DEoptim can be found in Mullen et al. (2011). In this chapter we evaluate its performance on a high-dimensional portfolio problem.In this chapter, we use of DEoptim to solve the portfolio optimization problem described Ardia et al. (2010), but expand the problem to include 100 free variables. As in Ardia et al. (2010), the portfolio CVaR is minimized under an upper bound constraint on the percentage CVaR contributions. See Boudt et al. (2010) for the rationale underlying this portfolio construction technique.The optimization of the objective function is a non-convex programming problem. Since DEoptim is a stochastic global optimization algorithm, it is more apt to offer a good solution than alternative local optimization methods. For instance, gradient-based methods such as the L-BFGS-B and Nelder-Mead methods in optim and nlminb will typically converge to suboptimal solutions on the problem considered here.The version of this problem described in Ardia et al. (2010) was stylized to describe many fewer variables to allow users to complete the optimization on a personal computer in a matter of minutes. Portfolio problems encountered in practice may require days to optimize on a personal computer, and involve several hundred variables. In the present chapter we examine a problem of complexity in-between the stylized, simple case considered by Ardia et al. (2010) and the most complex problems encountered in typical financial research.

We hope that the R package DEoptim will be fruitful for many users. If you use R or DEoptim, please cite the software in publications.

2. Setup

The results in this chapter are obtained using R version 2.13.0. The function getSymbols in quantmod (Ryan 2010) is used to obtain the data. The risk measures in the portfolio objective function are computed using PerformanceAnalytics (Carl and Peterson 2010). The initial population in DEoptim is generated using the function random_portfolios in PortfolioAnalytics (Boudt et al. 2011). Computations are performed on a Genuine Intel® dual core CPU P8400 2.26Ghz processor. DEoptim relies on repeated evaluation of the objective function in order to move the population toward a global minimum. Users interested in making DEoptim run as fast as possible should ensure that evaluation of the objective function is as efficient as possible. Using pure R code, this may often be accomplished using vectorization. Writing parts of the objective function in a lower-level language like C or Fortran may also increase speed.

3. Data

We take 100 randomly sampled stocks from the S&P 500 for which a sufficiently long data history is available. We first download ten years of monthly data using the function getSymbols of the package quantmod (Ryan 2010). Then we compute the log-return series and the sample mean and covariance matrix.

```
> tickers = c( "VNO" , "VMC" , "WMT" , "WAG" , "DIS" , "WPO" , "WFC" , "WDC" ,
+ "WY" , "WHR" , "WMB" , "WEC" , "XEL" , "XRX" , "XLNX" ,"ZION" ,"MMM" ,
+ "ABT" , "ADBE" , "AMD" , "AET" , "AFL" , "APD" , "ARG" ,"AA" , "AGN" ,
+ "ALTR" , "MO" , "AEP" , "AXP" , "AIG" , "AMGN" , "APC" ,"ADI" , "AON" ,
+ "APA" , "AAPL" , "AMAT" ,"ADM" , "T" , "ADSK" , "ADP" , "AZO" , "AVY" ,
+ "AVP" , "BHI" , "BLL" , "BAC" , "BK" , "BCR" , "BAX" , "BBT" , "BDX" ,
+ "BMS" , "BBY" , "BIG" , "HRB" , "BMC" , "BA" , "BMY" , "CA" , "COG" ,
+ "CPB" , "CAH" , "CCL" , "CAT" , "CELG" , "CNP" , "CTL" , "CEPH", "CERN" ,
+ "SCHW" , "CVX" , "CB" , "CI" ,"CINF","CTAS" , "CSCO" , "C" , "CLF" ,
+ "CLX", "CMS" , "KO" , "CCE" , "CL" , "CMCSA","CMA" , "CSC" , "CAG" ,
+ "COP" , "ED" , "CEG" ,"GLW" , "COST" , "CVH" , "CSX" , "CMI" , "CVS" ,          +
"DHR" , "DE")

> library(quantmod);
> getSymbols(tickers, from = "2000-12-01", to = "2010-12-31")
> P <- NULL; seltickers <- NULL
For (ticker in tickers) {
+    tmp <- Cl(to.monthly(eval(parse(text=ticker))))
+    if(is.null(P)){ timeP = time(tmp) }
+    if( any( time(tmp) !=timeP )) next
+    el se P<-cbind(P,as.numeric(tmp))
+    seltickers = c( seltickers , ticker )
+ }
> P = xts(P,order.by=time P)
> colnames(P) <- seltickers
> R <- diff(log(P))
> R <- R[-1,J
> dim(R)  [1]
120 100
> mu <- colMeans(R)
> sigma <- cov(R)
```

4. Portfolio objective function and constraints

The optimization problem consists of determining the portfolio weights for which the portfolio has the lowest CVaR and each investment can contribute at most 5% to total portfolio CVaR risk. Additionally, weights need to be positive and the portfolio needs to be fully invested. The level of portfolio CVaR and the CVaR contributions are computed conveniently with the function ES in the package Performance Analytics (Carl and Peterson 2010). For simplicity, we assume here normality, but also estimators of CVaR and CVaR contributions for non-normal distributions are available in the function ES.

The constraint that each asset can contribute at most 5% to total portfolio CVaR risk is imposed through the addition of a penalty function to the objective function. As such, we allow the search algorithm to consider infeasible solutions. A portfolio which is unacceptable for the investor must be penalized enough to be rejected by the minimization process and the larger the violation of the constraint, the larger the increase in the value of the objective function.

```
> library("PerformanceAnalytics")
> obj <- function(w) {
+       if (sum(w) == 0) {

+          w <- w + 1e-2
+       }
+    w <- w / sum(w)
+    CVaR <- ES(weights = w,
+                  method = "gaussian",
+        portfolio_method = "component",
+                          mu = mu,
+                    sigma = sigma)
+              tmp1 <- CVaR$ES
+tmp2 <- max(CVaR$pct_contrib_ES - 0.05, 0)
+              out <- tmp1 + 1e3 * tmp2
+ return(out)
+ }
```

The weights need to satisfy additionally a long only and full investment constraint. The current implementation of DEoptim allows for bound constraints on the portfolio weights. We call these lower and upper.

```
> N <- ncol(R)
> minw <- 0
> maxw <- 1
> lower <- rep(minw,N)
> upper <- rep(maxw,N)
```

The full investment constraint is accounted for in two ways. First, we standardize all the weights in the objective function such that they sum up to one. Second, we use the function random_portfolios in PortfolioAnalytics (Boudt et al. 2011) to generate random portfolios that satisfy all constraints. These random portfolios will be used as the initial generation in DEoptim.

```
> library("PortfolioAnalytics")

> eps <- 0.025
> weight_seq<-generatesequence(min=minw,max=maxw,by=.001,rounding=3)
> rpconstraint<-constraint(
+                  assets=N,  min_sum=(1-eps),  max_sum=(1+eps),
+       min=lower, max=upper, weight_seq=weight_seq)
assuming equal weighted seed portfolio
> set.seed(1234)
> rp<- random_portfolios(rpconstraints=rpconstraint,permutations=N*10)
> rp <-rp/rowSums(rp)
```

5. Failure of gradient-based methods

The penalty introduced in the objective function is non-differentiable and therefore standard gradient-based optimization routines cannot be used. For instance, L-BFGS-B and Nelder-Mead methods in optim and nlminb do not converge.

```
> out <- optim(par = rep(1/N, N), fn = obj,
+       method = "L-BFGS-B", lower = lower, upper = upper)
> out$value

[1] 0.05431692
> out$message
[1]  "ERROR: ABNORMAL_TERMINATION_IN_LNSRCH"
> out <- nlminb(start =rep(1/N, N), objective = bj,
+ lower = lower, upper = upper)
> out$objective
[1]             0.0547231
out$message
[1] "false convergence (8)"
```

6. Portfolio optimization with DEoptim

In contrast with gradient-based methods, DEoptim is designed to consistently find a good approximation to the global minimum of the optimization problem. For complex problems as the one considered here, the performance of DEoptim is quite dependent on the DE algorithm used. We first consider the current default DE algorithm in DEoptim, called the "local-to-best" strategy with fixed parameters. We define convergence when the percentage improvement between iterations is below reltol=1e-6 after steptol=150 steps. For some problems, it may take much iteration before the

DE algorithm converges. We set the maximum number of iterations allowed to 5000. Progress is printed every 250 iterations. As explained above, the initial generation is set to rp.

```
> controlDE <- list(reltol=.000001,steptol=150, itermax = 5000,      +trace = 250,
NP=as.numeric(nrow(rp)),initialpop=rp)
> set.seed(1234)
> start <- Sys.time()
> out <- DEoptim(fn = obj, lower = lower, upper = upper, control = controlDE)
Iteration: 250     bestvalit: 0.064652
Iteration: 500     bestvalit: 0.057199
Iteration: 750     bestvalit: 0.055774
Iteration:      1000   bestvalit:      0.055013
Iteration:      1250   bestvalit:      0.054581
Iteration:      1500   bestvalit:      0.054269
Iteration:      1750   bestvalit:      0.054146
Iteration:      2000   bestvalit:      0.054049
Iteration:      2250   bestvalit:      0.053706

Iteration:      2500   bestvalit:      0.053695
Iteration:      2750   bestvalit:      0.053351
Iteration:      3000   bestvalit:      0.053273
> out$optim$iter
[1] 3055
> out$optim$bestval
[1] 0.05327273
> end <- Sys.time()
> end – start
>
Time difference of 16.03645 mins
```

We thus see that, at iteration 5000, the "local-to-best" strategy with fixed parameters reaches a solution that is better than the one obtained using the gradient-based methods mentioned above.A recently proposed DE algorithm with better convergence properties on complex problems is the JADE algorithm proposed by Zhang and Sanderson (2009). JADE combines a "local-to-p-best" strategy with adaptive parameter control. The first building block of JADE is thus that the DE algorithm does not always use the best solution of the current generation to mutate the solutions, but one of the randomly chosen [100p%] best solutions, with $0 < p < 1$. The default value of p is 0.2. Even though this strategy is more greedy, it tends to converge faster because it diversifies the population.

The "local-to-p-best" strategy is chosen by setting strategy=6.
```
> controlDE <- list(reltol=.000001,steptol=150, itermax = 5000,       + trace =
250, strategy=6, c=0,
+ NP=as.numeric(nrow(rp)),initialpop=rp)
```

```
> set.seed(1234)
> start <- Sys.time()

> out <- DEoptim(fn = obj, lower = lower, upper = upper, control = controlDE)
Iteration: 250 bestvalit: 0.063848
Iteration: 500 bestvalit: 0.058090
Iteration: 750 bestvalit: 0.055960
Iteration: 1000 bestvalit: 0.055235
Iteration: 1250 bestvalit: 0.054884
Iteration: 1500 bestvalit: 0.054369
Iteration: 1750 bestvalit: 0.054269
Iteration: 2000 bestvalit: 0.054089
> out$optim$bestval
[1] 0.05408688
> end <- Sys.time()
> end - start
Time difference of 11.45833 mins
```

The second distinctive feature of Zhang and Sanderson (2009) is to introduce learning about successful parameters in the algorithm. Under this approach, the cross-over probability at generation $g + 1$ is set to $(1 - c)$ the cross-over probability at generation g plus c times the average of all successful cross-over probabilities at generation g. Similarly, the mutation factor at generation $g + 1$ is equal to $1 - c$ times the previous mutation factor plus c times the average mutation factor of all successful mutations. We take $c = 0.4$.

```
> controlDE <- list(reltol=.000001,steptol=150, itermax = 5000,trace = 250, +
strategy=2, c=.4,
+ NP=as.numeric(nrow(rp)),initialpop=rp)
> set.seed(1234)
> start <- Sys.time()

> out <- DEoptim(fn = obj, lower = lower, upper = upper, control = controlDE)
Iteration: 250 bestvalit: 0.074612
Iteration:    500    bestvalit:    0.068776
Iteration:    750    bestvalit:    0.067991
Iteration:    1000    bestvalit:    0.067894
Iteration: 1250 bestvalit: 0.067887
> out$optim$bestval
[1] 0.06788674
> end <- Sys.time()
> end - start
Time difference of 6.5763 mins
```

The "local-to-1-best" strategy with adaptive parameter control converges clearly too fast. It is the combination of "local-to-p-best" strategy with adaptive parameter control that is the most successful in solving our problem.

```
> controlDE <- list(reltol=.000001,steptol=150, itermax = 5000,        + trace =
250, strategy=6, c=.4,
+ NP=as.numeric(nrow(rp)),initialpop=rp)
> set.seed(1234)
> start <- Sys.time()
> out <- DEoptim(fn = obj, lower = lower, upper = upper, control = controlDE)
```

Iteration: 250	bestvalit: 0.087517

Iteration:	1000	bestvalit:	0.059015

Iteration: 250   bestvalit: 0.087517
Iteration: 500   bestvalit: 0.077481
Iteration: 750   bestvalit: 0.067673
Iteration: 1000   bestvalit: 0.059015

Iteration: 1250   bestvalit: 0.054758

Iteration: 1500   bestvalit: 0.053618

Iteration: 1750   bestvalit: 0.053290

Iteration: 2000   bestvalit: 0.053156

Iteration: 2250   bestvalit: 0.053099

Iteration: 2500   bestvalit: 0.053071

Iteration: 2750   bestvalit: 0.053059

Iteration: 3000   bestvalit: 0.053052

Iteration: 3250   bestvalit: 0.053049

```
> out$optim$iter
[1] 3451
> out$optim$bestval
[1] 0.0530483
> end <- Sys.time()
> end - start
Time difference of 18.57083 mins
```

We see that with JADE, DEoptim converges within 3451 iterations to 0.0530483, which is the lowest obtained by all methods considered in the chapter.

This chapter illustrates that for complex problems, the performance of DEoptim is thus quite dependent on the DE algorithm used. It is recommended that users try out several DE algorithms to find out which one is most adapted for their problem. Furthermore, DE is a stochastic optimizer and typically will only find a near-optimal solution that depends on the seed. The function optimize.portfolio.parallel in Portfolio Analytics allows to run an arbitrary number of portfolio sets in parallel in order to develop confidence bands around your solution. It is based on REvolution's for each package (REvolution Computing 2009).

References

[I] Ardia D, Boudt K, Carl P, Mullen KM, Peterson BG .2010. Differential Evolution (DEoptim) for Non-Convex Portfolio Optimization, URL http: //ssrn. com/abstract=1584905.

[II] Ardia D, Mullen K, Peterson BG, Ulrich J. 2011, DEoptim: Differential Evolution Optimization in R.R package version 2.1-0, URL http://CRAN.R-project.org/package=DEopt im

[III] Boudt K, Carl P, Peterson BG .2010, Portfolio Optimization with Conditional Value-at-Risk Budgets.

[IV] Boudt K, Carl P, Peterson BG. 2011, Portfolio Analytics: Portfolio Analysis, including numeric methods for optimization of portfolios package version 0.6, URL https://r-forge.r-project.org/R/?group_id=579.

[V] Carl P, Peterson BG. 2010, Performance Analytics: Econometric tools for performance and risk analysis. R package version 1.0.3.2, URL http://CRAN.R-project.org/package=PerformanceAnalytics

[VI] Mullen K, Ardia D, Gil D, Windover D, Cline J.2011.DEoptim: An R Package for Global Optimization by Differential Evolution, Journal of Statistical Software, 40(6), 1-26. URL http://www.jstatsoft.org/v40/i06/.

[VII] REvolution Computing.2009, foreach: Foreach looping construct for R. R package version 1.3.0, URL http://CRAN.R-project.org/package=foreach.

[VIII] Ryan JA. 2010, quantmod: Quantitative Financial Modelling Framework. R package version 0.3-15, URL http://CRAN.R-project.org/package=quantmod.

[IX] Zhang J, Sanderson AC .2009, JADE: Adaptive Differential Evolution with Optional External Archive, IEEE Transactions on Evolutionary Computation, 13(5), 945-958.

CHAPTER 6

Evaluation of Sectoral Success With Respect to Financial Ratio Analysis: Example From Turkish Sectors

Gül Tekin TEMUR,

Kaya TOKMAKÇIOĞLU

Istanbul Technical University

Evaluation of Sectoral Success With Respect to Financial Ratio Analysis: Example From Turkish Sectors

Abstract

Due to the dynamic and uncertain structure of business conditions, it becomes hard to develop a decision making tool for forecasting future trends of job creation potential. As one of critical decisions of entrepreneurs, to establish a new company within limited resources requires a comprehensive analysis in order to prevent risks as much as possible. Similarly, timing for closing decision is also critical for achievement of closing duration with minimum loss. Company establishment and liquidation quantities which are affected by sectoral financial performance can be referred as two of success indicators for defining job creation potential. Within this scope, this study aims to develop a forecasting methodology on sector success evaluation (SSE) regarding to job creation potential which is denoted with the difference of company establishment and liquidation quantities in this study. Artificial neural network system (ANNs) is used for identifying expected job creation potential of different sectors with respect to financial ratios such as liquidity, leverage, activity, profitability and growth ratios. The proposed system is carried out in three main sectors of Turkey (agriculture, construction and manufacturing). The relevant data concerning financial ratios is collected from Istanbul Stock Exchange data set, and data concerning job creation potential is gathered from the Union of Chambers and Commodity Exchanges of Turkey. The results reveal that ANNs is a successful decision making tool that can help managers have insight on expected success of sectors, compare expected and real job creations, and make their strategic planning more effectively. Furthermore, it is identified that "fixed assets turnover" as an activity ratio has the highest impact on sectoral success and the changes should be frequently followed. In contrast, "current assets/total assets (%)" and "net profit margin growth rate (%)" have the lowest effectiveness on sectoral success.

Keywords: Financial Ratio, Job Creation, Neural Network, Sectoral Success

1. Introduction

In today's competitive business environment, prediction of sector success is a very critical and challenging issue for governmental institutions, managers, stock holders, entrepreneurs, investors and researchers. The success of a sector (which also refers to job creation potential of sector) can be considered as an important key indicator when deciding on whether a strategic plan should be realized or not. Because strategic plans mostly require much time, resources and budget, they should be extensively analyzed in order to prevent unexpected results. It forces organizations attach more importance on the forecasting problem that can be named as "sector success evaluation (SSE)". Evaluating success of sectors is a useful tool to predict the risk when making strategic plans and prevent negative effects. The main goal of SSE is to make decision makers have insight on sector success in order to prevent falling into distress in future. It also makes financial or economic institutions compare real and expected success of sectors in order to effectively manage their credit risks exposure because nowadays, the domino effect of a sector failure is merely instantaneous and such an effect holds the potential of a financial crisis in a national economy.

Basically, SSE aims to evaluate the sufficiency of a sector repay its loans (credits) and the interests earned on the loan which is closely connected with its capacity to raise its savings while decreasing its expenses and payments. Thus, it can be asserted that the credibility of a sector has to be proportional to expected difference between the revenue and the expenditures of a sector over its credit life. Furthermore, in order to be profitable over the credit life, firms building up the sector should raise their earnings whereas they handle with their costs. Especially in instable economies, SSE becomes a more important task in both of academic and industrial environments. One of important indicator of sector success is job creation and destruction potential. From employment perspective, job creation can be defined as the total number of employment positions gained and job destruction can be defined as the total number of employment positions lost (Klein, et al. 2002). There are a large number of studies related with job creation issue in various countries. Hall (1986) reviewed four industrial countries (Great Britain, Federal Germany, USA and Japan) which showed shift from manufacturing sector to service sector. It is underlined that "in successful economies, employment gains in both good-handling and information-handling services compensate fore relatively modest manufacturing losses". Klette and Mathiassen (1995) carried out a job creation study in Norwegian labor market that is known as its incapability to changes in job opportunities. It is explored that entries and exits are important factors for creating and destructing job for long terms. Also, small enterprises have higher job creation and destruction levels, and if they have less employees, they become more capable to create new jobs. Picot and Dupuy (1996) addressed the influence of firm size effect on job creation in Canada. It is figured out that job creation and destruction have higher amount in small and medium sized companies. Acquisti and Lehmann (2000) studied on Russian job creation and destruction conditions by considering micro level data sets of the period 1996-1997. They revealed that small enterprises have the highest success at job creation. In the study of Barnes and Haskel (2002), job creation and destruction levels are analyzed and explored that how the small UK manufacturing enterprises contribute to the levels. It is found that large establishments have higher percentage for responsibility of job destruction and small firms have higher percentage for responsibility of job creation. Armington and Acs (2003) proposed a study on analyzing dynamics of job creation in service and manufacturing industries in order to have insight on industrial evolutions. They reveal that gross job flow quantity and additional job loss risk contributed by the newness of business of single unit establishments have higher volume than multi-unit establishments. Furthermore, job gain persistence from company establishments has larger amount than from expansion of existing establishments; and the persistence rates are not affected by the size of establishments.

Similar to different countries all around the world, job creation is one of important economic concerns also in Turkey. In Turkey, depending on demographic and economic conditions, the employment has been increased. With the results of the 2001 economic crisis, the unemployment rate increased to 8.4 percent. In further year, it is increased to 10.3 and did not decline until 2005. As World Bank's Report stated, in order to achieve European Union average employment rate in 2010, Turkey has to increase job creation quantity to 10 million. Consequently, job creation has become the most significant and challenge topic of Turkish economy (Bilgin and Kilicaslan, 2008). Furthermore, especially over the last fifty years, Turkey has enjoyed unsteady economic growth. In Turkey, the growth rate of per capita gross domestic product has shown nonstationary and rapidly changing behaviors (as seen at Figure 1). It can be caused from the feature of economic features which are easily affected by internal and/or external conditions. Therefore, one of critical problems of enterprises is not to be able to get knowledge of the possibility of sector success or failure, and assist themselves take appropriate action regarding to the sector failure potentials.

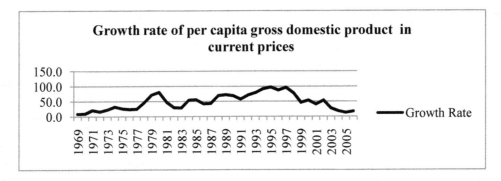

**Figure 1. Growth rate of per capita gross domestic product in current prices between 1969-2006
(x=years y=GDP price index per capita)**

In recent years, many supportive tools have been developed for dealing with uncertain structure of sector success and foreseeing sector failure potential. To the best of our knowledge, although the studies focusing on job creation and destruction issue increased, there is lack of studies proposing methodology for forecasting job creation potential. It is evident that sector success is cannot be thought independent from financial performance. Therefore, this paper contributes to an understanding of Artificial Neural Network System (ANNs) development for SSE by demonstrating the effect of financial ratios on job creation and job destruction in Turkish agriculture, construction and manufacturing industries for the period 1986 to 2010. Within this context, because the company establishments and liquidations have important role on job creation and destruction potential (Dawis and Haltiwanger, 1990), difference of company birth and death amounts can be taken into account as an important indicator for SSE. In the view of these goals, the rest of the paper is organized as follows: Section 2 gives the finance literature review on neural network implementations. Section 3 describes the theoretical background of ANNs. Section 4 depicts the implementation and presents the results. The study concludes with further directions.

2. Neural Network Implementation Trends in Finance

The number of studies using neural network techniques has been increased in finance research area. In finance applications, it is a critical task to benefit from decision making tools that give highly satisfactory results, especially for making classification and forecasting. There are many research areas range from operational to strategical. Wong and Selvi (1998) state that stock performance/selection prediction, bond rating, commercial loan analysis and future price forecasting are mostly studied personal support issues between 1990 and 1996. As group support researches; financial distress forecasting, investment management and financial statement analysis interpretation are the most famous research areas. Bankruptcy prediction of banks/thrifts, bankruptcy prediction of firms, futures trading volume forecasting and initial public offering pricing are famous study areas for organizational supports (Wong and Selvi (1998)). Vellido et al. (1999) indicate in which business problems different neural networks are used. They identify three researcher groups: business specialists who are interested in business related results, researchers who are interested in the capability of neural networks, and practitioners who are interested in both of results and capability of the proposed methodologies. Wong et al. (2000) present a comprehensive literature review on neural network based studies published between 1994 and 1998. It is found that bankruptcy prediction is the most commonly studied issue in finance, and there is a decrease in amount of studies focusing on stock performance/selection prediction. It is also noticed that because of complex and nonlinear features, finance will continue to be one the most common research area in the future studies of neural networks. Calderon and Cheh (2002) who focus on use of neural networks in auditing and risk assessment review studies on preliminary information risk assessment, control risk assessment, errors and fraud, going-concern audit opinion, financial distress and bankruptcy. The results of analysis reveal that neural networks are potentially effective method for predicting and classifying risk assessment data with a fairly high degree of accuracy. The main drawback of these studies is, they commonly do not focus on strategic planning issues (Wong and Selvi, 1998). In order to fill this gap, this study takes into account company establishment and liquidation decisions as two of strategic planning issues and develops a forecasting method by using ANNs in order to predict sector success.

3. Artificial Neural Network System (ANNs)

Actually, many forecasting methods (such as rule based forecasting, regression analysis, conjoint analysis, neural nets, causal models etc.) could be utilized for similar problems (Armstrong et al 2011). Because studies using neural network systems outperform traditional statistical methods in many cases (Mukta and Kumar 2009), this study uses ANNs as an intelligent system to develop sector success forecasting model. ANN is a system that simulates biological neural networks to get solution for hard, mathematically ill-defined, nonlinear or stochastic problems (Graupe 2007). In practical, ANNs is used in a wide range of studies and in various industries. Because, ANNs could learn the relationships between inputs and outputs from sample sets and generalize the results to other data sets. It does not require any modeling for matching inputs and outputs. It could also run by using noisy and missing data. ANNs is used especially in problems which include complex knowledge and has a complex decision process. In finance, it is also revealed that if the time series are analyzed, neural networks are more beneficial than statistical methods because of their ability to identify and simulate nonlinear relationships better. Financial environment consists of constantly changing variables and it becomes critical to adopt a robust system such as neural networks that has a lower prediction risks (Wong and Selvi, 1998).

The basic element of an ANNs is *neuron*. Each neuron receives input signals, and then produces an output signal that is typically sent as input to another neuron. A feed forward multi-layer perceptron (MLP) network system is used because of its success of solving complicated problems. A typical MLP network has a simple architecture that includes three main layers called as: input layer, hidden layer and output layer (as shown at Figure 2).

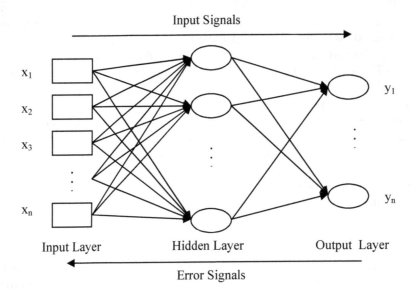

Figure 2. The general structure of MLP ANNs

After the values are received by input layer, they are multiplied with randomly chosen weights and total of weighted values are taken into activation function in hidden layer. The values resulted in hidden layers are sent to output layer and they are multiplied by randomly chosen weights and sent to activation function. One of the most commonly used activation function is hyperbolic tangent. Because it allows to model nonlinear mappings, tanh function can be preferred (as shown in Eq. 1). (x shows the total sum of inputs multiplied with randomly assigned weights).

$$\tanh(x) = \frac{e^x - e^{-x}}{e^x + e^{-x}} \qquad (1)$$

The main goal of establishing ANNs structure is to find the most satisfactory network structure. The ability of the structure to generalize for new data depends on the number of neurons at hidden layers (Schalkoff, 1997). Therefore, many trials are carried out in order to obtain best weights that give output value as close as the real values. As a performance indicator, the value of mean square error (MSE) function on cross validation set that shows the reasonability of each trial is calculated for each structure. When n is the observation number, MSE is the average of differences between expected values ($E(i)$) and the real values (x_i) of a variable (x) (as shown at Eq. 2.).

$$\text{MSE} = \frac{\sum_{i=1}^{n}(x_i - E(i))^2}{n} \qquad (2)$$

If a trial gives cross validation MSE value equal or less than 0,01; it is mostly considered as highly reasonable. The weights are changed according to results of learning rules in order to modify connections until the most satisfactory structure is built (Johnson and Picton, 1995).

4. Methodology of the Research

This section of research goals to develop an ANNs based methodology for SSE and investigating the impacts of financial ratios on the forecasting results by performing sensitivity analysis.
The steps of the methodology are shown in the below:

1. Identification of financial ratios and sector success indicator.
2. Creation of an ANNs implementation to evaluate and estimate the sector success with respect to financial ratios defined at step 1.
3. Performing sensitivity analysis in order to explore the effect of the factors on the results.

4.1.   Identification of Financial Ratios and Sector Success Indicator

In this study, two strategic planning decisions; company establishment and liquidation quantities are considered as important indicators for SSE. In this pursuit, the change on difference of company establishment and liquidation quantities is accepted as a sector success indicator. To evaluate the success of different sectors with respect to financial ratio analysis, important financial ratios of three sectors in Turkey, namely agriculture, manufacturing and construction are calculated. The period consists of years between 1986 and 2010, and the raw data of financial ratios is collected from sector balance sheets and income statements in the Istanbul Stock Exchange webpage (www.imkb.gov.tr). Company establishment and liquidation quantities are gathered from the Union of Chambers and Commodity Exchanges of Turkey. According to financial ratio analysis, there are five main ratio categories which affect the overall performance of a firm, sector or national economy, namely liquidity, leverage, activity, profitability and growth. Liquidity ratios reflect the ability of a sector to maintain positive cash flow, while satisfying immediate obligations whereas leverage ratios demonstrate its aptitude to pay its obligation to creditors and other third parties in the long-term. Moreover, activity ratios measure the effectiveness of the sectors use of resources. Contrarily, profitability ratios reveal the sector's use of its assets and control of its expenses to generate an acceptable rate of return. Finally, it can be asserted that growth ratios are crucial tools to exhibit a sector's ability to earn income and sustain growth in both the short- and long-term. The list of the financial ratios with their notations used in the paper is presented at Table 1

x_1: Liquidity Ratios	x_{11}: Current ratio (%)
	x_{12}: Acid test ratio (%)
	x_{13}: Cash ratio (%)
	x_{14}: Current assets/Total assets (%)
x_2: Leverage Ratios	x_{21}: Tangible fixed assets/Shareholder's equity (%)
	x_{22}: Fixed assets/Shareholder's equity (%)
	x_{23}: Shareholder's equity/Total assets (%)

x₃: Activity Ratios	x_{31}: Accounts receivable turnover
	x_{32}: Fixed assets turnover
	x_{33}: Equity turnover
	x_{34}: Asset turnover
x₄: Profitability Ratios	x_{41}: Net profit margin (%)
	x_{42}: Return on equity (ROE) (%)
x₅: Growth Ratios	x_{51}: Net profit margin growth rate (%)
	x_{52}: Net sales growth rate (%)
	x_{53}: Equity growth rate (%)

Table 1. Financial ratios in the analysis

4.2. ANNs Implementation

This part of the study includes the implementation of ANNs in order to predict success of three main sectors in Turkey. The success of ANNs depends on finding appropriate network structure giving the most satisfactory sector success results. Therefore, the results of the proposed system should be compared to see how they are close to real data. Basically, it is aimed to give insights into two main research items in this phase:

- To find the best MLP network structure for sector success prediction,
- To analyze the impact of different financial ratios on sector success evaluation.
Within this context, first of all, the data features variables will be identified and then implementation process will be explained.

4.2.1. Definition of data features

In sample set, the missing data is ignored and there are 69 data from three main Turkish sectors. The sample set includes financial ratios and sector category as factors impacting SSE. Because of nonlinear behaviors of inputs and outputs, ANNs is used. As an example, the fluctuations of current ratios for agriculture, construction and manufacturing sectors can be seen at Table 2.

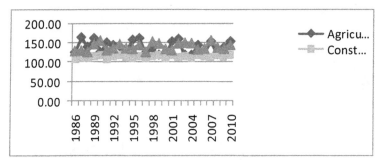

**Table 2. The fluctuations of current ratio for agriculture, construction and manufacturing sectors
(x=years y= current ratio (given in %))**

Similarly, the changes of sector success that is denoted as difference between company establishment and liquidation quantities also show unsteady behaviors. The fluctuations of changes in success for agriculture, construction and manufacturing sectors can be seen at Table 3.

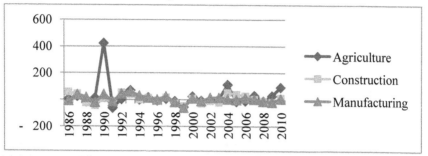

Table 3. The fluctuations of changes in success for agriculture, construction and manufacturing sectors (x=years y= changes in success (given in %))

As it is evident in both of Table 2 and Table 3, financial ratios and sector success are highly variable and show different trend behavior over years. Therefore, it is appropriate to use non-linear methods in the analysis of these time series. ANNs has high capability to get satisfactory solutions for non-linear problems. Consequently, data set includes financial ratios and sector category as input parameters and sector success as an output parameter. As an example, a part of normalized data set for three years can be seen at Table 4. That means input layer consists of sixteen financial ratios as numeric parameters and sector success as non-numeric parameter. For implementation, first of all, the data set is divided into three distinct sets called as training set, cross validation set and testing set. Training set is used to make the system learn the relationships of financial ratios with sector success. The cross validation set does not take place in the training set, but it is used to evaluate the generalization ability of the network at training running duration. The rest of data set includes testing data in order to compare capability of proposed ANNs structure. As a next step, it is necessary to decide on the number of hidden layers and neurons at each hidden layer. The successful accomplishment of this step directly affects ability of ANNs to learn from past.

x_{11}	x_{12}	x_{13}	x_{14}	x_{21}	x_{22}	x_{23}	x_{31}	x_{32}	x_{33}	x_{34}	x_{41}	x_{42}	x_{51}	x_{52}	x_{53}	Sector	Sector Success Indicator
0,63	0,63	0,32	0,51	0,39	0,23	0,88	0,99	0,21	0,54	0,41	0,35	0,52	0,49	0,66	0,25	Agriculture	0,13
0,95	0,29	1,00	0,32	0,71	0,18	0,65	0,75	0,72	0,36	1,00	0,33	0,81	0,55	0,88	0,75	Agriculture	0,15
0,30	0,03	0,72	0,08	0,75	0,04	0,84	0,68	0,59	0,37	0,87	0,27	0,75	0,53	0,60	0,28	Agriculture	0,14
0,03	0,93	0,05	0,34	0,55	0,89	0,07	0,04	0,34	0,36	0,43	0,73	0,92	0,43	0,75	1,00	Construction	0,15
0,12	0,89	0,05	0,53	0,39	0,69	0,16	0,20	0,12	0,08	0,32	0,93	0,80	0,48	0,88	0,29	Construction	0,07
0,09	0,96	0,07	0,52	0,06	0,45	0,13	0,06	0,22	0,21	0,20	0,58	0,50	0,38	0,74	0,64	Construction	0,09
0,39	0,60	0,41	1,00	0,94	0,07	0,53	0,34	0,44	0,39	0,82	0,24	0,40	0,55	0,78	0,05	Manufacturing	0,10
0,32	0,50	0,42	0,81	0,97	0,03	0,35	0,52	0,57	0,70	0,64	0,00	0,77	0,53	0,63	0,67	Manufacturing	0,16
0,36	0,66	0,43	0,60	0,71	0,28	0,88	0,42	0,11	0,79	0,40	0,01	0,95	0,50	0,80	0,64	Manufacturing	0,11

4.2.2. Training and testing the network

By training many networks with different hidden layer and neurons combinations, the best structure which has the minimum generalization error is found. It is important to notice that if the hidden layer has many neurons, it makes the network tend to memorize and always give
same results for each network. On the other hand, if the hidden layer has a few neurons, it makes the network cannot be able to learn from past. As an activation function, hyperbolic tangent is chosen for all combinations. For training process, nearly 70% of total data is randomly identified as a training set. The rest is set apart to be used for cross validation and testing. Furthermore, it should be noticed that there is a fully combined layers in the network. In other words, Neurons of layers are connected to every other neurons of the following layer.Firstly, in order to decide on the number of hidden layers and neuron numbers, the neural network is trained into stepwise training process for different combinations. These trials successively include 1 to 5 hidden layers and 1 to 10 nodes for each layer. If the MSE value of a trial found as acceptable, then testing process is started by running the rest of data and the structure with minimum MSE value is selected. Experiment results show that in the network structure with minimum MSE values on cross validation (MSE=0.00067) and maximum correlation value on test results (0.86), there is 1 hidden layer and 8 neurons in the layer. NeuroSolutions Software is used for ANNs development process. The best MLP model which consists of one input layer with seventeen inputs, one hidden layer with eight neurons and one output layer with one output is presented in Figure 3. The results of testing can be seen at Table 5.

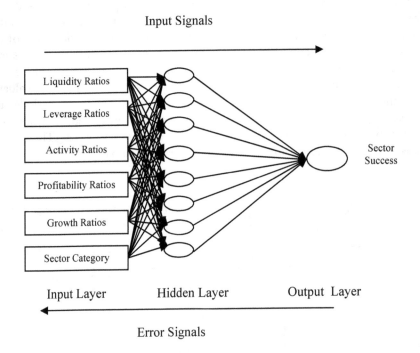

Figure 3. The general structure of MLP ANNs for sector success prediction

Indicators	Values
Hidden layer number	1
Neuron number at hidden layer	8
Trial number	2000
Minimum MSE	0,00067
Activation function	Hyperbolic tangent
Learning algorithm	Back propagation

Table 5 Features of the best ANNs structure

The closeness of test results with real sector success (that shows the change on difference of company establishment and liquidation quantities) can be seen at Figure 4. It reveals that the network is ready to use for prediction of sector success. If new sector success value that refers to change on difference of company establishment and liquidation quantities is entered to the proposed model, the decision maker can have idea about which potential success degree the sector will approximately have. On the other hand, in order to see whether a sector has expected success level for a defined period, the proposed model can be run and the results can be compared with the real events. That makes researchers and experts analyze the sector by using a supportive decision making tool.

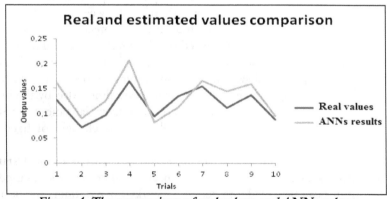

Figure 4. The comparison of real values and ANNs values.

In order to explore the impacts of input parameters on ANNs results, a sensitivity analysis is carried out. It is revealed that "fixed assets turnover" as an activity ratio has the highest impact on sectoral success and the changes should be frequently followed. In contrast, "current assets/total assets (%)" (as a liquidity ratio) and "net profit margin growth rate (%)" (as a growth ratio) have the lowest effectiveness on sectoral success. These findings indicate that it is vital for a sector how well it is using its fixed assets to generate sales. Especially in these three sectors, it can be asserted that less money has been tied-up in fixed assets for each unit of currency of sales revenue. On the contrary, the low effectiveness degree of "current assets/total assets" ratio reveals that there are no significant relationships on trade credit in there sectors. Moreover, working capital management as a financial issue is not an important tool for these sectors. Furthermore, "net profit margin growth rate" as an important growth ratio has no significant impact on evaluating the sectoral success. This may be due to the fragile nature of Turkish economy which makes it almost impossible to specify the sector's pricing strategies and how well it controls its costs. The impact levels of all financial parameters can be seen at Fig. 5.

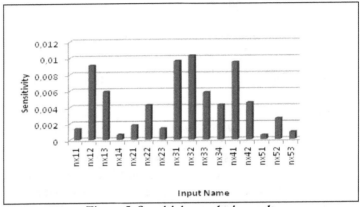

Figure 5. Sensitivity analysis results

5. Conclusion and Further Directions

This study adopts neural networks to develop SSE with respect to financial ratio analysis to be used in strategic planning decisions. The contribution of this study is to improve a support system that makes the process of SSE by considering the change on difference between company establishment and liquidation quantities as a key indicator. A case study for three main sectors in Turkey namely as agriculture, construction and manufacturing is carried out. The results reveal that ANNs is a powerful tool for being used as an alert system before company establishment or liquidation decision will be made. By benefiting from this proposed system, decision makers can discourage with the unexpected results that are caused from making strategic plans in inaccurate time. Also by the help of sensitivity analysis, it is explored that fixed assets turnover is a critical financial ratio for SSE. That means, decision makers should attach more importance on following the changes of fixed assets turnover rate closely.

Performances of the proposed networks can be compared with traditional statistical methods (such as multi discriminant analysis) as a future research. Also other heuristic methods such as fuzzy logic and genetic algorithms can be added into neural networks when defining the best structure.

5. References

[I] Acquisti A. and Lehmann H. 2000, Job Creation and Job Destruction in the Russian Federation, Trinity Economic Paper Series Paper No. 2000/1, JEL Classification: P52, J40.

[II] Armington C.and Acs Z. J. 2003, Job Creation and Persistence in Services and Manufacturing", Discussion Papers on Entrepreneurship, Growth and Public Policy. Max Plank Institute for Research into Economic Systems Group Entrepreneurship, Growth and Policy.

[III] Armstrong, J. S. and Green, K. C.2011,Demand forecasting: evidence-based methods,Thomas, C. R. and Shughart,W. F., (Ed), *Oxford Handbook in Managerial Economics*. pp. 123.

[IV] Barnes, M. and Haskel, J. 2002, Job Creation and Job Destruction in the Russian Federation, Trinity Economic Paper Series, Paper No. 2000/1, JEL Classification: P52, J40

[V] Bilgin, H. B. and Kilicarslan, I. N. 2008, An Analysis of the Unemployment in Selected MENA Countries and Turkey, *Journal of Third World Studies*, 25 (2), pp. 189.

[VI] Calderon, T. G. and Cheh, J. J. 2002, A Roadmap for Future Neural Networks Research in Auditing and Risk Assessment, International Journal of Accounting Information Systems, 3, pp. 203–236.

[VII] Dawis, S. J. and Haltiwanger, J. 1990, Gross Job Creation and Destruction: Microeconomic Evidence and Macroeconomic Implications, NBER Macroeconomics Annual 1990, Volume 5, Olivier J. Blanchard and Stanley Fischer (Eds), MIT Press.

[VIII] Graupe, D. 2007, Principles of Artificial Neural Networks, (2nd Edition), World Scientific Publishing, Singapore.

[IX] Hall, P. 1987, The Anatomy of Job Creation: Nations, Regions and Cities in the 1960s and 1970s, *Regional Studies*, 21 (2), pp. 95-106.

[X] Johnson, J. and Picton, P. 1995, Mechatronics: Designing Intelligent Machines, Concepts in Artificial Intelligence, Vol. 2, The Open University Press, Butterworth-Heinemann.

[XI] Klein, M. W., Schuh, S. and Triest, R. K. 2002, Job Creation, Job Destruction and the Real Exchange Rate, *Journal of International Economics,* 59 (2), pp. 239–265.

[XII] Klette, T. J. and Mathiassen, A. 1995 Job Creation, Job Destruction and Plant Turnover in Norwegian Manufacturing, Discussion Papers no.136. Statistics, Norway.

[XIII] Mukta, P. and Kumar, U.A. 2009, Neural Networks and Statistical Techniques: A Review of Applications, *Expert Systems with Applications*, 36 (1), pp. 2-17.

[XIV] Picot, G. and Dupuy, R. 1996, Job Creation by Company Size Class: Concentration and Persistence of Job Gains and Losses in Canadian Companies, Research paper 93. Business and Labour Market Analysis Division, Statistics Canada.

[XV] Schalkoff, R. 1997, Artificial Neural Networks, Mc Graw-Hill Professional, Toronto

[XVI] Vellido, A., Lisboa, P. J. G. and Vaughan, J. 1999, Neural Networks in Business: A survey of Applications (1992–1998)", *Expert Systems with Applications*, 17, pp. 51–70.

[XVII] Wong, B. K. and Selvi, Y. 1998, Neural Network Applications in Finance: A Review and Analysis of Literature (1990-1996), *Information & Management*, 34, pp. 129-139.

[XVIII] Wong, B. K., Lai, V. S. and Lam, J.2000, Bibliography of neural network business applications research: 1994-1998, Computers & Operations Research, 27, 1045-1076.

CHAPTER 7

Pricing Brazilian Fixed Income Options with Feedforward and Recurrent Neural Networks

Leandro Dos Santos Maciel

Economics Institute, State University of Campinas (UNICAMP)
Campinas, São Paulo, Brazil

Pricing Brazilian Fixed Income Options with Feedforward and Recurrent Neural Networks

Abstract

Pricing interest rate derivatives is a challenging task that has attracted the attention of many researches recently. From a practical point of view a plenty of reasons can justify this interest. Portfolio and risk managers, policymakers, traders and more generally all market participants find valuable information in forward, swap and option contracts. This information plays an important role in their strategies and decision making process. Thus, this paper compares the performance of Black (1976), Vasicek (1977) and CIR (1985) models, as benchmarks', with feedforward and recurrent artificial neural networks (ANNs) in pricing Brazilian IDI calls options using daily data for the period from January 2003 to September 2008. It is the first study that evaluates the performance of ANNs in pricing Brazilian interest rate options, one of the major emerging markets. We measure forecast performance for all the estimated models based on summary measures of forecast accuracy. Nevertheless, we performed parametric and nonparametric statistical tests as AGS, MGN and SIGN for competing forecast models. According to the statistical tests and summary forecast measurements, ANN is superior to Black, Vasicek and CIR models in IDI calls option pricing and, there are no differences between feedforward and recurrent architectures in terms of accuracy when pricing these options. Our results suggest that ANNs may have an important role to play in pricing interest rate options for which there is either no closed-form model, or the closed-form model is less successful as in Brazilian case.

Keywords: Neural Networks; Interest Rate Options; Options Pricing; IDI Options; Recurrent Neural Networks.

1. Introduction

Pricing interest rate derivatives is a challenging task that has attracted the attention of many researchers in recent decades. From a practical point of view many reasons can justify this interest. Portfolio and risk managers, policymakers, traders and more generally all market participants find valuable information in forward, swap and option contracts. This information plays an important role in their strategies and decision making process. On the other hand, the yield curve is undoubtedly one of the most important economic variables.

In Brazilian derivatives market, IDI options reflecting the behavior of interest rates between the trade date and the maturity of the option. Thus, traditional pricing models developed for other markets should be adjusted to evaluate them. Some recent studies have addressed this issue using different term structure models. Junior et al. (2003) fitted the spot rate term structure with the Hull-White model (Hull and White, 1993). Vieira Neto and Pereira (1999), assuming that short-term rates follow a Vasicek (1977) process, obtained a closed-form to price IDI options. Barbachan and Ornelas (2003) adopted CIR (Cox, Ross and Ingersoll, 1985) model and, Almeida and Vicente (2006) used affine models (see Duffie and Kan, 1996) to evaluate IDI options. However, all these models have showed that theoretical prices are very different in a comparison with market prices and, it can explain the poor liquidity verified in this market.

As option pricing theory typically derives non-linear relations between an option price and the variables determining it, a highly flexible model is required to capture the empirical pricing mechanism. Artificial Neural Networks (ANNs) are well suited for this purpose due to their ability to approximate virtually any (measurable) function up to an arbitrary degree of accuracy. First empirical results given in Malliaris and Salchenberger (1993), Hutchinson et al. (1994), and Geigle and Aronson (1999) for S&P 500 futures options showed promising for the neural network approach, though further research is needed, mainly in emergent markets as Brazilian Stock Market Exchange. A number of empirical studies that include Zurada et al. (1999) show that ANNs are better than several time series models. Likewise, Coats and Faut (1993), Leonard et al. (1991), and Fletcher and Goss (1993) reveal that neural networks are superior to the conventional statistical models. However, Bortiz et al. (1995), and Yang et al. (1999) show that both approaches have a similar degree of accuracy. On the other hand Bortiz et al. (1995) show that performance of ANN is sensitive to the choice of the variables selected. These results demand more applications of ANNs in finance and economics.

In this paper, we apply feedforward and recurrent artificial neural networks models to price IDI calls options traded on the Securities, Commodities and Future Exchange, BM&FBOVESPA, the Brazilian Stock Market Exchange, using daily data for the period from January 2003 to September 2008. The main difference from previous works, however, is the application of ANNs in the Brazilian interest rate options market, as well as the use of statistical tests to verify the accuracy among the evaluated methods. As a comparison, the closed-forms obtained by Black (1976), Vasicek (1977) and CIR (1985) models were applied to price IDI calls options, as benchmark models. We measure forecast performance for all these applications based on summary measures of forecast accuracy (RMSE, MAE and MAPE). Nevertheless, we performed parametric and nonparametric statistical tests as AGS, MGN and SIGN for competing forecast models.

The remainder of this paper is organized as follows: the next section briefly explains the IDI contracts and the benchmark models applied in this work. The third section describes the methodology, including the basic concepts of ANNs. The results and discussion is given in section four, followed by the conclusion in section five.

2. IDI Options and its Pricing Models

2.1. IDI Contracts

One of the most important Brazilian interest rate is the "CDI rate", or One-Day Interbank Deposit Contract rate. This rate is calculated by the average rate of all inter-bank overnight transactions in Brazil. It is published daily by ANBIMA (Brazilian National Association of Investment Banks), and has been the underlying asset of most Brazilian interest rate derivatives.

The Brazilian banks usually express their costs of funding in percentage of the published CDI terms, and it can be said that the CDI is the relevant cost of opportunity for Brazilian banks. The One-Day Interbank Deposit Contract Index, or IDI index, is calculated by BM&FBOVESPA as the result of the accrual of the daily CDI rate. The IDI index was set to 100,000 on January 2, 2003. In discrete-time, a correct representation of the IDI index is:

$$IDI_t = 100,000 \cdot \prod_{u=1}^{t}(1 + CDI_u) \tag{1}$$

where the index $u = 0$ refers to the date when the IDI was set to *100,000*, and CDI_u is the *CDI* rate of day *u*.

95

Expiration dates are the first business day of every month (however, the market has awarded more liquidity to the months of January, April, July and October, in addition to the month following the current). Each contract entitles to the payoffs described below.A call option on IDI is a European-style cash-settled options that entitles the owner to receive, at expiry, an amount equal to:

$$c(IDI_T, T) = max\ (0, IDI_T - X) \tag{2}$$

where T is the maturity date, IDI_T is the value of IDI index on the expiration date, and X is the strike price.

A put option on IDI is similar a call option that entitles the owner to receive, at expiry, an amount equal to:

$$p(IDI_T, T) = max\ (0, X - IDI_T) \tag{3}$$

2.2. Interest Rate Pricing Models

IDI option pricing has been related in the literature recently. One reason for that is about their particular features, as described above, which differs for the commons interest rate options traded over the global markets. In USA and European derivative markets, standard interest rate options has as underlying asset a fixed income equity with maturity so far than the option maturity. The peculiarity of Brazilian IDI interest rate options became its price, as well as the factors that affect them, different of those related to the standard models. In this case, researchers have employed particular attention in this derivative contract. The seminal works in this field are Vieira Neto and Pereira (1999) and Barbachan and Ornelas (2003). The authors derived a closed-form to price IDI options, based on a Vasicek and CIR process, respectively. In this work we perform these models to price IDI calls options, as well as the Black model, because the last one is widely applied for players on the Brazilian Stock Market Exchange, but, reasonably, this model is theoretically inappropriate for IDI interest rate options. These methods are described below.

2.2.1. IDI Black Option Pricing

Utilized by the players on the BM&FBOVESPA, the model based on Black (1976) give the price of an IDI call option, according to the formula as follows:

$$c_t = IDI_t N(d_1) - XP(t, T)N(d_2) \tag{4}$$

Where:

$$d_1 = \frac{ln\left(IDI_t / XP(t,T)\right) + \frac{\sigma^2 (T-t)^3}{6}}{\sigma\sqrt{(T-t)^3/3}} \quad \text{and} \quad d_2 = \frac{ln\left(IDI_t / XP(t,T)\right) - \frac{\sigma^2 (T-t)^3}{6}}{\sigma\sqrt{(T-t)^3/3}}$$

such that $N(\cdot)$ represents the normal cumulative distribution function, IDI_t is the value of IDI at time t; $P(t, T)$ is a price at time t of a discounted equity with maturity T, τ is the difference between T and t, and σ is the short-term interest rate volatility.

2.2.2. IDI Vasicek Option Pricing

Vieira Neto and Pereira (1999) derived a closed-form to IDI options based on a Vasicek (1977) process to the interest rate structure term, according to the following stochastic differential equation for the short-term interest rate:

$$dr(t) - \alpha(\theta - r(t))dt - \sigma dW(t) \tag{5}$$

where α represents the short-term interest rate mean reversion, σ is the short-term interest rate volatility, θ is the long-term interest rate and W is a Weiner process.

According to the martingale theory and the stochastic calculus, the authors derived the formula to IDI call option (c_t) as follows:

$$c_t = IDI_t \cdot N(d_1) - XP(t,T)N(d_1 - \sigma_p) \tag{6}$$

And d_1 is defined as:

$$d_1 = \frac{ln\left(\frac{IDI_t}{XP(t,T)}\right)+\frac{\sigma_p^2}{2}}{\sigma_p} \quad \text{and} \quad \sigma_p^2 = \frac{\sigma^2}{2\alpha^3}\left[2\alpha\tau + 4e^{(-\alpha\tau)} - e^{(-2\alpha\tau)} - 3\right]$$

where IDI_t is the value of IDI at time t; $P(t,T)$ is a price at time t of a discounted equity with maturity T, τ is the difference between T and t, and σ_p can be considered the short-term interest rate volatility obtained by a GARCH-D process (Vieira Neto and Pereira, 1999).

2.2.3. IDI CIR Option Pricing

In the model derived by Vieira Neto and Pereira (1999), short-term interest rate can assume negative values, which is not verified on the reality. CIR model solves this problem proposing the following diffusion equation to the short-term interest rate:

$$dr(t) = \alpha(\theta - r(t))dt - \sigma\sqrt{r(t)}dW(t) \tag{7}$$

According to this model, Barbachan and Ornelas (2003) developed a close-formula to price IDI options. For pricing an IDI call option we have:

$$c_t = c^* IDI_t\left(1 - \chi^2\left[ln\left(\frac{X}{IDI_{t+1}}\right);n^*,p^*\right]\right) - \frac{Xc^*3^{-\frac{n^*}{2}}e^{-p^*}\left(1-\chi^2\left[\frac{ln\left(\frac{X}{IDI_{t+1}}\right)}{3};n^*,p^*\right]\right)}{(1+CDI_t)} \tag{8}$$

where:

$$p^* = \frac{4CDI_t}{\sigma^2}\left(ln\left(\frac{1-e^{(\alpha-\lambda)\tau}}{1-e^{-(\alpha-\lambda)}}\right)\right); \; n^* = \frac{4(\alpha-\lambda)\left(\frac{6\alpha}{\alpha-\lambda}\right)\tau}{\sigma^2}; \; \text{and} \; c^* = \frac{\sigma^2}{4\,(\alpha-\lambda)} + \frac{\sigma^2}{4\tau e^{(\alpha-\lambda)}}\left(e^{\tau}-1\right)$$

such that λ represents the market price of risk and CDI_t represents the *CDI* index at day *t*.

3. Methodology

3.1. Data

Data consists of time series of IDI options for different strikes and maturities. The data covers the period from January 02, 2003 to September 02, 2008[1]. For the options data, we select the most liquid IDI call within each day with negotiated contracts greater or equal to 800. Nevertheless, the *CDI* daily index was selected for all business days covered by this work.

3.2. Benchmark Models

In order to evaluate the neural networks capability of interest rate option pricing, we used as benchmark models the equations (4), (6) and (8), because they are the models that more given theoretical prices close to real prices according to the literature and, they incorporate some characteristics of Brazilian interest rate term structure[2].

In the Black model, equation (4), sort-term interest rate volatility was estimated according with a GARCH (1,1) process based on *CDI* rate returns. In equation (6), we have all parameters in data base, except the sort-term interest rate volatility and the mean reversion parameter. These parameters were obtained by a GARCH-D (1,1) process, which according to Vieira Neto and Pereira (1999) we obtained the short-term interest rate volatility in terms of the interest rate mean reversion parameter[3].

However, in equation (8) we have four parameters to be estimated, the last two as well as in equation (6), and the other ones are: the market price of risk and the long-term interest rate. According to CDI historical evolution, the long-term interest rate was 18% per year (the same analysis can be verified in Barbachan and Ornelas, 2003). In this paper we admitted that the value of market price of risk is -1, it means that for each additional unit of risk, the stakeholder demands an additional unit of return and, it is negative because we assume risk aversion. With all parameters, we estimated the benchmark's closed-form models to price IDI calls options.

---

[1] The data was obtained with the BM&FBOVESPA.

[2] IDI put options are not evaluated in this work because this contracts do have a low liquidity on BM&FBOVESPA.

[3] According to Vieira Neto and Pereira (1999) this is the exogenous estimation of the parameters, such that GARCH-D (1,1) is formed by a common GARCH (1,1) process that consider the duration effects, feature verified in interest rate term structure.

3.3. Neural Networks Models

A Neural Network is a collection of interconnected simple processing elements structured in successive layers and can be depicted as a network of arcs/connections and nodes/neurons. In the muli-layer percetron (MLP) neural networks, the neurons are organized in different layers. The inputs are fed to an input layer, the outputs of the network are given in the output layer, and in between, there is an arbitrary number of hidden layers.

A feedforward artificial neural network consists of a number of interconnected elements called neurons or nodes. ANNs are powerful computational devices because they can process information based on learning from examples and to generalize it to solve problems never seen before. A neural network can be said to be a regression function that characterizes the relationship between the dependent variable and the explanatory variables. An ANN is constructed from a number of basic nonlinear functions via a multilayer structure. ANNs are nonlinear, nonparametric statistical methods that are independent of distributions of the underlying data generating processes.

The functionality of the individual neurons is simple. Each neuron sums up the signals leading to it, adds a bias term, and makes a non-linear transformation (Haykin, 2001). The transfer function is typically a smooth monotonically increasing function, a sigmoid, such as the hyperbolic tangents or the logistic function. The transformed signal of the neuron is passed on to neurons in subsequent layers, and the procedure is then repeated. The connections between the neurons are represented by weights. When the MLP is presented to input vectors, these are fed forward through the network via the neurons. The network outputs are compared to known targets and an error function, typically the sum of squared errors is computed.

The error is propagated backwards through the network and the weights are adjusted to minimize de error function. The same procedure is repeated over and over until the network outputs match the targets with an acceptable accuracy. The training algorithm in adjusting the weights is called backpropagation and was originally derived by (Rumelhart et al., 1986). Backpropagation finds the optimal, at least the locally optimal, weights for a given MLP architecture.

The MLP model is a universal approximator (Hornik, 1993). The implication is that given enough hidden neurons, any function can be modeled arbitrarily well. This is a very strong result, but in a presence of noise and outliers, too many neurons are likely to result in overfitting, and we end up in a situation characterized by a good fit of input vectors, but with large fluctuations in between. The network has been trained to copy the input data instead of generalizing, so when the network is presented to unseen data, its performance is low. A popular approach to avoid overfitting is to split the data into three parts: training, test and validation sets (see Hertz et al., 1991). The training set is used for estimating the weights, the test set is used for model selection, and the validation set is used for out-of-sample evaluation. Lagged dependent variables are included in feed forward neural networks to capture the dynamics of the model; however, the correct number of lags needed in a network is normally unknown. Therefore, a lagged dependent structure in a network may not be able to characterize the behavior of the dependent variable in some applications. To obviate this problem, researchers have devised various networks where feedbacks have been proposed. These types of neural networks are called recurrent neural networks (RNN). An RNN has a richer dynamic structure, but one that is similar to that of a linear time series model with a moving average term. Recurrent architectures consist of two separate components. The first part is comprised of one or more recurrent layers that encompass short-term memory, which is denoted by the lagged dependent variable and the past history of the network by the activation variable. The other part of the network, which is known as the predictor, is usually a feed forward part, similar to that of an ANN. The short-term memory part of the model captures the network's prior activation history services relevant to the prediction tasks. Therefore, the appropriate response at a particular point in time could depend not only on the current input, but also potentially on all previous inputs. A recurrent network appears to be able to capture dynamic characteristics of networks over and above that of the feed forward neural network because RNN is able to work with the contemporaneous and lagged values of the independent variables. In RNNs, the input layer's activity patterns pass through the network more than once before generating a new output pattern. This allows RNNs to learn extensively complex sequential patterns. In this work, we apply two different models of recurrent neural networks: Elman and Jordan models. The difference between these models is about the recurrence in the layers. Elman recurrent networks have recurrence for each hidden layer, although Jordan recurrent networks present recurrence just in the output layer.

The main issue in MLP models is how to find the optimal architecture, that is, the optimal number of hidden layers and neurons. For inputs we used first of all a model with all parameters that can influence the IDI call option price: *IDI* index at day t, long-term interest rate θ, short-term interest rate volatility σ (obtained by a GARCH-D (1,1) process), market price of risk (-1), mean reversion parameter (0.006, according to Barbachan and Ornelas, 2003), strike price X, and the time to maturity for each option, $\tau = T - t$.

Inputs, hidden layer(s) and hidden neurons numbers were selected according to a selection procedure BIC (Schwarz, 1978) based on root mean squared error (RMSE), comparing the theoretical prices with real prices, observed on the market movements. The optimal neural network architectures applied in this work to price IDI call options are illustrated in Figures 1, 2 and 3.

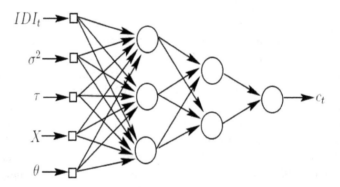

Fig. 1. Feedforward Neural Network (FNN) to IDI call options pricing

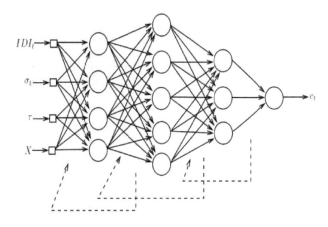

Fig. 2. Elman Recurrent Neural Network (ERNN) to IDI call options pricing

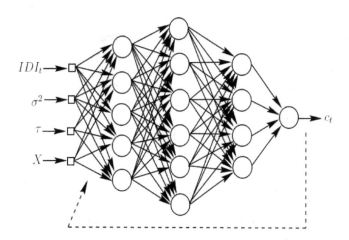

Fig. 3. Jordan Recurrent Neural Network (JRNN) to IDI call options pricing

The data partitioning were performed into three sets: training set, testing set and validation set, with 70%, 20% and 10% of data, respectively. In the results analysis, the most important set is the validation set, because it should consists the most recent contiguous observations. It is a final test to evaluate the generalization capability of a neural networks performed.

The learning algorithm applied was the backpropagation, as described in this section. Iterations converge in order to 500, which minimizes the error function, and it composes a forward and backward movement over the network. Finally, the learning rate, that determines the size of the step that we use for "moving" towards the minimum of error function, was set on 0.6.

3.4. Performance Measurement

To determine the pricing accuracy of each model's estimates, we examine the Root Mean Squared Error (RMSE), the Mean Absolute Error (MAE) and the Mean Absolute Percentage Error (MAPE):

$$RMSE = \sqrt{\left(\frac{1}{N}\right) \sum_{t=1}^{N} \left(c_t^{mkt} - c_t^{m}\right)^2} \tag{9}$$

$$MAE = \frac{1}{N} \sum_{t=1}^{N} \left|c_t^{mkt} - c_t^{m}\right| \tag{10}$$

$$MAPE = \sum_{t=1}^{N} \left|\frac{c_t^{mkt} - c_t^{m}}{c_t^{mkt}}\right| \tag{11}$$

where c_t^{mkt} denotes the real IDI call price observed on option market at time t, c_t^{m} is the IDI call price obtained by the estimated models, i.e., theoretical prices, and N is the sample size. Although all these summary measures discussed above, they are useful measures of forecast accuracy that have been employed by empirical researches extensively, they do not reveal whether the forecast from one model is statistically superior to the other model. Therefore, it is imperative to employ some other commonly used tests that could help compare two or more competing models in terms of forecasting accuracy. For this reason, in addition to the summary measures of price evaluations, we employ two parametric tests of pair-wise price/forecast evaluations, i.e., the AGS test and MGN test, and one nonparametric test of equivalence between two competing models, the SIGN test. These tests are based on hypothesis tests, which have as null hypothesis the equivalence between the competitive models against the alternative hypothesis that indicates the superiority of a model against a benchmark. In this work, we evaluated the superiority of neural network model against the standard models, based on equation (4), (6) and (8)[4].

4. Results and Discussion

We measure pricing performance for all the models estimated in this study based on summary measures and traditional accuracy tests that have been employed by many researches (Mathews, 1994). The results are based only on the validation set, once it is not necessary to evaluate the other sets. Table 1 summarizes the traditional error measures. According to the RMSE, MAE, and MAPE measurements, the best model is the Elman recurrent neural network. We can see that benchmark models showed the higher values to all measures of forecast.

---

[4] For AGS, MGN and SIGN tests descriptions see Ashley el al. (1980), Granger and Newbold (1977) and Lehman (1988), respectively.

Table 1. Summary measures of forecast evaluations

Models	RMSE	MAE	MAPE
Black	6.3768	2.3982	6.3263
Vasicek	4.8767	2.0213	5.5959
CIR	4.0935	1.9872	5.0121
FNN	1.0922	0.8752	1.7732
ERNN	0.8724	0.3142	1.2652
JRNN	0.9998	0.3736	1.3251

It is clear that the neural network models applied in this work results in IDI call prices more close to real prices, in a comparison with the closed-form models. In a comparison with the architectures of networks, the results do not showed a significant difference among them, in terms of error measurements.With the results above, we can say that, according to the traditional forecast measurements, neural network models outperform the traditional methods. The next step is to verify the statistical difference among the methods performed. Table 2 shows all the results of statistical tests for forecast prediction. The results from AGS, MGN and SIGN tests that are shown in Table 2 examine pair-wise comparisons between forecasts of two competing models (benchmark and ANNs models) reveal that feed forward and recurrent neural network architectures show statistically significant evidence of superior performance in pricing IDI call options.

Table 2. AGS, MGN and SIGN tests for pair-wise forecast evaluations

Models	AGS	MGN	SIGN
Black Vs. FNN	123.876	67.976	-7,875
	(0.0000)	(0.0001)	(0.0000)
Black Vs. ERNN	146.973	87.863	-8.765
	(0.0000)	(0.0000)	(0.0000)
Black Vs. JRNN	132.962	99.987	-9.765
	(0.0000)	(0.0000)	(0.0000)
Vasicek Vs. FNN	119.826	71.762	-8.090
	(0.0000)	(0.0000)	(0.0000)
Vasicek Vs. ERNN	123.753	76.862	-9.021
	(0.0000)	(0.0000)	(0.0000)
Vasicek Vs. JRNN	144.823	87.653	-9.001
	(0.0000)	(0.0000)	(0.0000)
CIR Vs. FNN	199.987	70.982	-8.872
	(0.0000)	(0.0000)	(0.0000)
CIR Vs. ERNN	187.751	74.973	-9.144
	(0.0000)	(0.0000)	(0.0000)
CIR Vs. JRNN	167.972	79.001	-9.472
	(0.0000)	(0.0000)	(0.0000)

Notes: The relevant p-values for each test are shown beneath each test statistic in parenthesis.

Figures 4 to 9 illustrate our results taking IDI call options with the most liquid strike price, i.e., 200.000 IDI points and, with maturity on February 2008. These results are selected by the validation set.

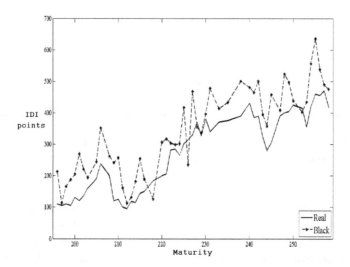

Fig. 4. Evolution of IDI calls market prices and obtained by Black model

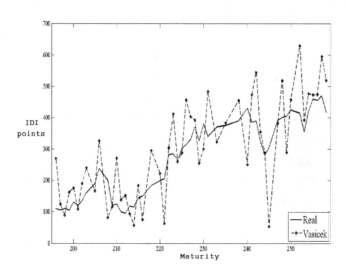

Fig. 5. Evolution of IDI calls market prices and obtained by Vasicek model

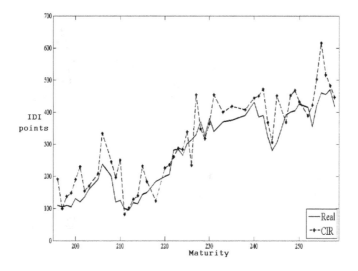

Fig. 6. Evolution of IDI calls market prices and obtained by CIR model

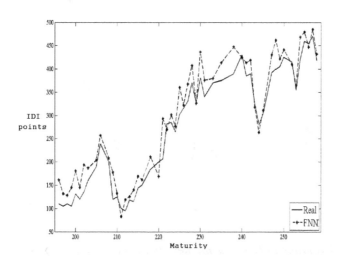

Fig. 7. Evolution of IDI calls market prices and obtained by FNN model

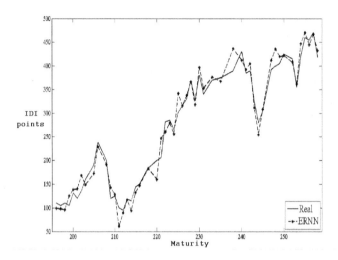

Fig. 8. Evolution of IDI calls market prices and obtained by ERNN model

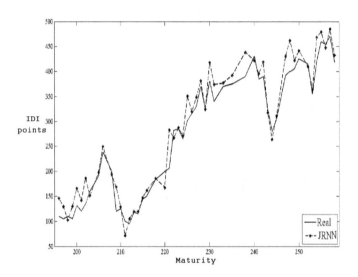

Fig. 9. Evolution of IDI calls market prices and obtained by JRNN model

By examining the figures above its clear the good performance of ANNs models. Nevertheless, we can see that among the artificial intelligence models, Elman's architecture shows the best performance in a comparison with the other models.

5. Conclusions

In this paper, we have evaluated the capability of neural networks to price Brazilian fixed income options, more specifically, IDI calls options. This works presents a contribution to the literature in this field, because approaches the Brazilian fixed income options using neural networks and, mainly, applied statistical tests to verify the performance among the competitive models. We price the IDI calls options, traded on BM&FBOVESPA, using the benchmark models (Black (1976), Vasicek (1977) and CIR (1985) models) and a feedforward and recurrent neural networks archtectures from January 2003 to September 2008. We evaluate predictions from these models using summary measures of forecast accuracy such as root mean squared error (RMSE), mean absolute percentage error (MAPE) and mean absolute error (MAE). In addition, we compare predictions from these models with the benchmark models according to the forecast accuracy, i.e., using parametric and nonparametric tests of forecast equivalence such as AGS, MGN and SIGN tests. From the results based on the summary measures of forecast accuracy, it reveals that the neural network models appears to be superior candidate to price IDI calls options. The results based on AGS and MGN tests show that ANN model outperforms the benchmarks in statistical terms. Finally, the SIGN test confirms our conclusions, that is, the neural network models employed show statistically significant evidence of predictability in IDI call options pricing.

Future research might be focused to employ such other structures of neural networks architectures as well as the option evaluation according to the moneyness. And, our results can be a possible solution to the liquidity problem in IDI options in Brazilian derivatives market. Nevertheless, others methods as Fuzzy Inference Systems and Genetic Programming can be performed in this field.

References

[I] Almeida, C. I., Vicente, J. V.: The Role of Fixed Income Options on the Risk Assessment of Bond Portfolios. In: Annals of the 6th Brazilian Financial Meeting (2006).

[II] Barbachan, J. S. F., Ornelas, J. R. H.: IDI Option pricing using CIR model. Estudos Econômicos 33(2), pp. 287-323 (2003) (In Portuguese).

[III] Bortiz, J. E., Kennedy, D. B., de Miranda e Albuquerque, A.: Predicting corporate failure using neural network approach. International Journal of Intelligence Systems in Accounting Finance and Management, 4, pp. 95-111 (1995).

[IV] Coats, P. K., Faut, L. F.: Recognizing financial distress patterns using neural network tool. Financial Management, 22, pp. 142-155 (1993).

[V] Cox, J. C., Ingersoll, J. E., Ross, S. A.: A Theory of the Term Structure of Interest Rates. Econometrica 53, pp. 385-407 (1985).

[VI] Duffie, D., Kan, R.: A Yield Factor Model of Interest Rates. Mathematical Finance, 6(4), pp. 379-406 (1996).

[VII] Fletcher, D., Goss, F.: Forecasting with neural networks: An application using bankruptcy data. Information and Management, 24, pp. 159-167 (1993).

[VIII] Geigle, D. S., Aronson, J. E.: An Artificial Neural Network Approach to the Valuation of Options and Forecasting of Volatility. Journal of Computational Intelligence in Finance, 7(6), pp. 19-25 (1999).

[IX] Haykin, S.: Neural Networks: A Comprehensive Foundation. New York: IEEE Press (2001).

[X] Hertz, J., Krogh, A., Palmer, R.G. Introduction to the Theory of Neurocomputation. Addison-Wesley, Reading MA (1991).

[XI] Hornik, K.: Some New Results on Neural Networks Approximation. Neural Networks, 6, pp.1069-1072 (1993).

[XII] Hull, J., White, A.: One-Factor Interest-Rate Models and the Valuation of Interest-Rate Derivative Securities. Journal of Financial and Quantitative Analysis, 28, pp. 235-253 (1993).

[XIII] Hutchinson, J. M., Lo, A., Poggio, T.: A Nonparametric Approach to Price and Hedging Derivatives Securities via Learning Networks. Journal of Finance, 49(3), pp. 851-889 (1994).

[XIV] Junior, A. F., Greco, F., Lauro, C., Francisco, G., Rosenfeld, R.,Oliveira, R.: Application of Hull-White Model to Brazilian IDI Options. In: Annals of the 3rd Brazilian Financial Meeting (2003).

[XV] Leonard, G., Alam, P., Medy, G. R.: Application of neural network and quantitative response model to the author's going concern uncertainty decisions. Decision Science, 23, pp. 896-916 (1991).

[XVI] Malliaris, M., Salchenberger, L.: A Neural Network Model for Estimating Option Prices. Journal of Applied Intelligence, 3(3), pp. 193-206 (1993).

[XVII] Mathews, B.P.: Towards a taxonomy of forecast error measures. Journal of Forecasting, 13, pp. 409-416 (1994).

[XVIII] Rumelhart, D., Hinton, G., Williams, R.: Learning Internal Representation by Error Propagation. In: Parallel Distributed Processing: Explorations in the Microstructure of Cognition, MIT Press, Cambridge, MA (1986).

[XIX] Schwarz, G.: Estimating the dimension of a model. Annals of Statistics, 6(2), pp. 461-468 (1978).

[XX] Vasicek, O.: An Equilibrium Characterization of the Term Structure. Journal of Financial Economics, 5, pp. 177-188 (1977).

[XXI] Vieira Neto, C., Pereira, P. L.V.: Closed Form Formula for the Arbitrage Free Price of an Option for the One Day Interfinancial Deposits Index, IBMEC Working Paper, Econpapers (1999).

[XXII] Yang, Z. R., Platt, M. B., Platt, H. D.: Probabilistic neural network in bankruptcy predictions. Journal of Business Research, 44, pp. 67-74 (1999)

[XXIII] Zurada, J. M., Foster, B. P.,Ward, T. J., Barker, P. M.: Neural networks versus logit regression models for financial distress response variables. The journal of Applied Business Research, 15, pp. 21-29 (1999)

CHAPTER 8

Chinese Stock Price and Volatility Predictions with Multiple Technical Indicators

Qin Qin, Qing-Guo Wang, Shuzhi Sam Ge, & Ganesh Ramakrishnan

National University of Singapore,
Singapore City, Singapore

Chinese Stock Price and Volatility Predictions with Multiple Technical Indicators

Abstract

While a large number of studies have been reported in the literature with reference to the use of Regression model and Artificial Neural Network (ANN) models in predicting stock prices in Western countries, the Chinese stock market is much less studied. Note that the latter is growing rapidly, will overtake USA one in 20-30 years time and thus becomes a very important place for investors worldwide. In this paper, an attempt is made at predicting the Shanghai Composite Index returns and price volatility, on a daily and weekly basis. In the paper, two different types of prediction models, namely the Regression and Neural Network models are used for the prediction task and multiple technical indicators are included in the models as inputs. The performances of the two models are compared and evaluated in terms of directional accuracy. Their performances are also rigorously compared in terms of economic criteria like annualized return rate (ARR) from simulated trading. In this paper, both trading with and without short selling has been considered, and the results show in most cases, trading with short selling leads to higher profits. Also, both the cases with and without commission costs are discussed to show the effects of commission costs when the trading systems are in actual use.

Keywords: Regression Model, Artificial Neural Network Model, Chinese Stock Market, Technical Indicators, Volatility.

1. Introduction

From the beginning of time it has been man's common goal to make his life easier. The prevailing notion in society is that wealth brings comfort and luxury, so it is not surprising that there has been so much work done on ways to predict the markets. Various technical, fundamental, and statistical indicators have been proposed and used with varying results. However, no one technique or combination of techniques has been successful enough to consistently "beat the market". As a result, there is a huge motivation to develop new forecasting techniques that can unravel the market's mysteries and obtain greater profits.

The stock market is known as the "cradle of capitalism". It is a place where companies come to raise their share capital and investors go to invest their surplus funds. Vast amounts of capital are invested and traded in everyday all over the world. The prediction of the stock market movements, however, poses a challenge to academicians and practitioners. The reason is that stock market movements are characterized as being uncertain and complex as it can be affected by virtually any economic, social or political development that has a bearing on the economy. This uncertainty and complexity is undesirable for any trader who is attempting to make profits from the stock market. Therefore, there is a need to reduce this uncertainty by making accurate predictions.

Initially, stock market research encapsulated two elemental trading techniques namely the Technical and Fundamental approaches. [1] In Technical and analysis, it is believed that market timing is keypoint. It involves the study of historical data of the stock market to predict trends in price and volume. In other words, there is heavy reliance on historical data in order to predict future outcomes. Fundamental analysis, on the other hand involves making estimates on the intrinsic value of a stock.

This technique uses information such as earnings, ratios, and management effectiveness to predict future outcomes.As the level of investing and trading grew, there began a pursuit for better tools and methods that could not only increase gains but also minimize the risks undertaken by the investor. Tools that used modeling techniques to discover patterns within the historical data of the stock market were put to test, with an attempt to predict and benefit from the market's direction. One such example is the Linear Time Series Models, where univariate and multivariate regression models [2] were used to identify patterns in the historical data of the stock market. For nonlinear patterns, Machine Learning Models, [3] in particular neural networks, were commonly used. For example, one sees that:

- In [4], the authors used a mean reverting characteristic to model and estimate the stock markets. The authors stated that the random walk which is used to describe the stock markets may not be correct when the process of stock markets diverge over time. The mean reverting characteristic is a good way to model and estimate the stock markets. The authors used two methods to estimate the parameters, which are Least Square Estimation and Maximum Likelihood Estimation. In this paper, the authors focused on the monthly data of Dow Jones Industrial Average and the Singapore Straits Times Index and got some interesting conclusion.

- In [5], the authors predicted the mid-term price trend for Taiwan stock market. The authors firstly extracted the features from ARIMA analyses, then the authors used the features which are produced in the first step to train a recurrent neural network. The Taiwan stock market series is regarded by the authors as a nonlinear ARIMA (1,2,1). The conclusion of this paper is that the prediction system can predict the Taiwan stock market trend of up to 6 weeks based on four years weekly data with an acceptable accuracy.

- In [6], the authors focused the research work on Shanghai stock market for Chinese stock market is one of fast growing stock markets in the world. The authors used two types of models which are the model of stochastic SARIMA and the model of backpropagation network. The author used the actual data of Shanghai Composite Index to do the prediction and found that SARIMA model is more optimistic.

- In [7], the authors took advantage of the nonlinear dynamical theory to use the multivariate nonlinear prediction method. The prediction system is based on the reconstruction of multidimensional phase space. The authors set the model using multivariate nonlinear prediction method and got the experiment results using the data of Shenzhen Index. The authors compared the results obtained using multivariate nonlinear prediction method with the results obtained using unvariate nonlinear prediction method and found that the performance of multivariate nonlinear prediction method is better than the performance of unvariate nonlinear pre-diction method.

- In [8], the author stated that the stock market is a very complicated nonlinear system, the artificial neural network also has nonlinear characteristic. It is proper to use artificial neural network to do the prediction of stock market. The authors used the artificial neural network to imitate the trading process of stock market. Because the convergent speed of backpropagation algorithm is low, the authors enhanced the convergent speed of

- backpropagation algorithm by proposing the rate of deviation. The authors used the data of both Shanghai and Shenzhen to do the prediction.

- In [9], the authors explored a new method to estimate the systematic risk (which is called as beta) in China stock market. A technique is involved in this new method, which is maximal overlap discrete wavelet transform (MODWT). The technique will not lose any information when it is investigating the behavior of beta at different time frames. The experimental results showed that China stock market is quite different from other stock markets. The authors drew a conclusion that the difference between China stock market and other stock markets is due to the character and behavior finance.

- In [10], the authors analyzed the volatility of a stock in China on its returns series using the models of GARCH family. They found that the series of stock returns is stationary, and it has a significant ARCH effect, a volatility cluster exists in China stock market. The authors also found that a return of negative shock produces more volatility than the positive one of equal magnitude. They finally drew a conclusion that there is a leverage effect in stock returns volatility.

- In [11], the authors used the daily data of Shanghai stocks to do the prediction based on the family GARCH models. The paper used ME, MAE and R- MSE for error measurement. From the results, the authors found that in the training period, EGAR- CH-

- M model can generate best performance, while in testing period, simple GARCH model or asymmetric model can produce best performance.

In general, most of stock market studies in the literature have been focused on developed markets while emerging markets are much less studied. Note that the latter is growing rapidly, and in particular, China market will overtake USA one in 20 - 30 years time and it has becomes a very important place for investors worldwide. It is thus timely to study this market's performance and efficiency based on recent data. This paper attempts to predict the Shanghai Composite Index return and volatility on a daily and weekly basis with use of multiple technical indicators. Specifically, the present work contributes to the literature in the following ways:

1) An attempt is made to understand the efficacy of an emerging market such as China. Today, China is one of the fastest growing emerging economies in the world. Not only is there a significant growth in the demand for investment funds but the growth in capital markets is also expected to play an increasingly important role in the process. At this transitional stage, it is necessary to assess the level of efficiency of the Chinese Stock Market in order to establish its longer term role in the process of economic development. However as studies on Chinese Stock Markets are very few and also dated and mostly inconclusive, the objective of this study in this paper is to test whether predictability of return rates and price volatility is possible.

2) An attempt is made to predict stock market price volatility. Volatility is an important indicator for investors. Results from this study do show that neural network models have their merits and perform better than regression models.

3) Multiple technical indicators are used in modeling. We also use different combinations of different technical indicators to do the prediction to see the performance. Some combinations improve the performance of the prediction.

The rest of the paper is organized as follows. Section 2 gives an overview of the stock market prediction methods. Section 3 presents the methodology and shows the results for the predictability of Shanghai Composite Index return. Section 4 presents the methodology and shows the results for the predictability of Shanghai Composite Index price volatility. Finally, Section 5 gives a conclusion of the work that has been done, as well as possible areas of improvements in future work.

2. Stock Market Prediction Methods

In this section, we will consider the different prediction methods that are available for predicting stock market movements and returns. Some of these methods that will be covered in depth in this section are Technical Analysis, Linear Time Series Models and Machine Learning Models.

2.1. Technical Analysis

The idea behind technical analysis is that stock prices move in trends dictated by the constantly changing attitudes of investors in response to different forces. Future stock movements are predicted by using price, volume and observing trends that are dominating the market. Technical analysis rests on the assumption that history repeats itself and that future market direction can be determined by examining past prices [1]. The groups of professionals who subscribe to this method are the technical analysts or the chartists, as they are more commonly known. To them all information about earnings, dividends and future performance of the company is already reflected in the stock's price history. Therefore the historical price chart is all a chartist needs to make predictions of future stock price movements.

This method of predicting the market is highly criticized because it is highly subjective. Two technical analysts studying the same chart may interpret them differently, thereby arriving at completely different trading strategies. Also a chartist may only occasionally be successful if trends perpetuate. Technical analysis is also considered to be controversial as it contradicts the Efficient Market Hypothesis. Despite such criticism and controversy, the method of technical analysis is used by approximately 90% of the major stock traders.

In this paper, several technical indicators are used. I will show the details of the technical indicators blow:

1) **Moving Average:** This indicator returns the moving average of a field over a given period of time. This is done primarily to avoid noise in the daily price movements. The formula of MA used in this chapter is showed below:

   $MA_n=$ mean (last n close prices)   (1)

The *n* is the parameter. We set *n* as 10 and 25 in this paper.

2) **Oscillator:** This function compares a security's closing price to its price range over a given time period. The formula of SO used in this chapter is showed as

$$\%K = 100 \times \frac{Close\ price - L_n}{H_n - L_n} \qquad (2)$$

$$\%D = 3 - period\ moving\ average\ of\ \%K \qquad (3)$$

Where H_n and L_n are respectively the highest and the lowest price over the last n periods. The n is the parameter. We set n as 10.

3) **Volatility:** Volatility can either be measured by using the standard deviation or variance between returns from the stock or market index. Commonly, the higher the volatility, the riskier the stock or market. The formula of volatility used in this chapter is showed below:

Volatility = std (last n close prices) $\qquad (4)$

The n is the parameter. We set n as 10.

Beside the technical indicators above, we also used some simple technical indicators: return, actual price change, volume and volume difference.

2.2. Linear Time Series Models

Linear time series models are often used to predict future values of the time series by detecting linear relationships between the historical data of the stock and the time series under consideration. [2] Depending on the number of different variables used as factors of the time series, two different types of linear time series models are used. For the case where only one factor is used to predict the time series, univariate regression is employed. If more variables are used to predict the time series, then the model of multivariate regression is used. The regression method works by having a set of independent variables, whole linear combination gives the predicted value of the time series under consideration. The predicted value of the time series is thus called the dependant variable. The model associated with such a regression method is given by the Equation (5) below:

$$Y_t = \sum_{n=1}^{m} a_n x_{n,t}$$

$$(5)$$

Where y_t is the dependent variable of the time series at time t, a_n is the regression coefficient and $x_{n,t}$ is the independent variable(s). For univariate regression, $m = 1$, whereas for multivariate regression, $m > 1$.

In this paper, linear regression model will be used. Regression models are statistical models that are used to predict one variable from one or more other variables. Inference based on such models is called Regression analysis, which is the technique for modeling and analyzing several variables, when the focus is on the relationship between a dependent variable and one or more independent variables. More specifically, the regression model helps in understanding how the typical value of the dependent variable changes when any one of the independent variables is varied.

Given a data set $\left\{ y_i, x_{i1}, \ldots, x_{ip} \right\}_{i=1}^{n}$ of n statistical units, a linear regression model assumes that the relationship between the dependent variable y_i and the p-vector of regressors x_i approximately linear. This approximate relationship is modeled through a "disturbance term" ε_i —an unobserved random variable that adds noise to the linear relationship between the dependent variable and regressors. The model is described by the function given below:

$$y_i = \beta_1 x_{i1} + \ldots + \beta_p x_{ip} + \varepsilon_i \qquad i = 1, \ldots, n \quad (6)$$

Here y_i is the forecasted return or volatility that is based on p independent variables, x_{i1} to x_{ip} and β_1 to β_p the coefficients of the linear regression model.

These n equations are often stacked together and written in vector form as:

$$y = X\beta + \varepsilon \qquad\qquad\qquad (7)$$

where

$$y = \begin{pmatrix} y_1 \\ y_2 \\ \vdots \\ y_n \end{pmatrix}, X = \begin{pmatrix} x'_1 \\ x'_2 \\ \vdots \\ x'_n \end{pmatrix} = \begin{pmatrix} x_{11} & \cdots & x_{1p} \\ x_{21} & \cdots & x_{2p} \\ \vdots & \ddots & \vdots \\ x_{n1} & \cdots & x_{np} \end{pmatrix},$$

$$\beta = \begin{pmatrix} \beta_1 \\ \beta_2 \\ \vdots \\ \beta_p \end{pmatrix}, \varepsilon = \begin{pmatrix} \varepsilon_1 \\ \varepsilon_2 \\ \vdots \\ \varepsilon_p \end{pmatrix}.$$

The study using the linear regression model is achieved using the "regress" function in MATLAB, which takes in the inputs to the model and the desired output from the model and returns the coefficients of the linear regression model. The coefficients of the linear regression model are obtained by the least mean squares method, which minimizes an error function which is the square of the error of each predicted value.

2.3. Machine Learning Models

Machine learning models [3] are a class of models which can study the underlying relationships between the independent variables and the dependent variables of the time series by being "trained" on a sample set of data which should ideally be representative of the actual environment. The most popular machine learning model used for stock market prediction is that of neural networks (NNs), thus my research work will be focusing on the use of NNs in predicting the Shanghai Composite Index returns. NN is a powerful data modeling tool that is able to capture and map an input (independent variable) set to a corresponding output (dependent variable) set. The motivation for the development of the NN technology stemmed from the desire to develop an artificial system that could perform
"intelligent" tasks similar to those performed by the human brain. A NN can resemble the human brain in two ways:
1) A NN acquires knowledge through learning.
2) A NN's knowledge is stored within inter-neuron connection strengths known as synaptic weights.

The NN architecture can be used to represent both linear and non-linear relationships. For data that contains non- linear characteristics, traditional linear models are simply inadequate. The most common neural network model is that of the Multi-Layer Perceptron (MLP) and this study on the Chinese stock market prediction will focus on the MLP. The MLP is also known as the supervised network because it requires a desired output in order to learn. The goal of this type of network is to create a model that correctly maps the input to the output using historical data so that the model can then be used to produce the output when the desired output is unknown. A graphical representation of an MLP with two hidden layers is shown in **Figure 1** below: The MLP is in fact a distributed processing network, comprising of numerous neurons, with each neuron as the most basic processing element within the network [12]. A neuron is a processing unit that takes in a number of inputs and gives a distinct output for the input it receives. The inputs are fed to each neuron through links between the different layers. An MLP only allows links between successive layers of neurons. Each link is characterized by a weight value, and it is this weight value where the "memory" or knowledge of the problem is stored. The output of each neuron is determined jointly by the weighted sum of the inputs, as well as the activation function, *f*, used in the neuron. The most commonly used activation functions are the hardlimit, linear, sigmoid and tansigmoid activation functions. As depicted in **Figure 1**, the MLP is made up of a number of layers of neurons. The input layer defines the inputs to the MLP. The inputs are then passed on to the first hidden layer of the MLP. For an MLP, the number of hidden layers must be at least one. After propagating through all the hidden layers, the input finally reaches the output layer, which then gives the final output of the whole network for the given set of inputs. A common notation to represent the architecture of the MLP is to use the string R-S1-S2-S3, where R is the number of inputs to the MLP, S1 and S2 indicates the number of neurons in the first and second hidden layer respectively, and S3 indicates the number of neurons in the output layer, which is also the number of outputs in the output set of the network. After the architecture of the MLP has been decided, the network will have to be trained before it can be used in any application. This procedure of training involves modifying the weights of the links within the MLP so that the MLP will store the correct knowledge of the system which it is modeling. The training procedure for

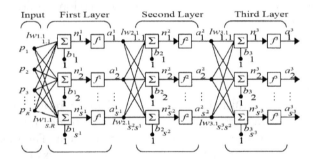

Figure 1. Architecture of MLP with two hidden layers [3].

an MLP can be done using a back-propagation algorithm to update the all the weights of the neurons in order to derive a good 'fit' on the training data, but at the same time not sacrificing performance on the unseen data. This means that a well-trained MLP must be able to generalize well from the training data that is presented to it.

3. Predictability of Shanghai Composite Index Return

In this section, we firstly introduce the simulation design which consists of data collection, data pre-processing, three comparison experiments and the metrics for performance evaluation, then the simulation results and discussions are showed.

3.1. Simulation Design
3.1.1. Data Collection

We collected the historical data of Shanghai Composite Index for both daily data and weekly data from the year 2000 to the year 2010 from the stockstar website [13].

3.1.2. Data Pre-Processing

Because we want to see whether the return is random or not, we calculate the daily returns from the daily data, the weekly returns from the weekly data for the Shanghai Composite Index. The entire set is divided into a three separate data sets for different usage. The first data is called the "Training" data set and is used for training and adjusting the coefficients or weights of the systems. The second is the 'Verification' data set which is used for verifying the predictive performance of the trained systems and evaluating the choice of parameters for a good trading system. Finally the third data set or 'Test' data set is used for an actual trading test to determine the trading performance of the chosen trading system. We set the training data from 2000 to 2006, the verification data from 2007 to 2008 and the test data from 2009 to 2010.

3.1.3. Predictability Experiments of Shanghai Composite Index return

The study for the predictability of daily and weekly Shanghai Composite Index return is tested using three experiments:
1) In Experiment I, 10 lags of Shanghai Composite Index returns are used for the prediction of the subsequent period's return.
2) In Experiment II, the actual Shanghai Composite Index returns of up to 10 lags, 10-period moving average of closing Shanghai Composite Index values, 25-period moving average of the same and a 10-period oscillator is used for the prediction of the subsequent period's return.
3) In Experiment III, the actual Shanghai Composite Index returns of up to 10 lags, 10-period moving average of closing Shanghai Composite Index values, 25-period moving average of the same and a 10-period volatility indicator is used for the prediction of the subsequent period's return.

In Experiments II and III, the term "period" refers to daily or weekly based on the context of the experiment. In each of the three experiments, the efficacy of the regression and neural network models in predicting the sub-sequent period's Shanghai Composite Index return is evaluated.

3.1.4. Metrics Used for Performance Evaluation

The performance of all the trading systems used in this paper will be accessed using two metrics:

3.1.4.1. Directional Accuracy

The first metric is the percentage of correct signs of predicted returns as compared to the actual returns. This is termed as directional accuracy in this paper. It has been argued in literature that for prediction on the stock market, the signs of returns are more important than the actual magnitude of returns. Also, it has been shown by Pesaran and Timmermann [2] that directional accuracy measures has a higher correlation with returns compared to using the mean square error.

3.1.4.2. Annual Return Rate

The second metric is the annual return rate (ARR) from simulated trading. The ARR indicates the annual returns from trading with an initial investment of 1 (ARR of 1.1 indicates a 10% profit). In this paper, both trading with and without short selling has been considered. Also, both the cases with and without commission costs are discussed to show the effects of commission costs when the trading systems are in actual use. As mentioned earlier, commission costs play a significant role when the number of transactions gets large.

In this paper, the commission cost is assumed to be 0.2% per trade (a single trade indicates either a buying or selling decision), which is a rather conservative amount. In computing the ARR for trading performance evaluation, the cumulative returns for the whole period (training or verification) is calculated first. After which, the ARR is obtained by taking the nth root of the cumulative returns, where n is the number of years in the period. In calculating the cumulative returns, two possibilities exist depending whether a long or short position is held. In the case of a long position, the cumulative return after period t is calculated as:

$$f(Cumulative \operatorname{Re}turns)_t = (Cumulative \operatorname{Re}turns)_t \times (1 + Actual \operatorname{Re}turns_t) \quad (9)$$

For a short position, the cumulative return in period t is :

$$(Cumulative \operatorname{Re}turns)_t = (Cumulative \operatorname{Re}turns)_t \times (1 - Actual \operatorname{Re}turns_t) \quad (10)$$

For the trading decision made in this chapter, the threshold based trading rule is used. The threshold based trading rule is based on both the magnitude and signs of predictions made by the systems. This decision-making trading rule is used to make trading decisions via the following clauses:
1) If the predicted return rate is positive and its magnitude greater than the threshold value, then a long (buy) position is recommended.
2) Alternatively, if the predicted return rate is negative and its magnitude greater than the threshold, then a short (sell) position is recommended.
3) If the above conditions fail, 3 scenarios are possible whereby the recommendation is to stay away from the market. If already in a long position, withdraw from market if the predicted return rate is negative. On the other hand, if already in a short position, withdraw from market if the return rate is positive. Else, the current position is maintained.

The use of this threshold-based trading rule leads to the need to vary the threshold value used in order to find an appropriate value for the trading system which leads to good trading performances.

3.2. Simulation Results
3.2.1. Predictability Experiments of Shanghai Composite Index Return

For convenience, in the presentation of tables, we denote directional accuracy as DA, annual return rate as ARR and commission fee as CF.
For daily data, we firstly use the regression model to do the prediction. We show the experiment results in **Tables 1-3**:

Table 1. Performance of regression model in experiment I (daily).

Period	DA	ARR (No Short sell)		ARR (Short sell)	
		No CF	0.2%CF	No CF	0.2% CF
Training	54.21%	1.2879	1.2760	1.2579	1.2330
Verification	54.81%	1.0698	1.0511	1.7173	1.6586

Table 2. Performance of regression model in experiment II (daily).

Period	DA	ARR (No Short sell)		ARR (Short sell)	
		No CF	0.2%CF	No CF	0.2% CF
Training	52.90%	1.2154	1.1960	1.2855	1.2462
Verification	55.65%	0.9676	0.9620	1.4507	1.4336

In experiment I, the threshold for trading is 0.0008. In experiment II, the threshold for trading is 0.0002. In ex-periment III, the threshold for trading is 0.0006. From the **Tables 1-3**, we can see that the experiment I showed the best performance of regression model. So we choose the method in experiment I for test period. We show the result in **Table 4**.

In experiment I, the threshold for trading is 0.0018 and the number of nodes is 18. In experiment II, the threshold for trading is 0.0016 and the number of nodes is 18. In experiment III, the threshold for trading is 0.0014 and the number of nodes is 12. From the **Tables 5-7**, we can see that the experiment II showed the best performance of NN model. So we choose the method and parameters in experiment II for test period. We show the result in **Table 8**.

Table 3. Performance of regression model in experiment III (daily).

Period	DA	ARR (No Short sell)		ARR (Short sell)	
		No CF	0.2%CF	No CF	0.2% CF
Training	53.68%	1.2690	1.2581	1.3955	1.3714
Verification	57.11%	0.9434	0.9380	1.1235	1.1116

Table 4. Performance of regression model in experiment I (daily).

Period	DA	ARR (No Short sell)		ARR (Short sell)	
		No CF	0.2%CF	No CF	0.2% CF
Testing	56.63%	1.2638	1.2572	1.3351	1.3299

119

Table 5. Performance of NN model in experiment I (daily).

Period	DA	ARR (No Short sell)		ARR (Short sell)	
		No CF	0.2%CF	No CF	0.2% CF
Training	55.89%	1.4654	1.4458	1.8384	1.7981
Verification	55.86%	1.1324	1.1118	1.7182	1.6624

Table 6. Performance of NN Model in experiment II (daily).

Period	DA	ARR (No Short sell)		ARR (Short sell)	
		No CF	0.2%CF	No CF	0.2% CF
Training	58.88%	1.7051	1.6812	2.1571	2.1003
Verification	55.60%	1.0135	1.0032	1.2261	1.2026

Table 7. Performance of NN model in experiment III (daily).

Period	DA	ARR (No Short sell)		ARR (Short sell)	
		No CF	0.2%CF	No CF	0.2% CF
Training	55.37%	1.3453	1.3325	1.4782	1.4493
Verification	55.81%	0.9581	0.9527	1.2554	1.2419

For the weekly data, we firstly use the regression mo- del to do the prediction. We show the experiment results in **Tables 9-11**. In experiment I, the threshold for trading is 0.0014. In experiment II, the threshold for trading is 0.0008. In experiment III, the threshold for trading is 0.0002. From the **Tables 9-11** above, we can see that the experiment II showed the best performance of regression model. So we choose the method in experiment III for test period. We show the result in **Table 12** below.

Table 8. Performance of NN model in experiment II (daily).

Period	DA	ARR (No Short sell)		ARR (Short sell)	
		No CF	0.2%CF	No CF	0.2% CF
Testing	56.02%	1.2984	1.2569	1.3966	1.3517

Table 9. Performance of regression model in experiment I. (weekly)

Period	DA	ARR (No Short sell)		ARR (Short sell)	
		No CF	0.2%CF	No CF	0.2% CF
Training	62.86%	1.2441	1.2416	1.3613	1.3563
Verification	56.67%	1.0308	1.0287	1.4773	1.4711

Table 10. Performance of regression model in experiment II (weekly).

Period	DA	ARR (No Short sell)		ARR (Short sell)	
		No CF	0.2%CF	No CF	0.2% CF
Training	59.40%	1.2398	1.2356	1.3735	1.3646
Verification	66.67%	1.1800	1.1781	1.7099	1.7048

Table 11. Performance of regression model in experiment III (weekly).

Period	DA	ARR (No Short sell)		ARR (Short sell)	
		No CF	0.2%CF	No CF	0.2% CF
Training	59.06%	1.1035	1.0980	1.1013	1.0902
Verification	44.57%	0.8628	0.8590	0.9303	0.9221

Table 12. Performance of regression model in experiment II (weekly).

Period	DA	ARR (No Short sell)		ARR (Short sell)	
		No CF	0.2%CF	No CF	0.2% CF
Testing	55.25%	0.9054	0.9039	0.9020	0.8988

For the weekly data, we then use the NN model to do the prediction. We show the experiment results in **Tables 13-15**. In experiment I, the threshold for trading is 0.0010 and the number of nodes is 14. In experiment II, the threshold for trading is 0.0020 and the number of nodes is 12. In experiment III, the threshold for trading is 0.0014 and the number of nodes is 20. From the Table 13 ~ 15, we can see that the experiment II showed the best performance of NN model. So we choose the method and parameters in experiment II for test period. We show the result in **Table 16**.

From the results showed above, we can see that the performance of NN model is better than the performance of regression model. We also can find that for the daily data, the ARRs of both regression model and NN model are better than the ARRs of buy-and-hold strategy in testing period (testing period ARR is 1.2419). Unfortunately, for the weekly data, the ARRs of both regression model and NN model are worse than the ARRs of buy- and-hold strategy.

Table 13. Performance of NN model in experiment I (weekly).

Period	DA	ARR (No Short sell)		ARR (Short sell)	
		No CF	0.2%CF	No CF	0.2% CF
Training	66.29%	1.4186	1.4122	1.6872	1.6728
Verification	53.33%	1.0847	1.0795	1.5257	1.5108

Table 14. Performance of NN model in experiment II (weekly).

Period	DA	ARR (No Short sell)		ARR (Short sell)	
		No CF	0.2%CF	No CF	0.2% CF
Training	62.39%	1.3135	1.3081	1.4347	1.4242
Verification	56.67%	1.0496	1.0480	1.3380	1.3337

Table 15. Performance of NN model in experiment III (weekly).

Period	DA	ARR (No Short sell)		ARR (Short sell)	
		No CF	0.2%CF	No CF	0.2% CF
Training	65.63%	1.1271	1.1237	1.1744	1.1673
Verification	52.17%	1.0074	1.0039	1.1390	1.1313

Table 16. Performance of NN model in experiment II (weekly).

Period	DA	ARR (No Short sell)		ARR (Short sell)	
		No CF	0.2%CF	No CF	0.2% CF
Testing	62.77%	1.0613	1.0598	1.2287	1.2258

4. Predictability of Shanghai Composite Index Price Volatility

In this section, we firstly introduce the simulation design which consists of data collection, data pre-processing, three comparison experiments and the metrics for performance evaluation, then the simulation results and discus-sions are showed.

4.1. Simulation Design
4.1.1. Data Collection

We collected the historical data of Shanghai Composite Index for both daily data and weekly data from the year 2000 to the year 2010 from the stockstar website [13].

4.1.2. Data Pre-Processing

Because we want to see whether the return is random or not, we calculate the daily returns from the daily data, the weekly returns from the weekly data for the Shanghai Composite Index. The entire set is divided into a three separate data sets for different usage. The first data is called the "Training" data set and is used for training and adjusting the coefficients or weights of the systems. The second is the "Verification" data set which is used for verifying the predictive performance of the trained systems and evaluating the choice of parameters for a good trading system. Finally the third data set or "Test" data set is used for an actual trading test to determine the trading performance of the chosen trading system. We set the training data from 2000 to 2006, the verification data from 2007 to 2008 and the test data from 2009 to 2010.

4.1.3. Predictability Experiments of Shanghai Composite Index Price Volatility

The study for the predictability of daily and weekly Shanghai Composite Index price-changes is tested using three experiments:

1) In Experiment IV, 10 lags of actual Shanghai Composite Index closing price values and 10 lags of periodic price-changes are used for the prediction of the subsequent period's price-change.
2) In Experiment V, 10 lags of actual Shanghai Composite Index trading volume values AND 10 lags of periodic trading volume differences are used for the prediction of the subsequent period's price-change.
3) In Experiment VI, 10 lags of actual Shanghai Composite Index closing price values, 10 lags of periodic price-changes, 10 lags of trading volume values and 10 lags of periodic trading volume differences are used for the prediction of the subsequent period's price change.

4.1.4. Metrics Used for Performance Evaluation

The performance of all the trading systems used in this paper will be accessed only using one metric: Directional Accuracy .This metric is the percentage of correct signs of predicted returns as compared to the actual returns. This is termed as directional accuracy in this chapter. It has been argued in literature that for prediction on the stock market, the signs of returns are more important than the actual magnitude of returns. Also, it has been shown by Pesaran and Timmermann [2] that directional accuracy measures has a higher correlation with returns compared to using the mean square error.

4.2. Simulation Results
4.2.1. Predictability Experiments of Shanghai Composite Index Price Volatility

For daily data, we firstly use the regression model to do the prediction. We show the experiment results in **Tables 17-19**. From the **Tables 17-19**, we can see that the experiment VI showed the best performance of regression model. So we choose the method in experiment VI for test period. We show the result in **Table 20**. For the daily data, we then use the NN model to do the prediction. We show the experiment results in **Tables 21-23**.

Table 17. Performance of regression model in experiment IV (daily).

Period	Directional Accuracy
Training	52.96%
Verification	56.28%

Table 18. Performance of regression model in experiment V (daily).

Period	Directional Accuracy
Training	54.27%
Verification	54.39%

Table 19. Performance of regression model in experiment VI (daily).

Period	Directional Accuracy
Training	56.84%
Verification	55.02%

Table 20. Performance of regression model in experiment VI (daily).

Period	Directional Accuracy
Testing	57.36%

In experiment IV, the number of nodes is 16. In experiment V, the number of nodes is 10. In experiment III, the number of nodes is 10. From the **Tables 21-23**, we can see that the experiment VI showed the best performance of NN model. So we choose the method and parameters in experiment VI for test period. We show the result in **Table- 24**. For the weekly data, we firstly use the regression mo- del to do the prediction. We show the experiment results in **Tables 25-27**.

Table 21. Performance of NN model in experiment IV (daily).

Period	Directional Accuracy
Training	55.98%
Verification	54.23%

Table 22. Performance of NN model in experiment V (daily).

Period	Directional Accuracy
Training	53.14%
Verification	53.49%

Table 23. Performance of NN model in experiment VI (daily).

Period	Directional Accuracy
Training	57.29%
Verification	55.60%

Table 24. Performance of NN model in experiment VI (daily).

Period	Directional Accuracy
Testing	58.18%

Table 25. Performance of regression model in experiment IV (weekly).

Period	Directional Accuracy
Training	59.70%
Verification	54.39%

Table 26. Performance of regression model in experiment V (weekly).

Period	Directional Accuracy
Training	59.70%
Verification	54.35%

Table 27. Performance of regression model in experiment VI (weekly).

Period	Directional Accuracy
Training	61.10%
Verification	56.74%

From the **Tables 25-27,** we can see that the experiment VI showed the best performance of regression model. So we choose the method in experiment VI and the parameters for test period. We show the result in **Table 28**. For the weekly data, we then use the NN model to do the prediction. We show the experiment results in **Tables 29-31**. In experiment I, the number of nodes is 12. In experiment II, the number of nodes is 20. In experiment III, the number of nodes is 16. From the **Tables 29-31**, we can see that the experiment VI showed the best performance of NN model. So we choose the method and parameters in experiment VI for test period. We show the result in **Table 32.**

Similar with the conclusions of the experiment I, II and III, from the results showed above, we can see that the performance of NN model is better than the performance of regression model.

Table 28. Performance of regression model in experiment VI (weekly).

Period	Directional Accuracy
Testing	59.66%

Table 29. Performance of NN model in experiment IV (weekly).

Period	Directional Accuracy
Training	61.19%
Verification	58.70%

Table 30. Performance of NN model in experiment V (weekly).

Period	Directional Accuracy
Training	61.97%
Verification	56.70%

Table 31. Performance of NN model in experiment VI (weekly).

Period	Directional Accuracy
Training	65.79%
Verification	58.52%

Table 32. Performance of NN model in experiment VI (weekly).

Period	Directional Accuracy
Testing	59.70

5. Conclusions and Future Work

In this paper, we do the prediction of Shanghai Composite Index return and the prediction of Shanghai Composite Index volatility based on regression model and NN model using the daily and weekly data of Shanghai Composite Index. The directional accuracy of most of the experiments is beyond 55%. For the prediction of Shanghai Composite Index return, both trading with and without short selling has been considered, and the results show in most cases, trading with short selling leads to higher pro- fits. Also, both the cases with and without commission costs are discussed to show the effects of commission costs when the trading systems are in actual use. We find that the performance of NN model is better than the performance of regression model. We also find that for the daily data, the ARRs of both regression model and NN model are better than the ARRs of buy-and-hold strategy in testing period (testing period ARR is 1.2419). Unfortunately, for the weekly data, the ARRs of both regression model and NN model are worse than the ARRs of buy-and-hold strategy in testing

126

period. For the prediction of Shanghai Composite Index volatility, we can find similar conclusion that the performance of NN model is better than the performance of regression model.

For the future work, two aspects may be considered. The first aspect: it has been studied in literature that better performance can be achieved by using systems comprising of multiple models. For example, three or four models could be used within each system, and a trend classification algorithm can be use to classify the time series into a larger number of different trends. The second aspect: the input data used for predictions of markets can be extended by using macro-fundamental data such as interest rate and required reserve ratio. Such macro- fundamental data may contain useful information which can be used to predict market movements more accurately.

References

[I] B. G. Malkiel, "A Random Walk Down Wall Street," W. W. Norton & Company, New York and London, 1999.

[II] M. H. Pesaran and A. Timmermann, "Forecasting Stock Returns: An Examination of Stock Market Trading in the Presence of Transaction Costs," *Journal of Forecasting*, Vol. 13, No. 4, 1994, pp. 335-367. doi:10.1002/for.3980130402

[III] M. T. Mitchell, "Machine Learning," The McGraw-Hill Companies, New York, 1997.

[IV] M. H. Eng and Q.-G. Wang, "Modeling of Stock Markets with Mean Reversion," *The 6th IEEE International Conference on Control and Automation (IEEE ICCA 2007)*, Guangzhou, 30 May-1 June 2007, pp. 2615-2618.

[V] J.-H. Wang and J.-Y. Leu, "Stock Market Trend Prediction Using ARIMA-Based Neural Networks," *The 1996 IEEE International Conference on Neural Networks*, Washington DC, 3-6 June 1996, pp. 2160-2165.

[VI] W. Wang, D. Okunbor and F. C. Lin, "Future Trend of the Shanghai Stock Market," *ICONIP '02: Proceedings of the 9th International Conference on Neural Information Processing*, Singapore, 18-22 November, pp. 2320-2324.

[VII] L.-X. Liu and J.-H Ma, "Multivariate Nonlinear Prediction of Shenzhen Stock Price," *The 3rd International Conference on Wireless Communications, Networking and Mobile Computing (WiCOM 2007)*, Shanghai, 21-23 September 2007, pp. 4120-4123.

[VIII] S.-H. Chen, C.-Q Tao and W. He, "A New Algorithm of Neural Network and Prediction in China Stock Market," *Pacific-Asia Conference on Circuits, Communications and Systems, PACCS 2009*, Chengdu, 16-17 May 2009, pp. 686-689.

[IX] X. Xiong, X,-T, Zhang, W, Zhang and C,-Y, Li, "Wave- let-Based Beta Estimation of China Stock Market," *Proceedings of 2005 International Conference on Machine Learning and Cybernetics*, Guangzhou, 18-21 August 2005, pp. 3501-3505.

[X] W.-R. Pan, "Empirical Analysis of Stock Returns Volatility in China Market Based on Shanghai and Shenzhen 300 Index," 2010 *International Conference on Financial Theory and Engineering (ICFTE)*, Dubai, 18-20 June 2010, pp. 17-21.

[XI] X.-M. Song and H.-X. Pan, "Analysis of China Stock Market: Volatility and Influencing Factors," 2010 *Inter-national Conference on Management and Service Science (MASS)*, Wuhan, 24-26 August 2010, pp. 1-5. doi:10.1109/ICMSS.2010.5578224

[XII] S. Haykin, "Neural Networks: A Comprehensive Foundation", Prentice-Hall, Saddle River, 1999.

[XIII] Http://www.stockstar.com/

CHAPTER 9

Variants of Self Organizing Maps in Social Systems Simulation

Marina Resta

University of Genova

Variants of Self Organizing Maps in Social Systems Simulation

Abstract

This paper explores the use of variants of Self Organizing Maps to simulate agents interaction in social systems. Our efforts were mainly concentrated to model agents learning and psychological relationships, as well as the way those latter can affect the system general behavior. As main result, we developed a suitable environment to simulate economic systems dynamics, totally based on models inspired on the approach of self-organization in cortical brain models.

Keywords: Self Organization, Dichotomous Growth, Neighbor relationships

JEL classes: C45, C51, O15

1 Problem Statement

In recent years many intellectual efforts have been spent to simulate economic dynamics by way of soft computing tools. The current interest on such topic may find explanations under different points of view; however, this work takes as the most remarkable the one outlined in (Kirman, 1997), who emphasized the importance of viewing to the economy as an evolving network.

In such a context, interaction emerges as the leading aspect of modern economic systems, where the individual behavior is perceived like the synthesis of both previous personal experience and partnership effects: our actions affect those of other people; those, in turn, can affect our welfare.

Such interdependence, together with its implications have been powerfully summarized in the illustration of the so called "social dilemmas" (Hegselmann, 1998), as expressions of complex dynamic processes: interpersonal and inter-group situations can be altered when potentially advantageous patterns become unsatisfactory, because they drive the agents in the community to outcomes which should have been better off by individuals running separately.

This true, reasonable simulations of interaction should take into account at least three interrelated levels of issue:

the individual level, driven by personal interests;

the aggregate level, where global behavior not necessarily emerges as simply cumulation of individual activities;

the level of the bi-directional flow, linking individual to aggregate behavior, and vice-versa, so that the macro and micro levels may influence themselves reciprocally.

Apart from considerations about its efficacy, an exhaustive dynamical description would hence require the assumption of a system of Partial Differential Equations (PDEs), as wide as the number N of individuals in the model. This obviously makes the problem not easy to handle, especially for larger values of N.

In order to overcome this issue, over the past decade heavy computational methods have been introduced to model phase transition in economic systems: shell models, coupled map lattices and cellular automata have been suggested as suitable methods helping to understand social systems basic mechanisms, thus building a bridge between traditional statistical descriptions, and dynamical representation in phase space. The aforementioned methods, in fact, share the common feature to reproduce economic dynamics by means of some kind of discretization (varying depending on the methodology in use), where the PDEs governing the process are transformed into a set of Ordinary Differential Equations (ODEs).

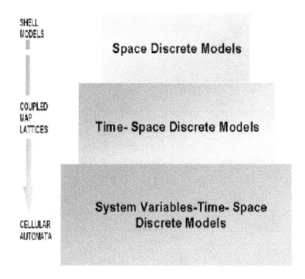

Fig. 1 Level of Discretization in Problem Management.

Figure 1 adds some additional remarks, showing (from top to bottom) how different capabilities of representation and generalization can be combined in order to get more or less simplified models of the observable world. The simplest and discretized the model is, the higher the related level of abstraction. Hence, while shell models are quite complicate but give a complete and detailed representation of the system under examination, cellular automata are at the opposite, giving a schematic representation of a system, but in a quite simplified fashion respect on how things really work.Starting from the pioneering work of (Hegselmann, 1998) the contemporary literature exhibited a great number of studies where cellular automata are used to simulate economic systems and interplays among individuals within them. However, since the comprehension of Cellular Automata still remains generally poor (Wuensche, 1999), there is a serious danger to confuse spontaneous switches, inherited in the algorithm, with endogenous ones.

On the other hand, the extensive use of Artificial Intelligence paradigms such as Genetic Algorithms (Arifovic, 1997), or their ibridisations ((McCain, 1998), (McCain, 1999)) was criticized already in (Geisendorf, 1998), who proved that sometimes results are due mostly to randomization issues of the Genetic Algorithm, rather than to mating or crossover features inherited into the model itself.Starting from this point, this paper analyzes a different approach to economic systems modeling, and addresses the specific field of simulation of interactions by means of spatial connections. This is possible thanks to the particular algorithm in use, which retrieves neighborhood interaction through traditional spatial relationships (induced by Moore, von Neumann neighborhoods), as well as by means of a Voronoi tessellation of system variables space. In such sense, connections have been assumed relevant both to condition the level of human capital (and hence production), and also propensities to save and to study. Besides, while the use of soft computing tools in robotics, medical imaging, characters recognition, to cite most important examples, is celebrated by a consistent literature corpus, economic simulations seem niche wise fields, relatively lesser explored, with some notable exceptions . Such lack is quite non-sense, provided the great potential that relies on this kind of technique.

The remaining of this paper is therefore organized as follows: Section 2 briefly introduces the theory of cortical brain maps, focusing on the way information is tuned by elementary artificial brain units (neurons), and on its mathematical formalization. Section 3 describes the assumptions for the economic model under examination. Section 4 discusses simulation results, and Section 5 contains some conclusive remarks and outlooks for future works.

2. Self organization and cortical brain models

Cortical brain models have gained increasing popularity over the past three decades, because of their ability to model input / output relationships through plastic linking, which can evolve and adapt over time. As widely known, their formalism seems to be inspired by the principles of nervous system architecture: nodes (i.e. neurons) are modeled as I/O elements, with connections (corresponding to biological synapses), which generally assume values in the open interval $(-1, 1)$, thus expressing both the strength and the significance of their activation with respect to input patterns.Nowadays there are hundreds of models merely inspired to such formalism, but we can roughly trace them back to two basic research streams: Feed Forward Neural Networks and Self Organizing Maps. We focus our discussion on those latter.

2.1 Self Organizing Maps

Self Organizing Maps (SOM)), also known as Kohonen maps, are unsupervised neural models, which consist of a number of neurons generally arranged into a two-dimensional grid, driven to preserve topological relationships over the input space, while performing at the same time a dimensionality reduction of the above representation space.The Kohonen algorithm assumes to iteratively modify the map nodes by way of a set of rules. On following we describe them, focusing on a slight modification of the original algorithm as suggested in (Martinetz et al 1994).

Consider first a finite set $X = \{\underline{u}(t)\}_{t=1,\dots,T}$ of d-dimensions input data items: $X \in \Omega \subset \mathbb{R}^d$. Besides, let us assume that M is the $m \times k$ bi-dimensional projection grid defined into a discrete bi-dimensional output space, Z^2, and $\underline{w_i} \in \Omega \subset \mathbb{R}^d$ to be the pointer associated to neuron (unit, node) i in the map ($i=1,\dots, m \times k$).The initial stage starts in the topological map M whose neurons are arranged in a disordered manner, i.e. at random.

At each step t, the input $\underline{u}(t)$ from a continuous space $\mathbb{R}^d$ is presented to the net, and the algorithm describes a mapping Φ from $\mathbb{R}^d$ to Z^2 , according to which a winner or leader neuron n is selected in the map when it satisfies to:

$$n = arg \min_{k \in M} \|\underline{w}_k - \underline{u}\|$$

This makes possible to order neurons according to their similarity with input as well as to similarity criteria among themselves:

$$p(i) > p(j) \Longleftrightarrow (\|\underline{u} - \underline{w}_i\| > \|\underline{u} - \underline{w}_j\|) \vee (\|\underline{u} - \underline{w}_i\| = \|\underline{u} - \underline{w}_j\|) \wedge (i > j) \tag{1}$$

where $p(i)$ is the position in M of neuron n_i at time $t+1$. Hence, both the pointer $\underline{w}_n$ associated to leader neuron, and all the pointers $\underline{w}_i$ belonging to a convenient (according to Eq. (1)) neighborhood in the map are modified with the following rule:

$$\wedge \underline{w}_j = h_{ij}[\alpha, d_{map}(p(i), j, i)](\underline{u} - \underline{w}_j) \tag{2}$$

with α being a fixed constant, $d_{map}(p(i), j, i)$ a distance function , and $(\underline{u} - \underline{w}_i)$ is the error between input and each pointer. Finally, $h_{ij}(\cdot)$ is the neuron interaction function between the nodes: it depends on the distance in the map d_{map} between each node, as well as by the constant α. On following, we will assume that:

$$h_{ij}[\alpha, d_{map}(p(i), j, i)] = e^{-\alpha * d_{map}(p(i), j, i)} \tag{3}$$

The learning phase is completed after presenting either a large number of inputs to the map (if the space they belong to is $\mathbb{R}^d$), or the whole dataset (if the number of input patterns is finite).

It is noteworthy to observe that the variant of SOM algorithm we have therein discussed takes into account spatial relationships at least twice and in quite different ways. At each step, in fact, neurons are ordered both according to Eq.(1), and to Eq.(2).While, in the former case, the Voronoi tessellation of input space (or better its evolution over time) is captured, in the latter the proper learning phase takes place, with information retrieval and exchange both between neurons and the input pattern, and among nodes themselves.

To make the concept clearer, consider Figure 2.

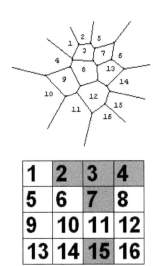

**Fig.2 From top to bottom: Voronoi tessellation, and
"traditional" neighborhood structure in a 4x4 net.**

Fig. 2 shows a sketch proof of the organization as resulting both from the Voronoi tessellation of neural space (Fig.2: top), and by applying a von Neumann (cross-shaped) neighborhood, when edges of the neural lattice are pasted together (Fig.2: bottom). It is easy to observe that the neighborhood structure deriving from Voronoi tessellation of neural space is generally quite different from the one which comes from ordinary proximity relationships. To make an example, consider the cross-shaped neighbor with radius one centered on the cell labeled by number 3: the map edges have been pasted together, to avoid border effects.

As one can see, the neighborhood of cell 3 includes neurons 2,4,7, and 15. On the other hand, the Voronoi tessellation of neural space assigns to cell 3 different neighbors from the ones previously indicated.A second remark is then noteworthy: if one looks at Eqs.(2)-(3) he might note that keeping α closer to 0 (e.g. $\alpha < 0.01$), the impact of additional information which comes from input tends to be widely spread from the leader nodes to nearest neurons. On the contrary, if α is maintained nearer to 1 (e.g. $\alpha > 0.7$), then neurons within a ϑ–wide ($\vartheta \in \mathbb{N}$) neighborhood amplitude from the leader will be less sensitive to new information than in previous case.

Figure 3 shows this idea in a more intuitive fashion.

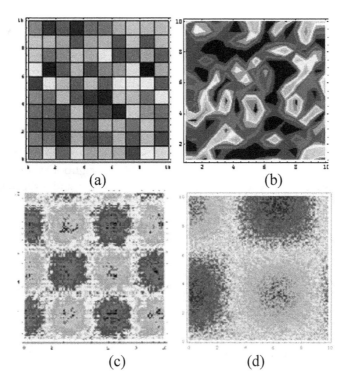

(a)   (b)

(c)   (d)

Fig.3 From top to bottom in clockwise sense, TOP: a 10x10 SOM map at initial step (a) and after 1000 iterations (b). BOTTOM: neighborhood effects in a 10X10 Self -Organizing Map when α is maintained closer either to 1 (c) or to 0 (d).

The aforementioned features make SOM a quite promising instrument to model human behaviour and interactions into an economic system. The extreme flexibility which is possible to gain by operating over α and $d_{map}(p(i), j, i)$, in fact, offers the opportunity to reproduce swarm effects, as well as its antonym i.e. the individual specification as sole identity. This in practice means that by properly varying either the value of α, or the shape of the function $d_{map}(p(i), j, i)$, it is possible to control the learning phase, so that either neighborhoods with same shapes (e.g. cross) have different sensitivity to information spread over them (α is varied) or equal information intensity (α unchanged) may be spread over different shaped areas, thus enforcing (or penalizing, depending of the constant value of α) the effect of original input over the map.

3 The computational model

3.1 Preliminar economic statements

We consider a two sector growth model, embedded into an overlapping generation system. This means that in our model each individual lives for two periods; at each step he/she chooses how to allocate potential labor between work and study, and hence how to divide wages between consumption and savings. Those, in turn, will be invested in physical capital, to be used in the second part of individuals life. New generations acquire from elders previous situation, and change it through learning and neighborhood effects.

The efforts of this study have been primarily focused to model such effects, as well as the impact over decision variables deriving from the existence of notable spatial connections. We have examined different neighborhood topologies, in order to represent both neighborhood effects in strictly geographical sense, and also collective behaviors, induced by affinity and by other psychological motivations. Giving a deeper look to the model, the function ruling the production of tangible good at time t is a Cobb-Douglas function of the type:

$$Q_t^{(i)} = \left| L_t^{(i)} \cdot K_t^{(i)} \cdot H_t^{(i)} \right|^{--}$$

(4)

where $Q_t^{(i)}$, $L_t^{(i)}$, $K_t^{(i)}$ and $H_t^{(i)}$ are, respectively, production, labor services, tangible and human capital for the i-th agent. We assumed that young individuals begin their life with an equal amount of potential labor σ, which has to be divided between work and study. Labor services $L_t^{(i)}$ depends then on initial potential labor disposal, as well as on individual propensity to study $v_t^{(i)}$:

$$L_t^{(i)} = \sigma \left[1 - v_t^{(i)} \right]$$

(5)

Analogously, physical capital $K_t^{(i)}$ is a function of propensity to invest into physical capital, $z_t^{(i)}$, and of residual propensity to study bring out from previous step:

$$K_t^{(i)} = \sigma^2 z_t^{(i)} \left[1 - v_t^{(i)} \right]$$

(6)

For what is concerning the human capital made available to each agent, it is given by:

$$H_t^{()} = (1 - \tau) H_{t-1}^{(i)} + g\left[v_t^{(i)} \right] H_t^{\bullet(i)}$$

(7)

where: τ is a constant value in the interval [0, 1); $H_t^{\bullet(i)}$ allows positive labor externalities into the model, being the average human capital into the spatial neighborhood of each agent, and $g\left[v_t^{(i)} \right]$ is a conditional function which associates diminishing returns to in incremental efforts in human capital formation. The function g must be a non-increasing continuous function: Fig. 3 shows an example concerning an admissible shape for function g).

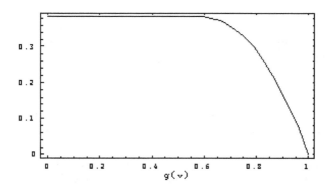

Fig. 3. An admissible shape for function *g*.

Finally, the individuals utility function for the generic agent *i* is given by:

$$U_t^{(i)} = \left[\sigma v_t^{(i)}\right]^{2/3} Q_t^{(i)} \left[z_t^{(i)}\left(1 - z_t^{(i)}\right)\right]^{1/2}$$

3.2. A model based on self-organization in cortical brain maps

Starting from the assumptions discussed in the previous section, a computational model involving Self-Organizing Maps has been developed.We build a rectangular grid of agents, with border joined together, so that to form a torus with agents lying over a continuous surface. Each individual is associated to a reference vector:

$$x_t^{(i)} = \left\{v_t^{(i)}, z_t^{(i)}, Q^{(i)}, H_i^{(\bullet i)}, H_t^{(i)}, U_i^{(i)}\right\} \tag{8}$$

representing agent condition respect on variables previously defined. In this context, *v* and *z* have been assumed as control variables, i.e. those parameters whose evolution can decisively influence the behavior of production, work, and hence the formation of individuals utility profile. At a generic step *t* the procedure works as follows:

STEP 1. Selection of the best performing unit according to the definition given below.

Definition 1. (Best performer). The best performer (BPF) unit of time *t* is said to be the agent whose utility has resulted at highest level at step t-1:

$$BPF_t = arg \max_{i \in M} U_{t-1}^{(i)}$$

STEP 2. A Voronoi tessellation of neural space is performed, by ordering neurons according to their distance from the couple $\{v_{BPF}, z_{BPF}\}$, of control parameters associated to the Best Performer. This order is then retrieved in the learning procedure through Eq.(3). In this way each agent will acquire new propensities to study and to save, which in turn are used to calculate step values for production *Q*, utility *U* and labor *H*.Besides, with respect to the formulation that we have described in Sec.2, we

137

added an additional random perturbation $\xi \in (-1,1)$, in order to avoid that tuning nodes position to that of the BPF might lead to super-positions among nodes: in the observable world, in fact, mimicking the behavior of other agents rarely lead to reach the goal exactly, but rather it is a task severely affected by noise. This is the ratio motivating the change of Eq.(3) now turned into:

$$\Delta \underline{w}_j = h_{ij}[\alpha, d_{map}(p(i), j, i)](\underline{u} - \underline{w}_j) + \xi \qquad (9)$$

Through Eq. (9) it is also clear that by properly choosing the shape of dmap, it will be possible to force the net to give more or less emphasis to the proximity of neurons. In order to model nodes (agents) proximity we considered three different types of neighborhood : (a) von Neumann or cross shaped, (b) Moore, and (c) "elastic" neighborhood. From now we will refer to those types of proximities by means of the labels: *VN(r)*, *MN(r)*, and *EN(r)* to indicate von Neumann, Moore, and elastic neighborhood respectively, with radius amplitude "*r*". Here the expression "elastic" means that we introduced a system of clique typologies, hence giving each neuron the chance to mutate the shape (and the amplitude) of its neighborhood, according to its fitness respect on the whole system. Within this context the meaning of fitness must be intended in the sense of level of welfare.

4. Case study and simulation results

Our simulation relied on a Self Organizing Map made by 400 neurons arranged into a rectangular 20x20 lattice, with edges pasted together to avoid border effects. Each neuron was structured as explained in Sec.3, i.e. it was associated to a 6th-uple like that of Eq.(8), originally set at random.
We examined various neighborhood types and amplitudes: for sake of comparison, we employed the same pseudo-random initialization for each type of neighborhood, and we reported average results for each case. System parameters have been maintained constant as shown in Table 1, while Fig. 4 shows the different kinds of neighborhood used

Table 1 Parameters set.

	σ	τ	α	ξ
Value	10	0.02	0.6	0.01

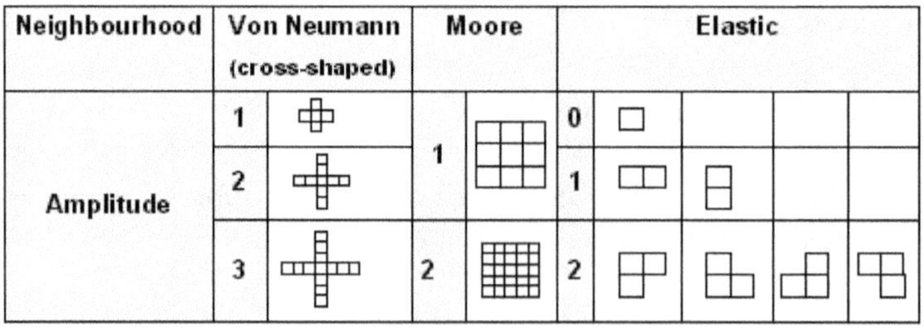

Fig. 4. Neighborhood used in the simulation.

Additionally, we monitored the dynamics of the average distribution of propensities to study v, and to invest into physical capital z: Fig. 5 shows their behavior when the control variables are forced to assume initial values around 0.5 (a), closer to one (b), or to zero (c).

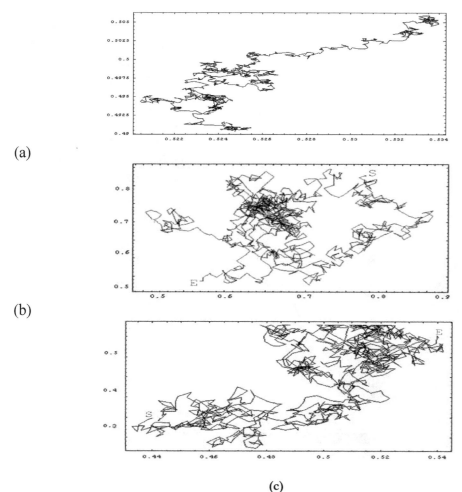

(a)

(b)

(c)

Fig. 5. Paths towards 1000 runs for the couples (v, z), when they are initialized at random (a) uniformly in the range (0, 1), (b) closer to 1, (c) closer to 0.

By considering the path of couples (v, z) along 1000 runs for different initialization values (Fig.5), one can note that when (v,z) are set as uniformly distributed random variables in the range (0, 1) their values tend to maintain closer to average values (i.e. 0.5) over the whole procedure (Fig.5 (a)). On the other side, whereas the couple (v, z) is forced to maintain closer either to one or to zero (Fig. 5 (b) and (c) respectively), the couple (v, z) spans a path which drives them to reach values around 0.5 − 0.52. These results appear stable, in the sense that they are limit values to which simulations converge independently by the kind of neighborhood adopted, or by the particular initial conditions.

Our preliminary conclusion we can then claim that neo-classical hypotheses agree with the empirical evidence, as obtained by soft-computing simulations. Moving to simulation results, for sake of simplicity we will show them separately, according to the kind of neighborhood in use: Figures 6 - 7 show the results for the Von Neumann neighborhood with radius amplitude 1 and 2; Figures 8- 9 show the results for Moore neighborhood with radius equal respectively to one and two; Figures 10 – 11 show the results for the elastic neighborhood. In this latter case, simulations were driven assigning to proximities with radius 0 and 1 much more probability to be chosen by agents, i.e. more attention has been focused on the simulation of "egoistic" politics. In this way, although in a still schematic fashion, it has been attempted to capture the capability of the model to emulate different human behaviour, when less or more structured crowd effects are present (like in the case of $VN(r)$ and $MN(r)$), or when the sole identity dominates over all possible behaviours $(EN(r))$.Each figure examines two different issues. The first one concerns the position in the map of agents with higher– low fitness in terms of production. The situation is fixed at initial step and after 1000 iterations (see subfigures labeled by (a) and (b)). Different tones of gray indicate different levels of production, black and white representing opposite situations, that is the highest and the lowest values of production reached by single cells;As second discussion issue (label (c) in each figure from Fig. 6 to Fig. 11) concerns the distribution (in percentage terms) of agents with high–low welfare levels. Agents are grouped according to their welfare: black stand for the poorest, white for the richest, gray levels for intermediate condition

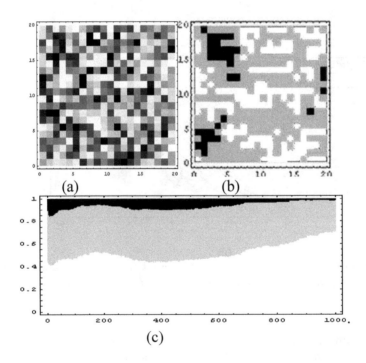

Fig. 6. Simulation results for Von Neumann Neighborhood with radius one.

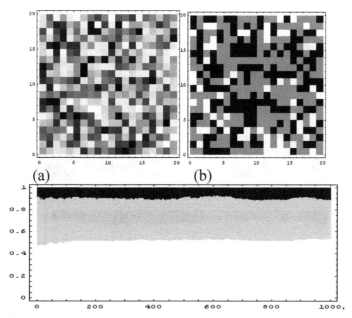

(a)   (b)

(c)Fig. 7. Simulation results for Von Neumann Neighborhood with radius two.

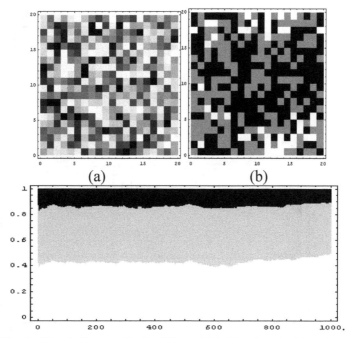

(a)   (b)

(c)Fig. 8. Simulation results for Moore Neighborhood with radius one.

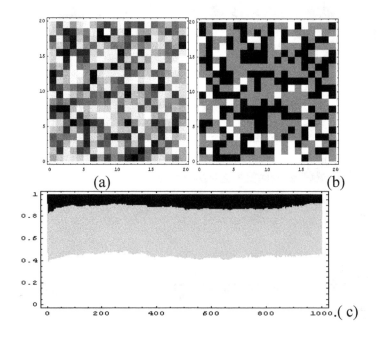

(a) (b)

(c)

Fig. 9. Simulation results for Moore Neighborhood with radius two.

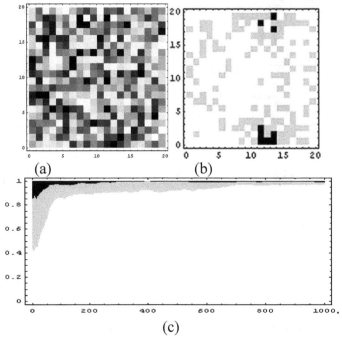

(a) (b)

(c)

Fig. 10. Simulation results for elastic Neighborhood with radius zero.

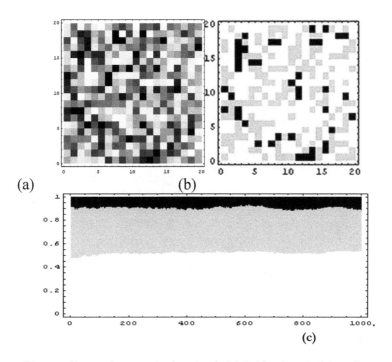

(a)   (b)

(c)

Fig. 11. Simulation results for elastic Neighborhood with radius one

A number of remarks can be drawn at this point.

By way of the Voronoi tessellation of input space we induced affinity relations rather than proximity ones. This is in agreement with the existence of agents sharing equal levels for propensities to study as well as to save although they are spatially placed on different regions. However, while (v, z) are driven over a path which bring them to converge on similar steady values, independently from initial conditions, this, on the other side, does not always holds for welfare. In almost 90% of monitored cases, in fact, the original distribution of welfare still maintains unchanged over the whole simulation: i.e. despite from changes in propensity to both study and work rich people remains rich and the same holds for poorer. We can then conclude that if the affinity is not accompanied by proper regional conditions, the affinity by itself is not able to modify existing situations. This brings to agree to what already stated in (McCain, 1998): equally trained agents tend to show different productivity, according to the particular regional context they are placed in. At the same time, the distribution of wealth appears variously structured, in accordance to the neighborhood shape which prevails in the simulation. In other words, the adoption of egoistic rules should produce limited imitation effects and dichotomization; since the regional dimension has been inflated in the model through the conditioning of labor externalities (namely through H*), it should be reasonable to deduce that , when the shape of neighborhood is wider enough, those play a major impact on the welfare level.

However, that is not ever true, and contradictory signals are offered from the presence of dichotomization in growth and development. For example, dichotomization appears strongly both in VN(1) and EL(1) and EL(2), where egoistic politics prevail, while it is not so evident in other cases, such as VN(2).An additional proof comes by looking at the ratio between different levels of individual welfare and correspondent contribution to overall production, as shown in Figure12.

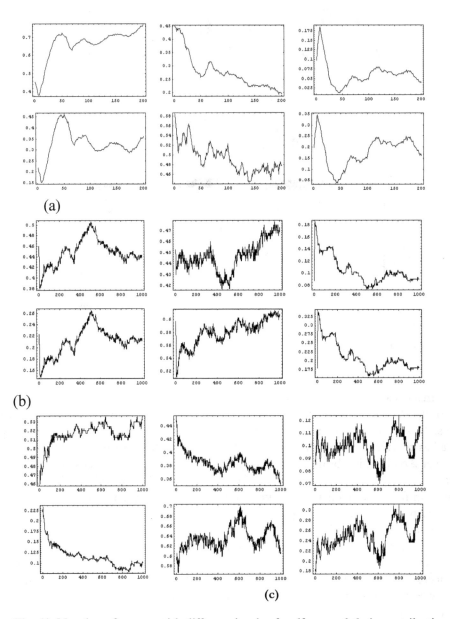

Fig. 12. Number of agents with different levels of welfare, and their contribution to the overall production

This should make possible to assert that there exist a sort of "optimality" in radius neighborhood amplitude, allowing for externality effects, and hence for the compression of dichotomous growth. More properly, dichotomization seems to appear in presence of really localized neighborhood (radius equal to one), but also when too wider proximities are considered: the spatial extension of relationships tend to soften (positive) externalities effects.

5. Conclusive remarks

This work has focused on the plausibility of computer simulation to reproduce the dynamic of economic systems.In particular, Self Organizing Maps have been introduced as operative tool to perform this task: thanks to their extreme flexibility, by properly varying control parameters, it is possible to drive them to reproduce a wide variety of situations, useful to emulate (obviously in a simplified way) real world dynamics.

To this purpose, it has been pointed on how Self Organizing Maps inherited features could be use to represent both affinity among individuals (and hence their psychology), and regional proximity.

Starting from this point, various simulations were implemented, using a variety of possible neighborhood, in order to test the emergence of dichotomous growth, and some possible explications of such phenomenon. From the simulations, it has emerged, that, although psychologically similar, agents may be strongly influenced by regional factors. Spatial connections, in turn, are not always significant at the same level, and either systems dominated by strongly community relationships, or systems where individual politics prevail may show dichotomization in growth and development.This makes possible to think to the existence of an "optimal threshold" for radius neighborhood amplitude, beneath which proximity effects tend to be soften. This conclusion has been supported by looking at the dynamics of the simulated artificial world with proximity affinities induced through propensities to study v and to invest into physical capital z, and regional neighborhood structure inflated through the presence of labor externalities.

The evidence of dichotomous growth has arisen in presence of really localized neighborhoods (unit radius for Von Neumann and Moore neighborhood), as well as at the presence of too spanned (obviously respect on overall system dimensions) neighborhoods. On the contrary, intermediate radius amplitudes (radius greater than two) has produced a better distribution of different levels in welfare and production.

Bibliography

[I] Antsaklis, P. J. Neural Networks In Control Systems IEEE Control Systems Magazine, 3–5, April 1990.

[II] Arifovic, J. Strategic Uncertainty And The Genetic Algorithm Adaption, In H. Amman, B. Rustem, A. Winston, Computational Approaches To Economic Problems, Kluwer, 1997.

[III] Cefis, E. and Espa, G. Modelli Di Interazione Spaziale: Presupposti Teorici E Aspetti Applicativi, Draft Paper, University of Trento, Italy, 1998

[IV] R. Conte, R. Hegselmann and P. Terna, Editors., Simulating Social Phenomena. Springer Lecture Notes In Economics And Mathematical Systems, 1997.

[V] Guez, A., Eilbert, J.L. and Kam M. Neural Network Architecture For Control IEEE Control Systems Magazine Vol. 8, pages 22–25, April 1988

[VI] Gaylord, R.J. and D'andra, L. Simulating Society: A Mathematica Toolkit For Modeling Socioeconomic Behavior, Springer, New York, 1998.

[VII] Geisendorf, S. Genetic Algorithms In Resource Economics Models, A Way To Model Rationality In Resource Exploitation?, Draft Paper.

[VIII] Hegselmann, R. Modelling Social Dynamics By Cellular Automata In B. G. Liebrand, A. Nowak, R. Hegselmann editors, Computer Modelling Of Social Processes, Sage Publications, 1998, pages 37–64.

[IX] Hors, I. and Lordon F. About Some Formalisms Of Interaction, Phase Transition Models In Economics?. Evolutionary Economics, Springer Verlag, 1997

[X] Johansson, E.M., Dowla, F.U., and Goodman, D. M., Backpropagation Learning For Multilayer Feed-Forward Neural Networks Using The Conjugate Gradient Method. International Journal Of Neural Systems, Vol. 2, 4, pages 291–301, World Scientific Publishing Company, 1992.

[XI] Kandel, R.E. and Hawkins, R.D., Apprendimento E Individualit: Le Basi Biologiche. Le Scienze N291, pages 48–59, Le Scienze Spa, Milano, November 1992.

[XII] Kirman, A. The Economy As An Evolving Network Journal Of Evolutionary Economics, Springer Verlag, 1997, 7.

[XIII] Kohonen, T . Self-Organizing Maps, Springer Series In Information Science, 2002.

[XIV] Linsker, R., Self-Organization In A Perceptual Network IEEE Computer, Vol. 21, 3, pages 105–117, March 1988.

[XV] Martinetz, T. and Schulten, K., Topology Representing Networks Neural Networks, Vol. 7, 3, 1994

[XVI] McCain, R. A., Localized Romer Externalities And Dichotomous Development: Simulations With A Cellular Genetic Automaton, Draft Paper, 1998.

[XVII] McCain, R. A., Backwash And Spread, Effects Of Trade Networks In A Space Of Agents Who Learn By Doing, Draft Paper, 1999.

[XVIII] Sakoda, J.M. The Checkerboard Model Of Social Interaction Journal Of Mathematical Sociology, 1, 1971, pages 119–132.

[XIX] Wuensche, A. Classifying Cellular Automata Automatically: Finding Gliders, Filtering, And Relating Space-Time Patterns, Attractor Basins, And The Z Parameter Complexity, Vol.4, 3, pages 47–66, 1999

CHAPTER 10

Applying GMDH-Type Neural Network and Genetic Algorithm for Stock-Price Prediction of Iranian Cement Sector

Saeed Fallahi, Meysam Shaverdi, & Vahab Bashiri

Islamic Azad University
Iran

Applying GMDH Type Neural Network and Genetic Algorithm for Stock-Price Prediction of Iranian Cement Sector

Abstract

The cement industry is one of the most important and profitable industries in Iran and great content of financial resources are investing in this sector yearly. In this paper a GMDH-type neural network and genetic algorithm is developed for stock price prediction of cement sector. For stocks price prediction by GMDH type-neural network, we are using earnings per share (EPS), Prediction Earnings Per Share (PEPS), Dividend per share (DPS), Price-earnings ratio (P/E), Earnings-price ratio (E/P) as input data and stock price as output data. For this work, data of ten cement companies is gathering from Tehran stock exchange (TSE) in decennial range (1999-2008). GMDH type neural network is designed by 80% of the experimental data. For testing the appropriateness of the modeling, reminder of primary data were entered into the GMDH network. The results are very encouraging and congruent with the experimental results.

Keywords: GMDH; Artificial neural networks; stock price index; Genetic algorithm; stock price prediction

MSC 2010 NO. : 90B15, 62P30

1. Introduction

Nowadays, cement demand has increased parallel to the increase in the construction sector. This increase is based on the economic stability, decrease in the interest and exchange rates and increase in the popularity of mortgage system (Ertugrul and Karakasoglu 2009). Cement is one of the main industries in the development and progress of a community plays a vital role. Cement is one of the significant industries which plays vital role in society's progress and development. With the potential existing, number of cement factories will be increased (www.apadanabana.com). Number of cement plants will be increased based on high existing potential. As reason of crucial progress and high impacts on economy, Iran's cement industry with 75 years experience and high potential capacity can be found special position in industry. Iran's cement industry with 75 years experience and high potential capacity to grow and for the most adequate influence in the economy has managed a special place in the country industry. At present, Iran with a production capacity of two hundred thousand tons of cement a day is the first manufacturer of the middle east and ninth of the world cement market. Currently, Islamic Republic of Iran with two hundred thousand tons capacity in per day is the largest cement producer in the Middle East.

Country's production capacity in 1978 was 8 million tons a year and now with 60 million tons per year of growth equal to 750% compared to the year 1978 and 300% in recent 10 years is allocated. Thus, the cement industry is allocated the largest share of the Growth country industry. The production capacity in 1978 was 8 million tons a year and now it improves to 60 million tons, it

148

means that it has 750% growth in comparison to 1978 and 300% growth in recent 10 years. Thus, the cement industry has allocated the largest growth share in industry. Foreign investment in cement industry has an appropriate situation and now the world's largest cement company Hlsym producers of six manufacturing units allocated to the Company and other big producers of cement in the world like Lafarzh and Smag and Smgz are under investigation process to enter the cement industry in Iran. Position of foreign investment in this industry has a good condition and now the Holcim cement company in the world is allocated largest producers in six manufacturing units and other big producers of cement in the world like Lafarj, and cemag and cemex are entering Iran's cement industry (www.Iranminehouse.org).Stock price prediction is one of the main tasks in all private and institution investors. It is an important issue in investment/ financial decision-making and is currently receiving much attention from the research society. However, it is regarded as one of the most challenging problems due to the fact that natures of stock prices/indices are noisy and non-static (Hall, 1994, Li et al 2003, Yaser and Atiya 1996).

The price changing of stock market is a very dynamic system that has drive from a number of disciplines. Two main analytical approaches are fundamental analysis and technical analysis. Fundamental analysis uses the macroeconomics factors data such as interest rates, money supply, inflationary rates, and foreign exchange rates as well as the basic financial status of the company. After scrutiny all these factors, the analyst will then make a decision of selling or buying a stock. A technical analysis is based on the historical financial time-series data. However, financial time series show quite complex data (for example, trends, abrupt changes, and volatility clustering) and such series are often non-stationary, whereby a variable has no clear tendency to move to a fixed value or a linear trend (Cheng and Liu 2008).The idea of setting up in Iran a well-established stock exchange goes back to the 1930s. In 1968, Tehran Stock Exchange (TSE) established and started trading shares of a limited number of banks, industrial companies and State-backed securities. TSE is a very small exchange compared to all well established Exchanges in terms of the size, turnover, and other indicators; mainly common shares and participation securities only are being traded and there are not any derivatives; nearly impossible to hedge and the risks are very high. In TSE there is a great lack of knowledge and expertise among the TSE's staff as well as the brokers and investors (Parchehbar, Shoghi and Talaneh 2010). The aim of this paper is application of GMDH type-neural network for prediction of stock price in cement industry. Within this work, we are using financial indices and closing prices in decennial range (1999-2008) that have taken from TSE. The new approach in this paper is using GMDH type-neural network in prediction of stock price for helping investor and financial analyst. The rest of this paper is organized as follows. Section 2 gives literature review of stock price prediction by neural network approach and GMDH methodology. The proposed forecasting model and the experimental findings from the research is thoroughly described in Section 3. The paper is concluded in Section 4.

2. Research Methodology
2.1. Literature Review

Prediction of stock price variation is a very difficult task and the price dynamism behaves more like a random walk and time varying. During the last decade, stocks and future businessman have come to rely upon different types of intelligent systems to make trading decisions. Lately, artificial neural networks (ANNS) have been applied to this task. (Atsalakis and Valavanis 2009, Cao and Parry 2009, Chang et al 2009, Chavarnakul and Enke 2008, Enke and Thawornwong 2005, Hassan et al 2007, Kim 2006, Tsang et al 2007, Vellido et al 1999, Yudong and Lenan 2009, Zhang et al 1998, Zhu et al 2008). These approaches have their limitations owing to the prodigious noise and complicated dimensionality of stock price data and besides, the quantity of data and the input variables may also intervene with each other. Therefore, the result may not be that unpredictable (Chang and Liu 2008). Other soft computing methods are also applied in the prediction of stock price and these soft computing approaches are to use quantitative inputs, like technical indices, and qualitative factors, like political effects, to more simplify stock market forecasting and trend analysis. Kuo et al. (2001) uses a genetic algorithm base fuzzy neural network (NN) to determine the qualitative effects on the stock price. Variable selection is sensitive to the success of any network for the financial utility of a company. They applied their method to the Taiwan stock market. Aiken and Bsat (1999) applied a FFNN trained by a genetic algorithm (GA) to forecast threemonth US Treasury Bill rates. They conclude that an NN can be used to truly predict these rates. Thammano (1999) used a neuro-fuzzy approach to predict future values of Thailand's largest governmental bank. The inputs of the model were the closing prices for the current and prior three months, and the profitability ratios. The output of the model was the stock prices for the following three months. Conclusion of this research was that the neuro-fuzzy architecture was able to identify the general traits of the stock market easier and more accurately than the basic back propagation algorithm. Also, it would obtain prediction possibility of investment opportunities during the economic crisis when statistical methods did not yield trusty results.Tansel et al. (1999) compared the ability of linear optimization, ANNs, and GAs in modeling time series data. In this study used the criteria of modeling accuracy, convenience and computational time. They concluded that the best estimates is related to linear optimization methods, although the GAs could gave the same values if the boundaries of the parameters and the resolution were selected suitably, but that the result of NNs had the worst estimations. However, they express that non-linearity could be adapted by both the GAs and the NNs and that the latter required minimal theoretical background. Baba et al. (2000) used NNs and GAs to create an intelligent decision support system (DSS) for analyzing the Tokyo Stock Exchange Prices Indexes (TOPIX). The necessary characteristic of their DSS was that it specified the high and low TOPIX values four weeks into the future and suggested buy and sell decisions based on the average projected value and the then-current value of the TOPIX.Kim and Han (2000) combine a modified NN and a GA to predict the stock price index. In this study, the GA was used to reduce the complexity of the feature space, by optimizing the thresholds for feature discretization, and to optimize the connection weights between layers. They concluded that the result of GA approach is better than the conventional models. Abraham et al. (2001) investigated hybridized SC approaches for prediction of automated stock market and trend analysis. They used principal component analysis to preprocess the input data, a NN for prediction of one-day ahead stock and a neuro-fuzzy approach for scrutiny the trend of the predicted stock values. Abraham et al. (2003) investigate how the seemingly erratic behavior of stock markets could be well formulated using several connectionist paradigms and soft computing techniques. To prove the proposed method, they analyzed the 7 year's Nasdaq-100 main index and 4 year's NIFTY index values. The result of their study was that all the connectionist paradigms considered could represent the stock indices behavior very accurately (Chang and Liu 2008).The group method of data handling (GMDH) (Ivakhnenko 1966) is aimed at identifying the functional structure of a model hidden within the empirical data. The main idea of the GMDH is the use of feed-forward networks based on short-term polynomial transfer functions whose coefficients are obtained using regression combined with emulation of the self-organizing activity behind NN structural learning (Farlow 1984). The GMDH was developed for complex systems for the modeling, prediction identification, and approximation of multivariate processes, diagnostics, pattern recognition, and clustering in data samples. It has been shown that, for inaccurate, noisy, or small data sets, the GMDH is the best optimal simplified model, with a higher accuracy and a simpler structure than traditional NNs models (Ketabchi et al 2010).Hwang (2006) used a fuzzy GMDH-type neural network model for prediction of mobile communication. They used input data within a possible extends as; the amount of portion of population, amount of households and the amount of average n expenditure per households. They showed the proposed neuro-fuzzy GMDH method was excellent for the complicated forecasting problems. Srinivasan (2008) using GMDH network for prediction of energy demand. This paper presented a medium-term energy demand forecasting method that helps utilities identify and forecast energy demand for each of the end-use consumption sector of the energy system, representing residential, industrial, commercial, non-industrial, entertainment and public lighting load. In this study a comparative evaluation of various traditional and neural networkbased methods for obtaining the forecast of monthly energy demand was carried out. This paper concluded GMDH very effective and more accurate in producing forecasts than traditional timeseries and regression-based models.

2.2. Definition of Stock Price Iindices

In this research input data include indices of EPS, PEPS, DPS, P/E and E/P. Stock price is defined as output data. All indices are defined below.

1- Earnings Per Share (EPS). Earnings per share are one of the most important measure of companies' strength. The significance of EPS is obvious, as the viability of any business depends on the income it can generate. A money losing business will eventually go bankrupt, so the only way for long term survival is to make money. EPS allows us to compare different companies' power to make money. The higher the EPS with all else equal, the higher each share should be worth. To calculate this ratio, divide the company's net income by the number of shares outstanding during the same period (http://investing-school.com).

2- Prediction Earnings Per Share (PEPS). PEPS is the last of Prediction Earnings Per Share. On the other hand, it is unrealized Earnings Per Share.

3- Dividend per share (DPS). DPS is the total dividends paid out over an entire year (including interim dividends but not including special dividends) divided by the number of outstanding ordinary shares issued (investopedia).

4- Price-earnings ratio (P/E). Value investors have long considered the price earnings ratio one of the single most important numbers available when evaluating a company's stock price. The P/E looks at the relationship between the stock price and the company's earnings and it is the most popular metric of stock analysis. The price earnings ratio is equal to the price of the stock divided by EPS of common stock (investopedia).

5- Earnings-price ratio (E/P). E/P is a way to help determine a security's stock valuation, that is, the fair value of a stock in a perfect market. It is also a measure of expected, but not realized, growth. It may be used in place of the price-earnings ratio if, say, there are no earnings (as one cannot divide by zero). It is also called the earnings yield or the earnings capitalization ratio. E/P is equal to the EPS of common stock divided by the price of the stock (financial dictionary).

6- Stock price. The Stock price is equal to the last of Stock price which trading at the one day.

2.3. Group Method of Data Handling (GMDH)

Using the GMDH algorithm, a model can be represented as a set of neurons in which different pairs of them in each layer are connected through a quadratic polynomial and, therefore, produce new neurons in the next layer. Such representation can be used in modeling to map inputs to outputs. The formal definition of the identification problem is to find a function, $\hat{f}$, that can be approximately used instead of the actual one, f, in order to predict output $\hat{y}$ for a given input vector $X = (x_1, x_2, x_3 ..., x_n)$ as close as possible to its actual output y. Therefore, given number of observations (M) of multi-input, single output data pairs so that

$$y_i = f(x_{i1}, x_{i2}, x_{i3} .... x_{in})(i = 1, 2, 3, ..., M). \tag{1}$$

It is now possible to train a GMDH-type-NN to predict the output values $\hat{y}_i$ for any given input Vector $X = (x_{i1}, x_{i2}, x_{i3}, ..., x_{in})$, that is

$$\hat{y}_i = \hat{f}(x_{i1}, x_{i2}, x_{i3}, ..., x_{in})(i = 1, 2, 3, ..., M). \tag{2}$$

In order to determine a GMDH type-NN, the square of the differences between the actual output and the predicted one is minimized, that is

$$\sum_{i=1}^{M} \left[\hat{f}(x_{i1}, x_{i2}, ... x_i) - y_i \right]^2 \rightarrow \min \tag{3}$$

The general connection between the inputs and the output variables can be expressed by a complicated discrete form of the Volterra functional series (Ivakhnenko 1966) in the form of

$$y = a_o + \sum_{i=1}^{n} a_i x_i + \sum_{i=1}^{n} \sum_{j=1}^{n} a_{ij} x_i x_j + \sum_{i=1}^{n} \sum_{j=1}^{n} \sum_{k=1}^{n} a_{ijk} x_i x_j x_k + \cdots, \tag{4}$$

where is known as the Kolmogorov-Gabor polynomial (Ivakhnenko 1966). The general form of mathematical description can be represented by a system of partial quadratic polynomials consisting of only two variables (neurons) in the form of

$$\hat{y} = G(x_i, x_j) = a_o + a_1 x_i + a_2 x_j + a_3 x_i x_j + a_4 x_i^2 + a_5 x_j^2 \cdots. \tag{5}$$

In this way, such partial quadratic description is recursively used in a network of connected neurons to build the general mathematical relation of the inputs and output variables given in Equation (4). The coefficients a_i in Equation (5) are calculated using regression techniques. It can be seen that a tree of polynomials is constructed using the quadratic form given in Equation (5). In this way, the coefficients of each quadratic function G_i are obtained to fit optimally the output in the whole set of input–output data pairs, that is

$$E = \frac{\sum_{i=1}^{M} (y_i - G_i())^2}{M} \rightarrow \min.$$

(6)

In the basic form of the GMDH algorithm, all the possibilities of two independent variables out of the total n input variables are taken in order to construct the regression polynomial in the form of Equation (5) that best fits the dependent observations $(y_i, i = 1, 2, ..., M)$ in a least squares sense (Nariman-Zadeh and Jamali 2007). Using the quadratic sub-expression in the form of Equation (5) for each row of M data triples, the following matrix equation can be readily obtained as

$$Aa = Y,$$

(7)

where a is the vector of unknown coefficients of the quadratic polynomial in Equation (5)

$$a = \{a_0, a_1, a_2, a_3, a_4, a_5\}$$

(8)

And

$$Y = \{y_1, y_2, y_3 ..., y_M\}^T.$$

(9)

Here, Y is the vector of the output's value from observation. It can be easily seen that

$$A = \begin{bmatrix} 1 & x_{1p} & x_{1q} & x_{1p}x_{1q} & x_{1p}^2 & x_{1q}^2 \\ 1 & x_{2p} & x_{2q} & x_{2p}x_{2q} & x_{2p}^2 & x_{2q}^2 \\ \vdots & \vdots & \vdots & \vdots & \vdots & \vdots \\ 1 & x_{Mp} & x_{Mq} & x_{Mp}x_{Mq} & x_{Mp}^2 & x_{Mp}^2 \end{bmatrix}$$

(10)

The least squares technique from multiple regression analysis leads to the solution of the normal equations in the form of

$$a = (A^T A)^{-1} A^T Y$$

(11)

3. The Stock Price Prediction Using the GMDH-type Neural Network

The feed-forward GMDH-type neural network for the stock price was constructed using an experimental data set of ten cement companies from Tehran stock exchange (TSE) in decennial range (1999-2008). For each cement companies, the data was divided into two parts: 80% was used as training data, and 20% was used as test data. The EPS, Prediction PEPS, DPS, P/E and E/P were used as inputs of the GMDH-type network. The Stock prices were used as desired outputs of the neural network.In order to estimate the stock prices for companies, using the GMDH type network, seven polynomial equations were obtained (Table 1). In this table, z1 is the DPS, and z2 , z3 ,z4 and z5 are the E/P, P/E, PEPS and EPS, respectively. The proposed model was used to calculate the stock prices (the output data).In the present study, the stock prices were predicted using GMDH-type- NNs. Such a NN identification process needs a suitable optimization method to find the best network architecture. In this way, genetic algorithm (GA) is arranged in a new approach to design the whole architecture of the GMDH-type-NNs. It provides the optimal number of neurons in each hidden layer and their connectivity configuration to find the optimal set of appropriate coefficients of quadratic expressions to model stock prices. The best structure in GMDH were reached by two hidden layers with 300 generations, cross over probability of 0.9 and mutation probability of 0.1, to model the stock prices.

The developed GMDH neural network was successfully used to obtain seven models for seven companies calculate Stock prices. The optimal structures of the developed neural network with 2-hidden layers are shown in Figure1 .For instance, "*abdecccd*" and "*ceaaeddd*" are corresponding genome representations for the Stock prices of Tehran and Sepahan companies, respectively. In which, *a* ,*b* , *c* , *d* and *e* stand for (DPS), (E/P), (P/E), (PEPS) and (EPS), respectively. All input variables were accepted by the models. In other words, the GMDH-type-NN provides an automated selection of essential input variables, and builds polynomial equations for the Stock prices modeling. These polynomial equations show the quantitative relationship between input and output variables (Table 1). Our proposed models behavior in prediction of the Stock prices is demonstrated in Figs. 2. The results of the developed models give a close agreement between observed and predicted values of the Stock prices.

In order to determine the accuracy of the models some statistical measures are given in Table 2. These statistical values are based on R^2 as absolute fraction of variance, RMSE as root-mean squared error, and MAD as mean absolute deviation which are defined as follows:

$$R^2 = 1 - \left[\frac{\sum_{i=0}^{M} \left(Y_{i(model)} - Y_{i(actual)}\right)^2}{\sum_{i=1}^{M} \left(Y_{i(actual)}\right)^2} \right], RMSE = \left[\frac{\sum_{i=0}^{M} \left(Y_{i(model)} - Y_{i(actual)}\right)^2}{M} \right]^{1/2,}$$

$$MAD = \frac{\sum_{i=0}^{M} \left|Y_{i(model)} - Y_{i(actual)}\right|}{M}$$

4. Conclusion

Today cement industry is an attractive market. The main reason of this is the increase in house and infrastructure investments. It is obvious that cement production will rise commensurate to the increase in the house demand. Also implementation of mortgage system, and increase in investments will affect the cement demand. The main reason of this is the increase in infrastructure investments. In this paper we examine the relationship between stock prices indices and stock prices. Modeling a soft computing system for stock price prediction in cement industry is very useful for all traders and financial consultant to decreasing investment risk kinds and rising profit of stockholders. In future study more price indices or other factor that effect on stock price can be used for accurate stock price prediction. Also other stock price prediction methods can be comparison with proposed model and the proposed model can be applied for the firms in other sectors.

References

[I] Abraham, A., Baikunth, N. & Mahanti, P.K. (2001). Hybrid intelligent systems for stock market analysis. Lecture Notes in Computer Science 2074: 337–345.

[II] Abraham, A., Philip, N.S. & Saratchandran, P. (2003). Modeling chaotic behavior of stock indices using intelligent paradigms. Neural Parallel and Scientific Computations 11: 143– 160.

[III] Aiken, M. & Bsat, M. (1999). Forecasting market trends with neural networks. Information Systems Management 16(4): 42–48.

[IV] Atsalakis, G. S. & Valavanis, K.P. (2009). Surveying stock market forecasting techniques Part II: Soft computing methods. Expert Systems with Applications 36(3): 5932–5941.

[V] Baba, N., Inoue, N. & Asakawa, H. (2000). Utilization of Neural Networks and GAs for Constructing Reliable Decision Support Systems to Deal Stocks. IEEE–INNS–ENNS International Joint Conference on Neural Networks (IJCNN'00) 5: 5111–5116.

[VI] Cao, Q. & Parry, M.E. (2009). Neural network earnings per share forecasting models: A comparison of backward propagation and the genetic algorithm. Decision Support Systems 47(1): 32–41.

[VII] Chang, P.C. & Liu, C.H. (2008). A TSK type fuzzy rule based system for stock price prediction. Expert Systems with Applications 34: 135–144.

[VIII] Chang, P.C., Liu, C.H., Lin, J.L., Fan, C.Y. & Ng, C.S.P. (2009). A neural network with a case based dynamic window for stock trading prediction. Expert Systems with Applications 36(3): 6889–6898.

[IX] Chavarnakul, T. & Enke, D. (2008). Intelligent technical analysis-based equivolume charting for stock trading using neural networks. Expert Systems with Applications 34(2):1004–1017.

[X] Enke, D. & Thawornwong, S. (2005). The use of data mining and neural networks for forecasting stock market returns. Expert Systems with Applications 29(4): 927–940.

[XI] Ertugrul, I. & Karakasoglu, N. (2009). Performance evaluation of Turkish cement firms with fuzzy analytic hierarchy process and TOPSIS methods. Expert Systems with Applications36(1):702–715.

[XII] Farlow, S.J. (1984). Self-Organizing Method in Modelling: GMDH-Type Algorithm, Marcel Dekker, New York.

[XIII] Financial dictionary. http://financial-dictionary.thefreedictionary.com

[XIV] Hall, J.W. (1994). Adaptive selection of US stocks with neural nets. In G. J. Deboeck (Ed.), Trading on the edge: Neural, genetic and fuzzy systems for chaotic financial markets, pp 45–65. New York: Wiley.

[XV] Hassan, M.R., Nath, B. & Kirley, M. (2007). A fusion model of HMM, ANN and GA for stock market forecasting. Expert Systems with Applications 33(1): 171–180.

[XVI] Hwang, S.H. (2006) Fuzzy GMDH-type neural network model and its application to forecasting of mobile communication. Computers & Industrial Engineering 50: 450–457.

[XVII] Investing-school (2008). http://investing-school.com Investopedia. www.investopedia.com

[XVIII] Ivakhnenko, A.G. (1966). Polynomial theory of complex systems. IEEE Transactions on Systems.

[XIX] Ketabchi, S., Ghanadzadeh, H., Ghanadzadeh, A., Fallahi, S. & Ganji, M. (2010). Estimation of VLE of binary systems (tert-butanol + 2-ethyl-1-hexanol) and (n-butanol + 2-

ethyl-1- hexanol) using GMDH-type neural network. J. Chem. Thermodynamics 42: 1352–1355.

[XX] Kim, KJ. (2006). Artificial neural networks with evolutionary instance selection for financial forecasting. Expert Systems with Applications 30(3): 519–526.

[XXI] Kim, KJ. & Han, I. (2000). Genetic algorithms approach to feature discretization in artificial neural networks for the prediction of stock price index. Expert Systems with Applications 19: 125–132.

[XXII] Kuo, RJ., Chen, C.H. & Hwang, Y.C. (2001). An intelligent stock trading decision support system through integration of genetic algorithm based fuzzy neural network and artificial neural network. Fuzzy Sets and Systems 118: 21–24.

[XXIII] Li, T., Li, Q., Zhu, S. & Ogihara, M. (2003). A survey on wavelet applications in data mining. SIGKDD Explorations 4(2):49–68.

[XXIV] Nariman-Zadeh, N. & Jamali, A. (2006). Pareto genetic design of GMDH-type neural networks for nonlinear systems. int J. Drchal, J. Koutnik (Eds.), Proceedings of the International Workshop on Inductive Modelling, Czech Technical University, Prague, Czech Republic, pp.96–103.

[XXV] Parchehbar, S., Shoghi, M. & Talaneh, A. (2010). An Analysis of Emerging Markets Returns Volatility: Case of Tehran Stock Exchange. Working Paper Series.

[XXVI] Srinivasan, D. (2008). Energy demand prediction using GMDH networks. Neurocomputing 72 625–629.

[XXVII] Tansel, I.N., Yang, S.Y., Venkataraman, G., Sasirathsiri, A., Bao, W.Y. & Mahendrakar, N. (1999). Modeling Time Series Data by Using Neural Networks and Genetic Algorithms. In Dagli CH, AL Buczak, J Ghosh, MJ Embrechts, O Ersoy (Eds.) Smart Engineering System Design: neural networks, fuzzy logic, evolutionary programming, data mining, and complex systems. In Proceedings of the Artificial Neural Networks in Engineering Conference (ANNIE '99). New York ASME Press: 1055–1060.

[XXVIII] Thammano, A. (1999). Neuro-fuzzy Model for Stock Market Prediction. In Dagli, CH, AL Buczak, J Ghosh, MJ Embrechts, O Ersoy (Eds.) Smart Engineering System Design: neural networks, fuzzy logic evolutionary programming, data mining, and complex systems. In Proceedings of the Artificial Neural Networks in Engineering Conference (ANNIE '99). New York: ASME Press: 587–591

[XXIX] Tsang, P.M., Kwok, P., Choy, S.O., Kwan, R., Ng, S.C. & Mak, J., et al. (2007). Design and implementation of NN5 for Hong Kong stock price forecasting. Engineering Applications of Artificial Intelligence 20(4): 453–461.

[XXX] Vellido, A., Lisboa, P.J.G., Vaughan, J. (1999). Neural networks in business: A survey of applications (1992–1998). Expert Systems with Applications 17: 51–70.

[XXXI] Yaser, S.A.M. & Atiya, A.F. (1996). Introduction to financial forecasting. Applied Intelligence 6: 205–213.

[XXXII] Yudong, Z. & Lenan, W. (2009). Stock market prediction of S&P 500 via combination of improved BCO approach and BP neural network. Expert Systems with Applications 36(5): 8849–8854.

[XXXIII] Zhang, G., Patuwo, B.E. & Hu, M.Y.(1998). Forecasting with artificial neural networks: The state of the art. International Journal of Forecasting 14: 35–62.

[XXXIV] Zhu, X., Wang, H., Xu, L. & Li, H. (2008). Predicting stock index increments by neural networks: The role of trading volume under different horizons. Expert Systems with Applications 34(4): 3043–3054.

Table 1. Polynomial Equations of the GMDH Model for the cement Companies Stock Price of Ilam company

---

Stock Price of Ilam company

$Y_1 = 14335.1317 - 191405848z_5 - 0.3774z_4 + 91.2376z_5^2 + 0.0053z_4^2 + 0.0739z_5z_4$

$Y_2 = 11485.5557 - 3.6704z_1 - 3.8540z_2 - 2.3817z_1^2 - 2.3061z_2^2 - 4.6942z_1z_2$

$Y_3 = 11485.5557 - 3.6704z_1 - 3.8540z_2 - 2.3817z_1^2 - 2.3061z_2^2 - 4.6942z_1z_2$

$Y_4 = 0.0001 + 0.0763Y_1 + 0.7900Y_2 + 0.00003Y_1^2 - 0.00003Y_2^2 + 0.000008Y_1Y_2$

$Y_5 = 0.0090 + 0.3653z_4 + 0.1142Y_3 + 10.0803z_4^2 - 0.00003Y_3^2 + 0.0613z_4Y_3$

$Value = 0.0001 + 1.0292Y_4 + 0.0221Y_5 - 0.0003Y_4^2 - 0.0003Y_5^2 + 0.0007Y_4Y_5$

Stock Price of Tehram Company

$Y_1 = 607.8173 - 3690.5823z_1 + 3545.3949z_2 - 3.2209z_1^2 - 4.8347z_2^2 + 8.1310z_1z_2$

$Y_2 = 2182.7494 - 139.1586z_4 + 0.3136z_5 + 53.0293z_4^2 + 0.0005z_5^2 + 0.3632 z_4z_5$

$Y_3 = -8.76645 + 3796.3023 z_3 + 7910.3860z_4 - 50.4918 z_3^2 - 124.4239z_4^2 - 876.4355z_3z_4$

$Y_4 = 0.000007 + 0.1018Y_1 + 0.8895Y_2 - 0.000002Y_1^2 + 0.0000004Y_2^2 - 0.000002Y_1Y_2$

$Y_5 = -0.0111 - 0.0125z_3 + 15989 Y_3 + 6.8815z_3^2 - 0.000008Y_3^2 - 0.0576z_3 Y_3$

$Value = -0.00007 + 1.4419Y_4 - 0.4224Y_5 - 0.00006Y_4^2 - 0.00003 Y_5^2 + 0.00009Y_4Y_5$

Stock Price of Irangach Company

$Y1 = -21.5977 + 1078.8286z_4 - 5.7736z_5 - 51.1767z_4^2 + 0.0054z_5^2 + 0.3074z_4z_5$

$Y_2 = 8174.0716 - 272.1459z_3 - 2.1345z_5 + 2.8032z_3^2 + 0.0046z_5^2 - 0.0386z_3z_5$

$Y_3 = -0.4929 - 25.3797z_3 + 2666.4638z_4 + 1.0292z_3^2 - 158.4473z_4^2 - 49.3238z_3z_4$

$Y_4 = -1573.6637 + 19.1327z_3 - 49.9142z_2 - 0.0066z_3^2 + 1.6899z_2^2 - 0.2814z_3z_2$

$Y_5 = 0.0036 + 19248Y_1 - 0.9972Y_2 - 0.0004Y_1^2 - 0.0003Y_2^2 + 0.0008Y_1Y_2$

$Y_6 = 0.0016 + 1.8334Y3 - 0.9274Y_4 - 0.0005Y_3^2 - 0.0002Y_4^2 + 0.0008Y_3Y_4$

$Value = 0.0003 - 0.3693Y_5 + 1.3992Y_6 - 0.0001Y_5^2 - 0.0003Y_6^2 + 0.0005Y_5Y$

Stock Price of Orumie company

$Y_1 = 0.0126 + 12.8808z_1 - 6.0043z_5 - 0.0020z_1^2 + 0.0022z_5^2 - 0.0008z_1z_5$

$Y_2 = 3.2523 - 264.6254z_1 + 275.8401z_2 + 0.0383z_1^2 - 0.0498z_2^2 - 0.0130z_1z_2$

$Y_3 = 0.00002 + 0.0001z_4 + 0.6017Y_1 + 0.0006z_4^2 - 0.000008Y_1^2 + 0.080z_4Y_2$

$Value = -0.000007 + 1.2552Y_3 - 0.2811Y_4 - 0.000002Y_3^2 - 0.0000001Y_4^2 - 0.000003Y_3Y_4$

Stock Price of Khazar company

$Y_1 = 9970.2069 - 1292.3273 z_3 + 24.4081z_5 + 56.3911z_3^2 - 0.0020z_5^2 - 1.1611z_3z_5$

$Y_2 = 6359.4509 - 2.2734z_1 + 6.6454z_2 - 0.0463z_1^2 - 0.0278z_2^2 + 0.0800z_1z_2$

$Y_3 = -23820.6500 + 16.0379z_1 + 2784.3134z_4 - 0.0040z_1^2 - 26.7419z_3^2 - 0.06988z_1z_4$

$Y_4 = 4080.6252 + 26.3012z_1 + 68.169z_3 + 0.0029z_1^2 + 51.1881z_3^2 - 2.4558z_1z_3$

$Y_5 = 0.00006 + 0.2157Y_1 + 0.7616Y_2 + 0.0000001Y_1^2 - 0.00002Y_2^2 + 0.00002Y_1Y_2$

$Y_6 = 0.00008 + 0.0006Y_3 + 0.8782Y_4 + 0.00001Y_3^2 - 0.00002Y_4^2 - 0.00001Y_3Y_4$

$Value = 0.00004 + 0.8815Y_5 + 0.1720Y_6 - 0.00002Y_5^2 - 0.00001Y_6^2 + 0.00003Y_5Y_6$

Stock Price of Sepahan company

$Y_1 = -29.2606 - 303.4102z_3 + 28.9018z_5 + 16.4888z_3^2 - 0.0022z_5^2 - 1.1148\ z_3z_5$

$Y_2 = 48.8993 + 310.2420z_5 + 5.0092z_4 + 53.0202z_5^2 - 0.0006z_4^2 + 0.1056z_5z_4$

$Y_3 = 0.0036 + 0.6570Y_1 + 3.2297z_1 + 0.000009Y_1^2 + 0.00006\ z_1^2 - 0.0001Y_1\ z_1$

$Y_6 = 0.00006 + 0.8893Y_2 + 0.0004z_4 - 0.00001Y_2^2 + 0.0002z_4^2 + 0.0382Y_2\ z_4$

$Value = 0.000006 + 0.6521Y_3 + 0.2798Y_4 - 0.00001Y_3^2 - 0.000005Y_4^2 - 0.00002Y_3Y_4$

Stock Price of Behbahan company

$Y_1 = -4.5609 - 488.6869\ z_3 + 7958.4327z_4 + 71.0835z_3^2 - 149.0807z_4^2 - 456.1076\ z_3z_4$

$Y_2 = 229.3744 + 8.8449z_2 + 17.5928\ z_5 - 0.0009z_2^2 + 0.0005\ z_5^2 - 0.0071z_2z_5$

$Y_3 = -18757.0150 - 2.7177z_1 + 5313.3035\ z_4 + 0.0025z_1^2 - 80.4349z_4^2 - 0.3913z_1z_4$

$Y_4 = -0.0069 - 10.3213\ z_2 + 1.2426Y_1 + 0.0046z_2^2 - 0.000003Y_1^2 - 0.000003z_2\ Y_1$

$Y_5 = 0.00002 + 0.2696\ Y_2 + 0.5759Y_3 - 0.000001Y_2^2 + 0.000007Y_3^2 - 0.000001Y_2Y_3$

$Value = 0.00001 + 0.8813Y_4 - 0.04865Y_5 + 0.0003Y_4^2 + 0.0003Y_5^2 - 0.0006Y_4Y_5$

Stock Price of Bojnurd company

$Y_1 = 593.7701 + 19.2261\ z_2 + 1455.6015z_3 - 0.0026z_2^2 - 137.9500z_3^2 - 0.9516\ z_2z_3$

$Y_2 = 3527.6854 - 100.0816\ z_1 + 91.3377\ z_2 + 2.3894\ z_1^2 + 1.9089z_2^2 - 4.2656z_1z_2$

$Y_3 = -370.1390 + 2620.2263\ z_3 + 20.9167z_5 - 245.6548z_3^2 - 0.0027z_5^2 - 1.2131z_3z_5$

$Y_4 = 2321.3117 + 1.4752z_2 + 3.2072z_5 + 0.0093z_2^2 + 0.0111z_5^2 - 0.0156z_2z_5$

$Y_5 = 0.0002 + 0.1931\ Y_1 + 1.0148Y_2 - 0.00007Y_1^2 - 0.0001Y_2^2 + 0.0002Y_1Y_2$

$Y_6 = 0.0001 + 0.1361Y_3 + 0.6103\ Y_4 - 0.00001Y_3^2 - 0.00003Y_4^2 + 0.00006Y_3Y_4$

$Value = 0.0001 + 0.6017Y_5 + 0.2675Y_6 + 0.00006Y_5^2 + 0.00007\ Y_6^2 - 0.0001Y_5Y_6$

Stock Price of Esfahan company

$Y_1 = 0.0159 - 16.5882z_2 + 28.5577z_5 + 0.0097z_2^2 + 0.0033z_5^2 - 0.0131\ z_2z_5$

$Y_2 = 639.5846 + 20.9844z_2 + 3491.2517\ z_3 + 0.0116\ z_2^2 + 912.1789z_3^2 - 9.4724z_2z_3$

$Y_3 = -269.5581 + 205070.5351z_3 + 150443.4550z_4 - 5544.4970z_3^2 - 2870.1483z_4^2 - 26947.5323z_3z_4$

$Y_4 = 0.00002 - 0.2871Y_1 + 1.1116Y_2 + 0.00002Y_1^2 + 0.000006Y_2^2 - 0.00002Y_1Y_2$

$Y_5 = -0.0003 - 2.9936z_5 + 0.9562Y_3 + 0.0008z_5^2 - 0.000003Y_3^2 + 0.0001\ z_5\ Y_3$

$Value = 0.00004 + 0.9166Y_4 + 0.0494Y_5 + 0.00003Y_4^2 + 0.00005Y_5^2 - 0.00009Y_4Y_5$

Stock Price of Ardabil company

$Y_1 = 269006.5601 - 41002.9613\ z_3 - 17430.1111z_4 + 1382.6842z_3^2 + 242.6875z_4^2 + 1747.3189\ z_3z_4$

$Y_2 = 61.3892 + 13.9339z_2 + 1122.6543z_4 - 0.0003\ z_2^2 - 1.6247\ z_4^2 - 0.6250z_2z_4$

$Y_3 = 0.0008 - 5.4160Y_1 + 6.3321Y_2 + 0.0003Y_1^2 + 0.0001Y_2^2 - 0.0004Y_1Y_2$

$Value = -0.0041 + 0.5784Y_3 + 0.2690\ z_4 + 0.00001Y_3^2 - 13.0345\ z_4^2 + 0.0131Y_3\ z_4$

Table 2. Model Statistics and information for the GMDH-Type NN Model for the Prediction of Stock Price.

Company	Set	R2	RMSE	MAD
Tehran	Training	0.99	1992.55	1463.52
	Testing	0.99	1782.47	1443.41
Sepahan	Training	0.99	3025.74	2138.48
	Testing	1.00	2439.06	1830.83
Ardabil	Training	1.00	982.39	630.22
	Testing	1.00	696.06	575.17
Bojnurd	Training	0.99	1286.61	978.03
	Testing	0.98	1589.11	1270.57
Behbahan	Training	0.99	3286.16	2273.14
	Testing	1.00	2914.21	2425.30
Orumie	Training	0.99	5352.00	3810.98
	Testing	0.99	5195.13	3705.33
Irangach	Training	0.99	566.23	424.40
	Testing	0.99	726.32	566.13
Khazar	Training	0.99	2650.62	1990.90
	Testing	0.99	2081.21	1733.22
Esfahan	Training	0.99	2829.08	2063.50
	Testing	0.99	3212.21	2167.11
Ilam	Training	0.99	1134.02	857.46
	Testing	0.99	733.44	594.87

(a)

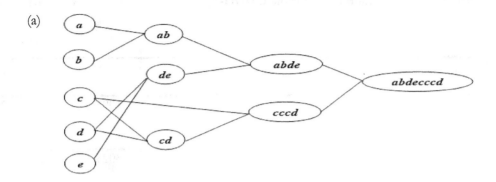

(b)

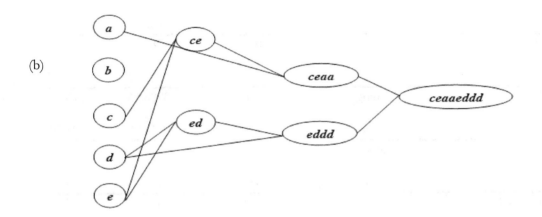

(c)

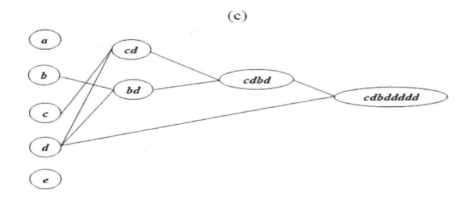

(d)

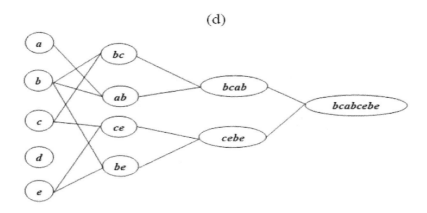

(e)

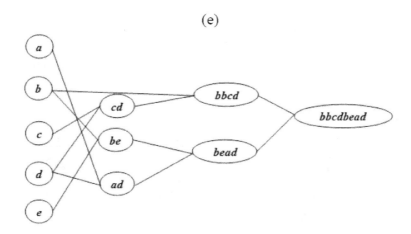

(f)

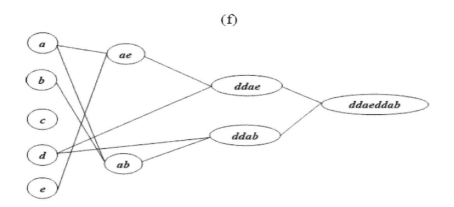

(g)

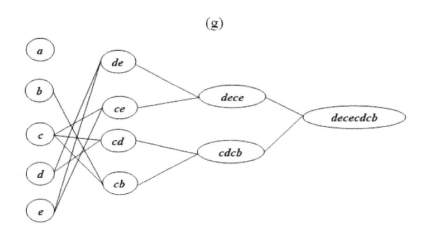

(h)

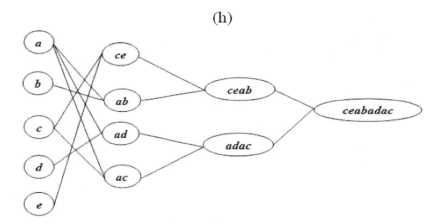

(i)

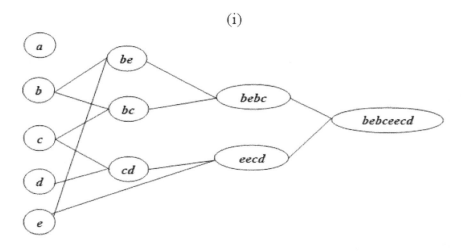

(j)

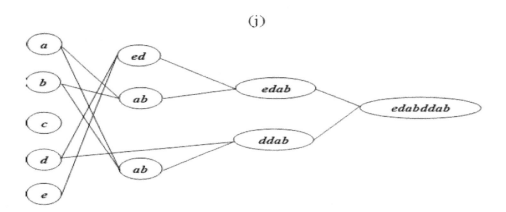

Figure 1.Developed strcture of GMDH-NN Model: a)Teheran, b)Sepahan. c) Ardabil. d) Bojnurd. e) Behbahan. f) Orumie. g) Irangach.h) Khazar. i)Esfahan. j) Ilam

(a)

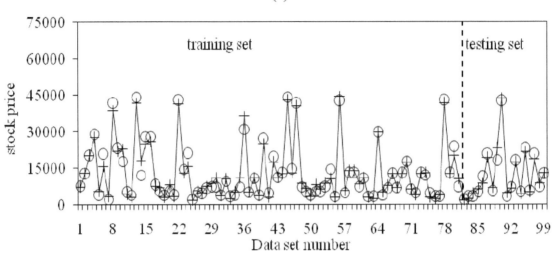

(b)

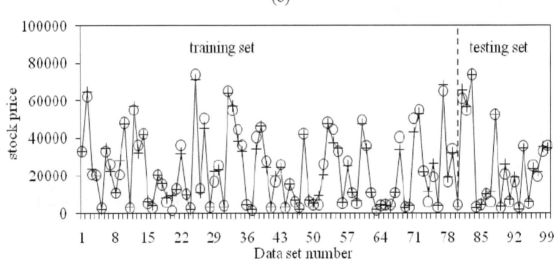

(c)

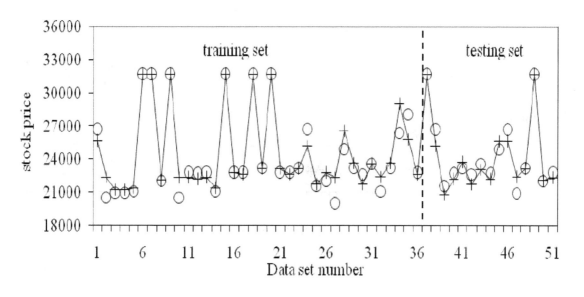

(d)

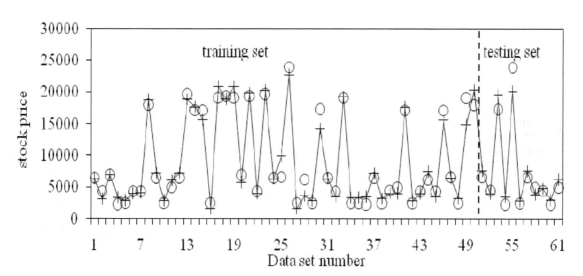

(e)

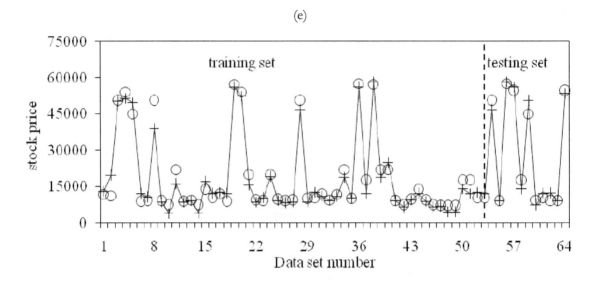

(f)

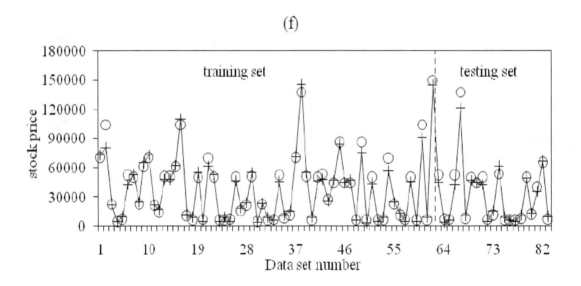

(g)

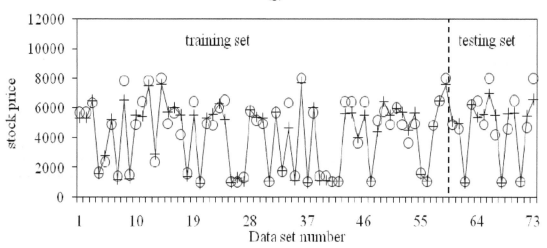

(h)

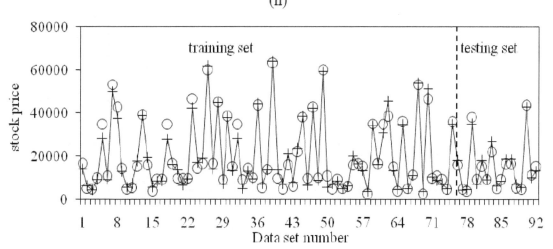

(i)

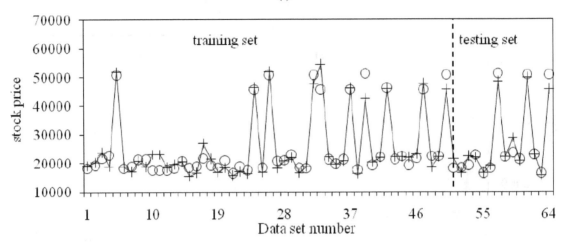

(j)

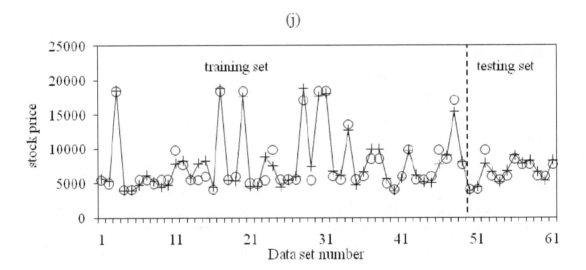

Figure 2 Plot of the stock price against data set number to illustrate the prediction ability of GMDH model : (0) Experimental Points: (+) Calculated Points, a)Teheran, b)Sepahan. c) Ardabil. d) Bojnurd. e) Behbahan. f) Orumie. g) Irangach. h) Khazar. i)Esfahan. j) Ilam

CHAPTER 11

Design Neural Network for Stock Market Volatility: Accuracy Measurement

J.K.Mantri, D.Mohanty, & Braja B Nayak

North Orissa University
India

Design Neural Network for Stock Market Volatility: Accuracy Measurement

Abstract

Artificial Neural Networks (ANNs) are very powerful tool in modern quantitative finance and have immerged as a powerful statistical modeling technology. This paper focuses on the problem of estimation of volatility of Indian Stock market. It begins with volatility calculation by Auto Regressive Conditional Heteroscedastic (ARCH), & Generalized Autoregressive Conditional Heteroscedasticity (GARCH) models of financial computation. At last the accuracy of using Artificial Neural Network for it is examined and concluded that ANN can be used as a best choice for measuring the volatility of stock market.

Keywords: ARCH, GARCH, ANN

Introduction

The main characteristic of any financial asset is its return. Return is typically considered to be a random variable. An asset's volatility, which describes the spread of outcomes of this variable, plays an important role in numerous financial applications. Its primary usage is to estimate the value of market list. Volatility is also a key parameter for pricing evaluation. It is also used for risk management applications and in general portfolio management. This is crucial for financial institutions not only to know the current value of the volatility of managed assets, but also to be able to estimate their future values. Volatility measuring & forecasting is especially important for institution involved in options trading and portfolio managementDifferent Mathematical Modeling Techniques are used by the researchers & practitioners to calculate it. But Artificial Neural Networks (or Neural Networks) are popular statistic techniques for machine learning. Originally, they were created as an attempt to model the biological neuron system. This attempt was made to create a new approach to the computing, and to possible mimic the behavior of human brain. This field of a science was created in a late 1950s, and was extensively developed in 1980s.Now a days ANNs techniques are used to calculate the value of volatility & forecasting for Stock Market.

Empirical Research on Volatility Modeling

Stock market analysis is an area of financial application. Detecting trends of stock market data is a difficult task as they have complex, nonlinear, dynamic and chaotic behavior.More specifically, at first Mandelbrot [1963] observed that volatility of stock prices exhibits 'clustering', where periods of large returns are followed by period of small returns. Later popular models of volatility clustering were developed by Engle [1982] and Bollerslev [1986]. The autoregressive conditional heteroskedastic (ARCH) models Engle, [1982] and generalized ARCH (GARCH) models Bollerslev et al [1986] have been extensively used in capturing volatility clustering in financial time series data. The superiority of GARCH of models in volatility predictions over naïve models like historical average, moving average and exponentially weighted moving average (EWMA) has been confirmed in several empirical studies Akgiray [1989], West et al [1993]. GARCH models are claimed to work better under the conditions of such non-normality. Working with daily data from 1990-1998, Varma [1999, 2002] showed the superiority of the GARCH (1,1) model over EWMA model for predicting volatility. [Dev et al [2003], Karmakar [2005] and Kakati and Kakati [2006] also confirm the superiority of GARCH (1,1) model for volatility prediction. Banerjee and Sarkar [2006] claim that Indian stock market exhibits volatility clustering and hence GARCH type models can better predict the market volatility. The GARCH models are however subject to certain weaknesses (Brooks, 2002). One of the primary restrictions imposed by the GARCH models is that they enforce a symmetric response of positive and negative shocks. However, it has been reported that volatility in a falling market is more than volatility in a rising market. This asymmetry is typically attributed to leverage effect (Black, 1976, Christie, 1982). Empirical evidence on leverage effect can also be found in Nelson (1991), Gallant et al (1992), Campbell and Kyle (1993) and Engle and Ng (1993). Nelson (1991) also proposed an Exponential GARCH (EGARCH) framework to model volatility under the conditions of leverage or asymmetry. Many financial time series data possess the characteristics of persistence. IGARCH (Integrated GARCH) model proposed by Engle & Bollerslev (1986) has taken care of the current shock on the conditional volatility which does not die out asymptotically. Pandey (2005), on the other hand claimed that extreme value estimators perform better than the conditional volatility estimators.But,White [1988] was the first who had used Neural Networks for forecasting stock market volatility. However, Ripley [1993] claims that although comparison of ANNs to other models are rare, however, when done carefully, often show that statistical methods can outperform the state-of the art ANNs. His paper includes a comment from Aharnian [1992] on ANNs as financial applications. Sarle [1994] concludes that ANNs will supersede statistical methodology as he believes that applied statistic is highly unlikely to be reduced to an automatic process or expert system.They were also successfully used for the prediction of the stock/index returns Sharada[1990], Kimoto[1990], Brown[1988], Gencay[1998];the economic time series forecasting Swanson[1995],Zhang[1994];interest rate prediction Swanson[1995],Kim [1997]; earning prediction Charitou[1996],fraud detection Fanning [1998];bond risk analysis Dutta[1988],Kim[1997],Maher[1997]; and other areas.

Volatility Estimation By Using ARCH ,GARCH Group & ANN Models
ARCH Model

The ARCH model was formulated by Robert F. Engle in 1982. The underlying principle of the model is that the variance of a dependent variable is expressed as a function of its own past value. The clustering of large moves and small moves of either sign in the price process was one of the first documented features of the volatility process of asset prices. Mandelbrot (1963) and Fama (1965) both reported evidence that large changes in the price of an asset are often followed by small changes. The principal implication of such volatility clustering is that volatility shock to-day will influence the volatility many periods in future. Accordingly, conditional variance under ARCH(q) model is a linear combination of squared past errors of specified lag.
This is

$$\sigma_t^2 = \alpha_0 + \sum_{i=1}^{q} \alpha_i u_{t-1}^2$$

σ_t^2 = Conditional variance of return at time 't' which depends on the squared disturbances at time lag of ' i' where i varies from 1,2,3……..

α_0 = Intercept

α_i = Coefficient of the lagged squared error terms

u^2_{t-i} = lagged lagged squared error terms

$\alpha_0 > 0; \alpha_i \geq 0,$

It is very difficult to decide the number of lags (q) of the squared residual in the model. But the study has used lagged squared residuals up to three periods.Other things being equal, the more the parameters in the conditional variance equations as stated above in equation , the more likely it is that one or more of them will have negative estimated value.

GARCH Model

ARCH model has the limitation with respect to the violation of non-negativity constraints. To overcome these limitation,GARCH model was developed independently by T. Bollerslev in 1986 and S. J. Taylor in 1987. They suggested that the conditional variance be specified through GARCH (q, p) model as

$$\sigma_t^2 = \alpha_0 + \sum_{i=1}^{q} \left(\alpha_i . u_{t-i}^2\right) + \sum_{j=1}^{p} \left(\beta_j . \sigma_{t-j}^2\right)$$

Where, σ_t^2 = conditional variance, with constraints

$\alpha_0 > 0; \alpha_i \geq 0$, for i= 1,2,…………..q

$\beta_j \geq 0,$ for j= 1, 2,………………..p

to ensure a positive conditional variance.Thus, the volatility is expressed as a function of α_0, a constant, u_{t-i}^2 news about volatility from the previous period 't:' (the ARCH term) and σ_{t-j}^2 , the previous periods forecast variance (The GARCH term). The unconditional variance can be expressed under GARCH (q, p) as

$$Var \ (u_t) = \frac{\alpha_0}{1 - \sum_{i=1}^{q} \alpha_i - \sum_{j=1}^{p} \beta_j}$$

Thus, for the unconditional variance to exist, the GARCH model requires a restriction on $\alpha_1 + \beta_1 < 1$ incase of GARCH(1,1)

If $\sum \alpha_i + \sum \beta_i = 1$, it is known as a 'unit root invariance' and is termed as Integrated GARCH..

If $\sum \alpha_i + \sum \beta_i \geq 1$, the unconditional variance of u$_t$ is not defined and this would be termed as non-stationarity in variance. Banarjee and Sarkar (2006) claim that the Indian stock market exhibits volatility clustering and hence, GARCH type of models can better predict the market volatility.In the present study, GARCH (1, 1), GARCH (2, 2) and GARCH (3, 3) are used to estimate the volatility of BSE SENSEX and NSE NIFTY.

ANN model

Neural Network learning methods provide a robust approach to approximating real-valued, discrete-valued and vector-value target functions. For certain types of problems, such as learning to interpret complex real-world sensor data, artificial neural networks (ANNs) are among the most effective learning methods currently known, Mitchell, [1997]. The study of ANNs has been inspired in part by the observation that biological learning systems are built of very complex webs of interconnected neurons. In rough analogy, ANNs are built out of a densely ,interconnected set of sample units, where each unit takes a number of real-valued inputs (possibly the outputs of other units) and produces a single real-valued output, which may become input to other units,Mitchell, [1997]. One motivation for ANN systems is to capture this kind of highly parallel computation based on distributed representations. Most ANN software runs on sequential machines emulating distributed processes, although faster versions of the algorithms have also been implemented on highly parallel machines and on specialized hardware designed specifically for ANN applications.Here we have used the Multilayer Perceptron Model(MLP) to calculate the volatility of stock market of India(BSE Sensex and NSE Nifty),Mantri etl[2010]

Comparison Analysis

Here we will go to present the ANN structure implemented for the Data(High,Low,Open & close indices of BSE SENSEX and NSE NIFTY) that resulted in a minimum error.Also the results of ARCH(1),ARCH(2),ARCH(3),GARCH(1,1),GARCH(2,2),GARCH(3,3),and ANN models are described to a comparison.At first,the study has three different specifications such as ARCH (1), ARCH (2) and ARCH(3). The study does not go beyond the order three because of the Parsi monious representation of higher order ARCH models. The order of the lag 'q' determines the length of time for which a shock persists in conditioning the variance of the subsequent errors.

Table- 1 shows year- wise volatility calculation of BSE SENSEX and NSE NIFTY using ARCH models.

Table-1

YEAR	ARCH (1)		ARCH (2)		ARCH (3)	
	SENSEX	NIFTY	SENSEX	NIFTY	SENSEX	NIFTY
2006	1.193	1.105	1.091	0.957	1.140	0.988
2007	1.561	1.626	1.561	1.626	1.342	1.427
2008	2.670	2.438	2.225	2.148	2.240	2.402
2009	2.215	2.168	2.205	2.165	2.214	2.157
2010	1.015	0.970	1.014	0.974	1.001	0.979

Table- 2 shows, GARCH (1, 1), GARCH (2, 2) and GARCH (3, 3) are used to estimate the volatility of BSE SENSEX and NSE NIFTY year wise.

Table-2

YEAR	GARCH (1,1)		GARCH (2,2)		GARCH (3,3)	
	Sensex	Nifty	Sensex	Nifty	Sensex	Nifty
2006	1.113	1.054	1.109	1.064	1.130	1.069
2007	1.562	1.626	1.562	1.626	1.471	1.503
2008	2.833	2.713	2.804	2.728	2.822	3.290
2009	3.449	3.293	3.449	3.293	3.349	3.293
2010	1.232	1.205	1.232	1.205	1.232	1.205

Finally, it is concluded from table-1 and table-2 that in both the indices, time varying volatility is present Also volatilities except 2009 and 2010 are nearly same for Sensex & Nifty by considering ARCH & GARCH models.Table-3 shows the volatility under ANNs model calculated under multilayer perceptron (MLP) model and R-squared value of ANN and GARCH models

Table -3

		Sensex Volatility			Nifty Volatility	
		ANN	GARCH		ANN	GARCH
Year	MISO	R-squared	R-squared	MISO	R-squared	R-squared
2006	1.256	0.9827	0.9765	1.294	0.9819	0.9711
2007	1.479	0.9903	0.9890	1.425	0.9894	0.9881
2008	2.510	0.9845	0.9830	2.340	0.9860	0.9713
2009	2.217	0.9911	0.9909	2.564	0.9928	0.9910
2010	1.015	0.9831	0.9824	0.943	0.9824	0.9785

MISO: Multiple Inputs Single Output.

The Volatility under ANN model is less than that of the volatility from GARCH model. The GARCH model is symmetric in nature and therefore gives equal weightage to both positive and negative shocks while calculating volatility. For this above reason, volatility under GARCH model may not appropriately find a place in option valuation and portfolio selection models. It is the volatility under ANN model which may be used for option pricing and portfolio selection as it takes care of non-linearity in data by removing outliers and sentiments of the traders.The graphical representation of the volatilities of SENSEX and NIFTY (Fig-1) using ARCH(1) ARCH(2),ARCH(3),GARCH(1,1),GARCH(2,2),GARCH(3,3),and ANN are shown below. It shows that except two years all the values nearly same for respective indices.Fig-1 Graphical Representation of SENSEX & NIFTY Using ARCH,GARCH & ANN Model.

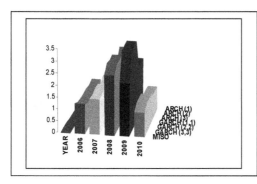 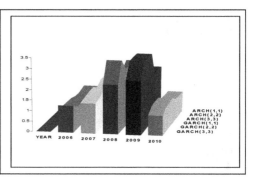

The R-squared value (in table 3) represents the proportion of variation in the dependent variable, that is explained by the independence variables. The better the model explains variation in the dependent variable, the higher the R-squared value. Without further comparision,the Neural network best explains variation in the dependent variable, followed by the GARCH model(the Regression Model).Hence ANN model though differs from the model ranking due to R squared values as it performs better than other model.

Conclusion

This research examined and analyzed the use of Artificial Neural Networks for calculating the volatilities of Indian stock market. We can conclude that ANNs has the capabilities to measure the volatilities more accurately than other mathematical models. For future research work, Fuzzy logic, Natural language processing, and Wavelet analysis, Pattern recognition can be used with ANN to calculate and forecast the volatility of Stock market.

Reference

[I] Aharonian, G., (1992) Comments on comp.ai.neural-nets, Items 2311 and 2386 Internet Newsgroup

[II] Akgiray, V. (1989), 'Conditional heteroskedasticity in time series of stock returns: evidence and forecasts,' Journal of Business, 62(1), 55-80

[III] Banerjee, A. and Sarkar, S. (2006), 'Modeling daily volatility of the Indian stock market using intra-day data,' working paper series No. 588/March, Indian Institute of Management Calcutta.

[IV] Bekaert, G., Garvey, C.R., and Lumsdaine, R.L (2002), 'Dating the Integration of world capital markets,' Journal of Financial Economics, 65, 203-247.

[V] Black, F. (1976), 'Studies in stock Price volatility changes,' Proceedings of the 1976 Business Meeting of the Business and Economic Statistics section, American Statistical Association, 177-181.

[VI] Bollerslev, T. (1986), 'Generalized autoregressive conditional heteroskedasticity,' Journal of Econometrics, 31, 307-327.

[VII] Brooks, C. (2002), Introductory Econometrics for Finance. Cambridge University Press, Cambridge, United Kingdom.

[VIII] Brown, S. G. (1998). The Dow theory: William Peter Hamilton's track Record Reconsidered. Journal of Finance, 1311-1333.

[IX] Campbell, J.Y. and Kyle, A.S. (1993), 'Smart money, noise trading and stock price behavior,' Review of Economic Studies, 60, 1-34.

[X] Charitou, A. a. (1996). The Prediction of Earnings Using Financial Statement Information: Empirical Evidence using Logit Models & Artificial Neural Networks. International Journal of Intelligent Systems in Accounting, Finance & Management

[XI] Christie, A.A. (1982), 'The Stochastic Behaviour of common stock Variances: value, leverage and Interest rate Effects,' Journal of Financial Economics, 10, 407-432.

[XII] Dev, S.S., Vuyyuri, S. and Roy, B. (2003), 'Modeling stock market volatility in India A comparison of univariate deterministic models,' ICFAI Journal of Applied Finance, 9(7), 19-33.

[XIII] Dutta G. Jha P. Laha A.K. Mohan N.(2006) " Artificial Networks Models for Forecasting Stock Price Index in the Bombay Stock Exchange", Journal Of Emerging Market Finance.207-215.

[XIV] Engle, R.F. (1982), 'Autoregressive conditional heteroskedasticity with estimates of the variance of UK inflation,' Econometrica, 41, 135-155.

[XV] Engle, R. F. (1983), "Estimates of the Variance of U.S. Inflation Based Upon the ARCH Model," Journal of Money, Credit, and Banking, 15, 286–301.

[XVI] Engle R and Bollerslev.T (1986) Modeling the persistence of conditional variances. Econometric Reviews, 5:1 50, 1986

[XVII] Engle, R.F. and Ng, V.K (1993), 'Measuring and Testing the impact of news on volatility,' Journal of Finance, 48, 1749-1801.

[XVIII] Fama, E.F. (1965), 'Behavior of Stock Market Prices,' Journal of Business, 38, 34-105.

[XIX] Gallant, A.R., Rossi, P.E. and Touchen, G. (1992), 'Stock prices and volume', Review of Financial Studies, 5, 199-242.

[XX] Gencay, R. (1998). The Predictability of Security Returns with Simple TechnicalTrading Rules. Journal of Empirical Finance , 347-359.

[XXI] Kakati, M. and Kakati, R. (2006), 'An Evaluation of the Volatility Forecasting Techniques in the Indian Capital Market', ICFAI Journal of Applied Finance, 12(3).

[XXII] Karmakar, M. (2005), 'Modeling conditional volatility of the Indian stock markets,' Vikalpa, 30(3), 21-37.

[XXIII] Kaur,H(2004) 'Time varying volatility in the Indian stock market' Vikalpa,29(4),25-42.

[XXIV] Kim, K. J. and I. Han. (2000) "Genetic algorithms approach to feature discretization in artificial neural networks for the prediction of stock price index." Published by Elsevier Science, Ltd., Expert Systems with Applications, 19, 125-132

[XXV] Kim, S. H. and S. H. Chun. (1998) "Graded forecasting using an array of bipolar predictions: application of probabilistic neural networks to a stock market index." International Journal of Forecasting. 14, 323-337

[XXVI] Kimoto, T. A. (1990). Stock Market Prediction System with Modular Neural
    a. Networks. Proceedings of the International Joint Conference .

[XXVII] Maher, J. J. (1997). Predicting Bond Ratings Using Neural Networks: A Comparison with Logistic Regression. International Journal of Intelligent Systems in Accounting, Finance & Management.

[XXVIII] Mandelbrot, B. (1963), 'The variation of certain speculative prices,' Journal of Business, 36(3), 394-419.

[XXIX] Mantri J.K., Gahan P and Nayak B B, "Artificial neural networks- an application to stock market volatility", International Journal of Engineering Science and Technology Vol. 2(5), 2010, 1451-1460.

[XXX] Mitchell, (1997) Mitchell, T.M., 1997. Artificial neural networks. In Mitchell, T.M. Machine learning. McGraw-Hill Science/Engineering/Math. pp.81-126.

[XXXI] Nelson, D., (1990) 'Conditional heteroskedasticity in asset retums: a new approach' Econometrica. 59 , 347-70

[XXXII] Pandey, A. (2005), 'Volatility models and their performance in Indian capital markets,' Vikalpa, 30(2), 27-46.

[XXXIII] Ripley, B. D., "Statistical Aspects of Neural Networks", Networks and Chaos: Statistical and Probabilistic Aspects edited by Barndoff-Nielsen, O. E., Jensen, J.L. and Kendall, W.S., Chapman and Hall, London, United Kingdom, 1993.

[XXXIV] Sarle, W.S., 1994, "Neural Networks and Statistical Models," Proceedings of the Nineteenth Annual SAS Users Group International Conference, Cary, NC: SAS Institute, April, 1538-1550.

[XXXV] Sharda, S. A. (1990). Neural Networks as Forecasting Experts: An Empirical test.Proceedings of the International Joint Conference on Neural Networks , 491-494.

[XXXVI] Swanson, N. R. (1995). A model selection approach to assessing the information in the term structure using linear models and artificial neural networks. Journal of Business and Economic Statistic, 265-275.

[XXXVII] Taylor, S.J. (1987). 'Forecasting the Volatility of Currency Exchange Rates'. International Journal of Forecasting, 3(1), 159-170.

[XXXVIII] Varma, J.R. (1999), 'Value at Risk models in the Indian Stock Market,' working paper 99-07-05, Indian Institute of Management, Ahmedabad.

[XXXIX] West K.D., Edison, H.J., Cho, D. (1993), 'A utility based comparison of some models of exchange rate volatility', Journal of International Economics, 35, 25-45.

[XL] White, H. (1988) "Economic Prediction Using Neural Networks: The Case of IBM Daily Stock Returns" in Proceedings of the Second Annual IEEE Conference on Neural Networks, II: 451-458.

[XLI] Zhang, X. (1994). Non-linear Predictive Models for Intra-day Foreign Exchange Trading. International Journal of Intelligent Systems in Accounting, Finance and Management, 293-302.

CHAPTER 12

Artificial Neural Networks: An Application to Stock Market Volatility

J.K.Mantri, P.Gahan, & Braja B. Nayak

North Orissa University
India

Artificial Neural Networks:
An Application to Stock Market Volatility

Abstract

The present study aims at applying different methods i.e GARCH, EGARCH, GJR- GARCH, IGARCH & ANN models for calculating the volatilities of Indian stock markets. Fourteen years of data of BSE Sensex & NSE Nifty are used to calculate the volatilities. The performance of data exhibits that, there is no difference in the volatilities of Sensex, & Nifty estimated under the GARCH, EGARCH, GJR GARCH, IGARCH & ANN models.

Keywords: GARCH, EGARCH, GJR GARCH, IGARCH, ANN, SISO.MIMO. &ANOVA Test

1.1 Introduction

Artificial Neural Networks (ANNs) is a statistical technique under the non-linear regression model, discriminant model, data reduction model and non-linear dynamic systems [Sarle -1994; Cheng and Tetterington -1994]. They are trainable analytic tools that attempt to mimic information processing patterns in the brain [Krishnaswamy, Gilbert, Paschley-2000]. ANNs do consider the non-parametric aspects like sentiments, emotions etc. for the estimation of volatilities.Since ANNs do not require assumptions about the normality of population distribution, financial analysts, economists mathematicians and statisticians are increasingly using ANNs for data analysts.

1.2 The Objectives of the chapter

1. A multilayer perceptron (MLP) neural network model is used to determine & explore the relationship between some variables as independent factors & the return of the indices as a dependent element.

2. The volatility of Sensex and Nifty under ANNs is compared with the volatility obtained under GARCH, EGARCH, GJRGARCH & IGARCH models.

1.3 Literature survey

The volatility of stock returns has been mainly studied in the developed economies. After the seminal work of Eagle [1982] on the ARCH model and its generalized form (GARCH) by Bollerslev [1986], much of the empirical work has used these models. The extension of GARCH models were used by French, Scwart and Stambaugh [1987]; Akgiray [1989]; Connolly [1989]; Ballie and DeGennaro [1990]; Lamoureux and Lastrapes [1990]; Geyer [1994]; Nicholls and Touri [1995]; Booth, Martikainen and Tse[1997], and White [1998]; Chong, Ahmad and Abdullah[1999], Alexander [2000, 2001]; Cont., Fanseca and Durrleman [2002] and many others till recently. In recent years, a number of studies on stock market volatility were done in emerging markets by using different parametric models. They are Mala and Reddy [2007]; Raju & Ghosh [2004]; Batra[2004]; Eckner [2006]; Andrade, Chang and Tabak[2003], Choudhury [2000]; Gulen and Mayhew[2000], Padhi [2004] and many others. White [1988] was the fist to be Neural Networks for stock market forecasting. Ripley [1993] claims that although compressions of ANNs to other methods are rare, however, when done carefully, often show that statistical methods can outperform the state-of the art ANNs. His paper includes a comment from Aharnian [1992] on ANNs as financial applications. Sarle [1994] concludes it is unlikely that ANNs will supersede statistical methodology as he believes that applied statistic is highly unlikely to be reduced to an automatic process or expert system.Many more works have done to forecast stock market volatility using Neural Networks. Such as Karadi [1997], Aikan [1999], Edolmen [1999], Kammana [1999], Trefalis[1999], Garliauskas, Abraham [2000], Sfetsos[2002], Keyong [2004], Lipinsk [2005], De Leone [2006], Xiaotan [2007], Al-Qahari [2008] and Bruce [2009], Mitra [2009]. Similarly Chiang [1996], Kuo [1996], thammaro [1999], Romahi [2000], Marcek Network for analysis stock market volatility. But the statistical approaches descriptive statistics, linear regression, framework GARH family are also used to compare the result of data analysis using NXI for stock market volatility by the researches such as Chan [2000], Resto [2000], Hwang[2001], Dunis[2002], Popesic [2003], Sohn[2005], Leone [2006].

1.4. Data & Methodology:
1.4.1 The Sample

The stock market indices are fairly representative of the various industry sectors and trading activity mostly revolves around the stocks comprising indices. Therefore, the sample of the study consists of the two most important stock indices of India viz. the BSE SENSEX INDEX (Sensex -30) and the NSE-NIFTY (Nifty – 50). Here we analyzed the data from January 1995 to December 2008

1.4.2Research Methodology
I. Volatility Estimation By Using GARCH Group of Models

The basic version of the least squares model assumes that the expected value of error terms, when squared, is the same at any given point of time. This assumption is called homoskedasticity, and it is this assumption which is the focus of GARCH models. Data in which the variances of the error terms are not equal, or in which the error terms may reasonably be expected to be larger for some points of time or smaller at some points, are said to suffer from heteroskedasticity. In the presence of heteroskedasticity, the ordinary least squares (OLS) method of regression solution calculates standard errors and confidence intervals which will be giving a false sense of precision. In stead of considering this as a problem to be corrected, GARCH models to be corrected, GARCH models developed by Engle (1982) and Bollerslev (1986) respectively treat heteroskedasticity as a variance to be modeled.
In financial applications, the return on an asset or portfolio acts as the dependent variable and the variance of the return represents the risk level of those returns. The heteroscedasticity is an issue of time series financial data. The financial data suggests that some time periods are riskier than others. That is, the expected value of the magnitude of error terms at some time period is greater than the others. These risky times are not scattered randomly across monthly, quarter or annual data. There is a degree of auto correlation in the riskiness of financial returns. The amplitude of the returns varies over time is described as volatility clustering GARCH models are designed to deal with just this set of issue. The goal of such models is to provide a volatility measure like a standard deviation – that can be used in financial decisions concerning risk analysis, portfolio selection and derivative pricing.

I.a. GARCH Model

ARCH model has the limitation with respect to the violation of non-negativity constraints. To overcome these limitation GARCH model was developed independently by T. Bollerslev in 1986 and S. J. Taylor in 1987. They suggested that the conditional variance be specified through GARCH (q, p) model as

$$\sigma_t^2 = \alpha_0 + \sum_{i=1}^{q} \left(\alpha_i . u_{t-i}^2 \right) + \sum_{j=1}^{p} \left(\beta_j . \sigma_{t-j}^2 \right) \quad \ldots\ldots\ldots\ldots\ldots equ.2$$

Where, σ_t^2 = conditional variance

With constraints

$$\alpha_0 > 0; \ \alpha_i \geq 0 \ , \text{ for i= 1,2,}\ldots\ldots\ldots\ldots q$$

$$\beta_j \geq 0, \text{ for j= 1, 2,}\ldots\ldots\ldots\ldots\ldots p$$

to ensure a positive conditional variance. Thus, the volatility is expressed as a function of α_0, a constant, u_{t-i}^2 news about volatility from the previous period 't$_i$' (the ARCH term) and σ_{t-j}^2 , the previous periods forecast variance (The GARCH term). The unconditional variance can be expressed under GARCH (q, p) as

$$Var \ (u_t) = \frac{\alpha_0}{1 - \sum_{i=1}^{q} \alpha_i - \sum_{j=1}^{p} \beta_j}$$

Thus, for the unconditional variance to exist, the GARCH model requires a restriction on $\alpha_1 + \beta_1 < 1$ incase of GARCH(1,1)

If $\sum \alpha_i + \sum \beta_i = 1$, it is known as a 'unit root invariance' and is termed as Integrated GARCH..

If $\sum \alpha_i + \sum \beta_i \geq 1$, the unconditional variance of u$_t$ is not defined and this would be termed as non-stationary in variance.

I.b. EGARCH (Exponential GARCH) model

GARCH model is based on the assumption of symmetric treatment of positive and negative shocks. However, it has been observed and reported that volatility in a rising market is less than the volatility in a falling market. This asymmetry is attributed to leverage effect, whereby a fall in the value of a firm's stock causes the debt to equity ratio to rise which in turn leads the share holders who undertake the unsystematic risk of the company to perceive their future cash flow stream as being more risky. This feature was first documented by Black (1976) and Christie (1982). Empirical evidence can also be found in Nelson (1991), Gallant et_al (1992), Campbell and Kyle (1993) and Engle and Ng (1993); Nelson (1991) also proposed an exponential GARCH (E GARCH) framework to model volatility under the conditions of asymmetric reaction of the investors / leverage effect. The present study and

EGARCH (3, 3) in order to estimate the volatility of Indian stock market under the condition of asymmetric behaviour of the investor in a rising and falling markets.

The EGARCH (p, q, r) model is specified below:

$$\ln\left(\sigma_t^2\right) = \alpha_0 + \sum_{i=1}^{q}\left[\alpha_i \frac{|u_{t-i}| + (\gamma_i u_{t-i})}{\sigma_{t-1}}\right] + \sum_{j=1}^{p}\left[\beta_j \ln\left(\sigma_{t-j}^2\right)\right]\dots\dots\dots equ.3$$

The log of the conditional variance implies the leverage effect is exponential. The last term of the above equation captures the asymmetric impact. α is the GARCH term that measures the impact of last period's forecast variance. A positive α indicates volatility clustering implying that positive stock price changes are associate with further positive changes and vice versa. γ is the ARCH term that measure that effect of news about volatility from the previous period on current period volatility. β measures the leverage effect. Ideally β is expected to be negative implying that bad news has a bigger impact on volatility than goods new of the same magnitude. A persisted volatility shock raises the unit price volatility.

I.c. I. GARCH (Integrated GARCH)

One of the restrictions in GARCH model is that the value of α and β equals unity, there would be an unit root variance and is termed as Integrated GARCH. I GARCH is used to estimate volatility if the current shocks persist indefinitely in conditioning future variances [Engle and Bollerslev, 1986; Nelson, 1990.

I.d. GJR GARCH Model (Glosten, Jagannathan and Runkle GARCH)

GJR –GARCH model is an extension of GARCH model with additional term added to account for possible asymmetries. The conditional variance is now given by:

$$\sigma_t^2 = \alpha_0 + \sum_{i=1}^{q} (\alpha_i u_{t-i}^2) + \sum_{i=1}^{q} (\delta_i I_{t-i} u_{t-i}^2) + \sum_{j=1}^{p} (\beta_j \sigma_{t-j}^2)$$

Where, $I_{t-1} = 1$ if $u_{t-i} < 0$

$= 0$,otherwise

For the leverage effect, $\beta > o$. The condition for non negativity will be $\alpha_0 > 0$, $\alpha_1 \geq 0$, $\beta \geq 0$ & δ_i is the asymmetric term.

I.e MLP Model

One of the most useful and successful applications of neural networks to data analysis is the multilayer perceptron model (MLP). Multilayer perceptron models are non-linear neural network models that can be used to approximate almost any function with a high degree of accuracy (white 1992). AN MLP contains a hidden layer of neurons that uses non-linear activation functions, such as a logistic function. Figure 1 offers a representation of an MLP with one hidden layer and a single input and output. The MLP in figure 1 represents a simple non-linear regression.

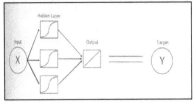

[Figure 1: Multi-layer Perceptron with Single input and outputs]
The number of inputs and outputs in the MLP, as well as the number, can be manipulated to analyze different types of data. Figure2 presents a multilayer perceptron with multiple inputs and outputs. This MLP represents multivariate multiple nonlinear regression.

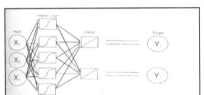

[Figure 2: Multi-layer Perceptron with Multiple inputs and outputs.]

1.4 Analysis of Results

Table -1 represents the year-wise daily volatility of Sensex and Nifty over January 1995 to December 2008 obtained from Single Input Single Output & Multiple Inputs Single Output of MLP technique of ANNs model

Year	Sensex Volatility		Nifty Volatility	
	SISO	MISO	SISO	MISO
1995	1.03515	1.12268	1.1349	1.10025
1996	1.01753	1.20147	1.14972	1.2309
1997	1.07989	1.31996	1.05076	1.30627
1998	1.41298	1.40189	1.22769	1.37131
1999	1.33452	1.43588	1.43588	1.42019
2000	1.74905	1.84146	1.60518	1.46947
2001	1.08309	1.31508	1.01619	1.28586
2002	0.72298	0.84885	0.65202	0.80301
2003	0.76205	0.98956	0.79634	0.96407
2004	0.75012	1.1907	0.90385	1.19244
2005	0.64083	0.95566	0.61568	0.96189
2006	0.85601	1.25608	1.51564	1.29434
2007	1.09288	1.47939	1.4174	1.42525
2008	1.98115	2.51065	1.75171	2.34098

Table-1-Daily Volatility of Sensex and Nifty under MLP Technique of ANNs Model (In percent)
NB: SISO: Single Input Single Output, MISO: Multiple Inputs Single Output.

The daily volatilities obtained in each year over 1995-2008 under single input as low index level and single out as high index lever are less than what has been obtained under multiple inputs as opening, high and low index levels and single output as the closing index level through the MLP of ANNs in case of Sensex. Volatilities during 1995-2000 are showing an increasing trend consistently in single layer as well as multilayer training method of MLP in ANNs in case of Sensex. In case of Single layer trainable system, volatility has increased to 1.749% in 2000 from a low volatility of 1.035% in 1995. In case of multilayer trainable system, volatility has risen to 1.841% in 2000 from a low of

1.123% in 1995. Volatility has started declining from the year 2001 to 2006 consistently in both the trainable systems (single and multiple). Hence, the period 2001 to 2006 can be considered as a period of relative calm which may be the result of financial derivatives like options and futures on indices. From a high value of 1.74% in 2000, volatility declined to 0.85% under single layer in 2006 and from a high value of 1-84% in 2000, it has declined to 0.956% in 2005 and 1.256% in 2006. After 2006, the volatility again has showed a rising trend. The rising trend in volatility is attributed to the global financial crisis and its impact on Indian stock market. Similar results are obtained in case of Nifty under both single layer and multi layer, trainable techniques of MLP of ANNs model. The volatility in Nifty has increased to 1.60% in 2000 from a low of 1.35% in 1995 in case of single input as low index level and single out as high index level of MLP. The period of relative calm as observed from 2001 to 2005 where the volatility has been drastically reduced to 0.615% in 2005 from a high of 1.605% in 2000. The reason is due to the aggressive use of derivatives in NSE in comparison to the BSE. But after 2005, again there is the rise of volatility and it has shot up to 1.75% in 2008 from a low of 0.615% which is almost 300% rise in volatility within three years. This is due to the world-wide financial crisis. Under multiple inputs and single output trainable technique of MLP of ANNs, similar results of rising and falling trends are observed. In this case, volatility in Nifty has risen to 1.47% in 2000 from a low of 1.1% in 1995. From 2001- 2005, volatility has showed a declining trend where volatility has been reduced to 0.96% in 2005 from a high of 1.47% in 2000.The volatilities obtained under single input and single out device of MLP of ANNs are less than that of the volatilities under multi input and single out device of MLP of ANNs in both the indices. It may be concluded that the volatility under multiple inputs and single out should be considered in the purpose of option valuation, portfolio construction and risk hedging as it is calculated by considering, high, low, opening & closing index data. Table 2 presents the volatility of ANN model along with GARH, EGARCH, GJR GARCH and IGARCH models for Sensex for the period January 1995 - December 2008.

Year	Volatility (ANN)	GARCH (1,1)	EGARCH 1,1)	GJR GARCH (1,1)	IGARCH (1,1)
1995	1.123	1.094	0.987	1.033	1.156
1996	1.201	1.485	1.483	1.483	1.292
1997	1.32	1.381	1.364	1.382	1.392
1998	1.402	1.884	1.879	1.884	2.045
1999	1.436	1.779	1.645	1.628	1.967
2000	1.841	1.869	1.903	1.849	1.948
2001	1.315	1.961	1.590	1.472	2.227
2002	0.849	1.098	1.035	1.056	0.893
2003	0.99	1.150	1.049	1.056	1.206
2004	1.191	1.370	0.959	1.050	1.155
2005	0.956	1.095	0.999	1.095	1.286
2006	1.256	1.11	1.180	1.0449	1.124
2007	1.479	1.552	1.212	1.549	1.666
2008	2.511	2.827	2.230	2.041	3.134

Table 2-Year wise Daily volatility of Sensex under ANN models and GARCH Family of Models (in percent)

The Volatility under ANN model is less than that of the volatility from GARCH model. The GARCH model is symmetric in nature and therefore gives equal weightage to both positive and negative shocks while calculating volatility. For this above reason, volatility under GARCH model may not appropriately find a place in option valuation and portfolio selection models. It is the volatility under ANN model which may be used for option pricing and portfolio selection as it takes care of non-linearity in data by removing outliers and sentiments of the traders.EGARCH and GJR GARCH models are best known as asymmetric models. These models are based on the fact that negative shocks bring more fluctuation (decline in value) than the positive events (increase in value) in indices or in individual securities. It's because the investors are more affected sentimentally due to the arrival of bad news to the market than that of the good news. Volatility calculation under ANN models since takes care of both sentimental factors as well as outliers. It is to be considered as a better model than the asymmetric models. Volatility obtained under ANN model is less than that of EGARCH and GJR GARCH models in most of the years as has been seen in Table 2 for Sensex. Volatility under IGARCH model deals with the persistence of shocks in the market. This model helps the trader to know whether the impact of the present shock on the price of the stock will remain for a short period/ long period/ infinite period. This type of information can't be obtained from the ANN model. The table 2 shows that the volatility of GARCH, EGARCH, GJR GARCH, IGARCH models is also more than the volatility of ANN model.In order to test whether there is difference in the volatilities estimated under ANN model and GARCH and its family of models, ANOVA test is done and its results are placed in Table3. The calculated value of 'F' is less than the critical value of 'F' at 52% significance level. Therefore, it is rightly concluded that there is no difference in the volatility given by different models under consideration here. Hence, the null hypothesis may be accepted. The traders/ financial analysts /economists may remain indifferent while choosing the model for the estimation of volatility

Anova: Single Factor SUMMARY						
Groups	*Count*	*Sum*	*Average*	*Variance*		
Column 1	14	18.87	1.347857	0.173961		
Column 2	14	21.655	1.546786	0.238717		
Column 3	14	19.515	1.393929	0.164705		
Column 4	14	19.6229	1.401636	0.126636		
Column 5	14	22.491	1.6065	0.362878		
ANOVA						
Source of Variation	*SS*	*df*	*MS*	*F*	*P-value*	*F crit*
Between Groups	0.690756	4	0.172689	0.809305	0.523765	2.51304
Within Groups	13.86965	65	0.213379			
Total	14.5604	69				

Table 3-ANOVA results Sensex volatility under ANN, GARCH, EGARCH, GJRGARCH and IGARCH models

Year	Volatility (ANN)	GARCH (1,1)	EGARCH (1,1)	GJR GARCH (1,1)	IGARCH (1,1)
1995	1.1	1.342	1.331	1.323	1.307
1996	1.231	1.516	1.293	1.483	1.567
1997	1.306	1.801	1.610	1.706	2.386
1998	1.371	1.789	1.707	1.781	2.211
1999	1.42	1.682	1.692	1.659	1.640
2000	1.469	1.879	1.836	1.760	1.922
2001	1.486	2.161	1.596	1.596	1.594
2002	0.803	1.05	1.014	1.024	0.864
2003	0.964	1.118	1.062	1.116	1.004
2004	1.192	1.413	0.981	1.060	0.916
2005	0.962	1.109	1.015	1.108	1.236
2006	1.294	1.052	1.031	0.951	1.062
2007	1.425	1.612	1.224	1.581	1.792
2008	2.341	2.705	2.040	1.893	2.984

Table 4-Year wise Daily volatility of Nifty under ANN models and GARCH Family of Models (in percent)

It is seen from the above table that the volatility of Nifty under ANN model is also less than the volatility obtained from GARCH, EGARCH, GJR GARCH AND IGARCH models. Similar interpretations can be made here like that of Sensex while comparing ANN model with that of GARCH, EGARCH, GJR GARCH and IGARCH model of volatility. Whether the above models are same with respect to volatility, ANOVA tests conducted and its results are given in table -5

Anova: Single Factor SUMMARY						
Groups	*Count*	*Sum*	*Average*	*Variance*		
Column 1	14	18.364	1.311714	0.131587		
Column 2	14	22.229	1.587786	0.221484		
Column 3	14	19.432	1.388	0.125391		
Column 4	14	20.039	1.431357	0.105575		
Column 5	14	23.305	1.664643	0.425112		
ANOVA						
Source of Variation	*SS*	*df*	*MS*	*F*	*P-value*	*F crit*
Between Groups	1.187291	4	0.296823	1.470659	0.221316	2.51304
Within Groups	13.11893	65	0.20183			
Total	14.30622	69				

Table-5---ANOVA results Nifty volatility under ANN, GARCH, EGARCH GJRGARH and IGARCH models

It is observed from the above table that the F-calculated value is less than the F-critical value at 22.13% significance level. From this, it is concluded that there is no difference in the volatilities estimated under the different models under consideration here. So, the traders, financial analyst and others should remain indifferent in using any method to estimate volatility Fig3& Fig4 presents a graphical view of the volatilities under all the models used here

Fig 3-Year wise Volatility of Sensex- MISO,GARCH(1, 1), EGARCH (1, 1),GJRGARCH (1, 1), and IGARCH(1, 1)	[Fig 4-Year wise Volatility of Nifty- MISO, GARCH(1, 1), EGARCH (1, 1),GJRGARCH (1, 1), and IGARCH(1, 1)
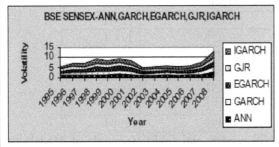	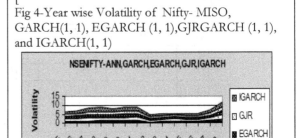

Conclusion

Here the volatility of Sensex and Nifty under ANN model are compared with the volatility obtained under GARCH, EGARCH, GJR GARCH AND IGARCH models. It is observed that though the volatilities obtained ANN model is less than that of the GARCH, EGARCH, GJR GARCH and IGARCH models, ANOVA test is being conducted to conclude that there is no difference in the volatility estimated by the different models. Hence, the traders, financial analysts and economists may remain indifferent while choosing the model and the estimation of volatility

References

[I] Abraham, A., B. Nath and P. K. Mahanti. (2001) "Hybrid Intelligent Systems for Stock Market Analysis," Computational Science, Springer-Verlag Germany, Vassil N. Alexandrov et. al. (Eds.), ISBN 3-540-42233-1, San Francisco, USA, 337-345

[II] Aharonian, G., (1992) Comments on comp.ai.neural-nets, Items 2311 and 2386 [Internet Newsgroup].

[III] Aiken, M. and M. Bsat. (1999) "Forecasting Market Trends with Neural Networks." Information Systems Management 16 (4)", 42-48.

[IV] Al-Qaheri H., Hassanien A. E., Abraham A(2008), "Discovering stock price prediction rules using rough sets, Neural Network World", Vol. 18, 181-198

[V] Black, F. (1976), 'Studies in stock Price volatility changes,' Proceedings of the 1976 Business Meeting of the Business and Economic Statistics section, American Statistical Association, 177-181

[VI] Banerjee, A. and Sarkar, S. (2006), 'Modeling daily volatility of the Indian stock market using intra-day data,' working paper series No. 588/March, Indian Institute of Management Calcutta

[VII] Bruce Vanstone &Gavin Finnie,- (2009) "An empirical methodology for developing stock market trading systems using artificial neural networks, An International Journal of Expert Systems with Applications", Volume 36 , Issue 3 , 6668-6680

[VIII] Chan, M-C, C-C Wong, and C-C Lam. (2000) "Financial Time Series Forecasting by Neural Network Using Conjugate Gradient Learning Algorithm and Multiple Linear Regression Weight Initialization," Department of Computing, The Hong Kong Polytechnic University, Kowloon, Hong Kong

[IX] Cheng, B. and D.M. Titterington, 1994, "Neural Networks: A Review from a Statistical Perspective," Statistical Sciences, 9(1), 2-54.

[X] Chiang, W.-C., T. L. Urban and G. W. Baldridge. (1996) "A Neural Network Approach to Mutual Fund Net Asset Value Forecasting." Omega, Int. J. Mgmt Sci. 24 (2), 205-215.

[XI] Christie, A.A. (1982), 'The Stochastic Behaviour of common stock Variances: value, leverage and Interest rate Effects,' Journal of Financial Economics, 10, 407-432

[XII] De Leone R., Marchitto E., Quaranta A. G. (2006), "Autoregression and artificial neural networks for financial market forecast, Neural Network World," Vol. 16, 109-128

[XIII] Deboeck G.J. ,Ultsch A. (2000), "Picking stocks with emergent self-organizing value maps, Neural Network World" , Vol. 10,203-216

[XIV] Dunis C.L. Laws J. Chauvin S. (2000), "FX volatility forecasts: a fusion-optimisation approach, Neural Network World", Vol. 10, 187-202

[XV] Edelman, D., P. Davy and Y. L. Chung. (1999) "Using Neural Network Prediction to achieve excess returns in the Australian All- Ordinaries Index". In: Queensland Financial Conference, Sept 30th & Oct 1st, Queensland University of Technology

[XVI] Engle, R.F. (1982), 'Autoregressive conditional heteroskedasticity with estimates of the variance of UK inflation,' Econometrica, 41, 135-155.

[XVII] Engle R and Bollerslev.T (1986) Modeling the persistence of conditional variances. Econo- metric Reviews, 5:1 50, 1986

[XVIII] Engle, R.F. and Ng, V.K (1993), 'Measuring and Testing the impact of news on volatility,' Journal of Finance, 48, 1749-1801

[XIX] Gallant, A.R., Rossi, P.E. and Touchen, G. (1992), 'Stock prices and volume', Review of Financial Studies, 5, 199-242.

[XX] Garliauskas, A. (1999) "Neural Network Chaos and Computational Algorithms of Forecast in Finance." Proceedings of the IEEE SMC Conference on Systems, Man, and Cybernetics 2, 638-643. 12-15 October

[XXI] Ghaziri H ,Elfakhani S. Assi J. , (2000), "Neural networks approach to pricing options, Neural Network World, Vol. 10,271-277

[XXII] Gilbert, E.W., C.R. Krishnaswamy, and M.M. Pashley, 2000, "Neural Network Applications in Finance: A Practical Introduction,".

[XXIII] Gleitman, H., (1991), Psychology, W.W. Norton and Company, New York.

[XXIV] Hwarng, H. B. (2001) "Insights into Neural-Network Forecasting of Time Series Corresponding to ARMA (p, q) Structures." International Journal of Management Science, Omega, 29, 273-289.

[XXV] Karali, O. Edberg, W. Higgins, J. Motorola Inc., Schaumburg, (1997)" Modelling volatility derivatives using neural networks, Computational intelligence for Financial Engineering (CIFEr), 1997, Proceedings of the IEEE/ IAFE 1997, 280-286.

[XXVI] Kollias, C. and A. Refenes, (1996), "Modeling the Effects of Defense Spending Reductions on Investment Using Neural Networks in the Case of Greece," Center of Planning and Economic Research, Athens.

[XXVII] Kuo, R. J., L. C. Lee and C. F. Lee. (1996) "Integration of Artificial Neutal Networks and Fuzzy Delphi for Stock Market Forecasting." IEEE, June, 1073-1078.

[XXVIII] Kyoung-Jae Kim ,Boo Lee (2004), "Stock market prediction using artificial neural networks with optimal feature transformation: Neural Computing and Applications" 255 - 260

[XXIX] Lipinski P. (2005), "Clustering of large number of stock market trading rules, Neural Network World", Vol. 15, 351-357

[XXX] Maasoumi, E., A. Khotanzad, and A. Abaye, (1994), "Artificial Neural Networks for Some Macroeconomic Series: A First Report," Econometric Reviews, 13(1), 105-22.

[XXXI] Majhi R., Panda G., Majhi B., Sahoo G., (2006), "Efficient prediction of stock market indices using artificial adaptive bacterial foraging optimization (ABFO) and BFO based techniques" Expert Systems with Applications: An international journal, pp.10097- 10104

[XXXII] Michalak K., Lipinski P.(2005), "Prediction of high increases in stock prices using neural networks, Neural Network World", Vol. 15, 359-366

[XXXIII] Mitra Subrata Kumar (2009), "Optimal Combination of Trading Ruls Using Neural Networks" International Business Research, Vol 2, No.1.pp. 86-99.

[XXXIV] Nelson, D., (1990) 'Conditional heteroskedasticity in asset retums: a new approach' Econometrica. 59 , 347-70

[XXXV] Nelson, D.B. (1991), 'Conditional heteroskedasticity in asset returns : a new approach,' Econometrica, 53, 347-370

[XXXVI] Popescu Th. D. (2003), "Change Detection in Nonstationary Time Series in Linear Regression Framework, Neural Network World", Vol. 13, 133-150

[XXXVII] Resto M. TRN; (2000), "Picking up the challenge of non linearity testing by means of topology representing networks, Neural Network World", Vol. 10,173-186

[XXXVIII] Ripley, B. D., "Statistical Aspects of Neural Networks", Networks and Chaos: Statistical and Probabilistic Aspects edited by Barndoff- Nielsen, O. E., Jensen, J.L. and Kendall, W.S., Chapman and Hall, London, United Kingdom, 1993.

[XXXIX] Roger, L CG, Satchell, SE (1991) " Estimating variance from High, Opening & Closing Price annals of applied probability,1(4),504- 512

[XL] Romahi, Y. and Q. Shen. (2000) "Dynamic Financial Forecasting with Automatically Induced Fuzzy Associations." IEEE, 493-498

[XLI] Sarle, W.S., 1994, "Neural Networks and Statistical Models," Proceedings of the Nineteenth Annual SAS Users Group International Conference, Cary, NC: SAS Institute, April, 1538-1550.

[XLII] Sfetsos A. (2002), "The application of neural logic networks in time series forecasting, Neural Network World", Vol. 12, 181-199

[XLIII] Sohn S. Y, Shin H. W. (2005), "EWMA combination of both GARCH and neural networks for the prediction of exchange rate, Neural Network World", Vol. 15, 375-380

[XLIV] Thammaro, A. (1999) "Neuro-fuzzy Model for Stock Market Prediction," in Dagli, C. H., A. L. Buczak, J. Ghosh, M. J. Embrechts, and O. Ersoy (Eds.) Smart Engineering System Design: neural networks, fuzzy logic, evolutionary programming, data mining, and complex systems. Proceedings of the Artificial Neural Networks in Engineering Conference (ANNIE '99). New York: ASME Press, 587-591

[XLV] Trafalis, T. B. (1999) "Artificial Neural Networks Applied to Financial Forecasting," in Dagli, C. H., A. L. Buczak, J. Ghosh, M. J. Embrechts, and O. Ersoy (Eds.) Smart Engineering Systems: Neural Networks, Fuzzy Logic, Data Mining, and Evolutionary Programming, Proceedings of the Artificial Neural Networks in Engineering Conference (ANNIE'99). New York: ASME Press, 1049-1054.

[XLVI] White, H. (1988) "Economic Prediction Using Neural Networks: The Case of IBM Daily Stock Returns" in Proceedings of the Second Annual IEEE Conference on Neural Networks, II: 451-458

[XLVII] White, H., 1992, Artificial Neural Networks: Approximation and Learning Theory, With A. R. Gallant, Cambridge and Oxford: Blackwell.

[XLVIII] Xiaotian Zhu, Hong Wang, Li Xuc and Huaizu Li: (2007) "Predicting stock index increments by neural networks: The role of trading volume under different horizons,Science Direct 3043-3054

Acknowledgements

I would like to express my thanks and gratitude to the authors who have contributed their article for the completion of this book.

1. *Reza Gharoie Ahangar*

2. *Sadam Al Wadi, Mohd Tahir Ismail and Samsul Ariffin Abdul Karim*

3. *Lamjed Ben Said, Zahra Kodia, and Khaled Ghedira*

4. *G. C. Imanov*

5. *Kris Boudt, David Ardia, Katharine M. Mullen, Brian G. Peterson*

6. *Gül Tekin TEMUR, Kaya TOKMAKÇIOĞLU*

7. *Leandro Dos Santos Maciel*

8. *Qin Qin, Qing-Guo Wang, Shuzhi Sam Ge, Ganesh Ramakrishnan*

9. *Marina Resta*

10. *Saeed Fallahi, Meysam Shaverdi & Vahab Bashiri*

11. *J.K.Mantri, D.Mohanty, Braja B Nayak*

12. *J.K.Mantri, P.Gahan, Braja B.Nayak*

Dr.Jibendu Kumar Mantri
Dept. of Comp.Sc and Application
North Orissa University, Orissa, INDIA, 757003

www.ingramcontent.com/pod-product-compliance
Lightning Source LLC
Chambersburg PA
CBHW060130060326

40690CB00018B/3820